HOW FAT
was
HENRY
VIII?

HOW FAT
was
HENRY VIII?

And 101 Other Questions
on Royal History

RAYMOND LAMONT-BROWN

Cover: an original illustration by Gwen Burns

First published 2008
This edition first published 2009

The History Press Ltd
The Mill, Brimscombe Port
Stroud, Gloucestershire, GL5 2QG
www.thehistorypress.co.uk

British Library Cataloguing in Publication Data.
A catalogue record for this book is available from the British Library.

ISBN 978 0 7524 5377 4

Typesetting and origination by The History Press
Printed in Great Britain

CONTENTS

AUTHOR'S PREFACE

Whenever God of his infinite goodness shall call me out of this world, the tongue of malice may not paint my intentions in those colours she admires, nor the sycophant extoll me beyond what I deserve. I do not pretend to any superior abilities, but will give place to no one in meaning to preserve the freedom, happiness and glory of my dominions and all their inhabitants, and to fulfill the duty to my God and my neighbour in the extended sense.

King George III (r. 1760–1820) making a self-assessment.

The mystique of royalty, in the sense of its remoteness from the ordinary, has vanished in the twenty-first century. This is partly because of the burgeoning technological media available to pry into every corner of existence, as well as the lowering of deference and respect for the Royal Family. The latter is greatly contributed to by the vulgar displays by younger members of the current ruling House of Windsor. The trend of lowering deference is nothing new. Such publications as *Tomahawk* and *Punch* were sending up Queen Victoria and her family in the nineteenth century, following the spirit of *Atlas* which offered to the public royal epigrams of Queen Victoria's ancestors by those such as Walter Savage Landor (1775–1864) in 1855:

George the First was always reckoned
Vile, but viler George the Second;
And what mortal ever heard
Any good of George the Third?
When from the earth the Fourth descended
God be praised, the Georges ended!

In the twentieth century the Georges were back again. By and large George V and George VI received a better press. Although George V's court was described by the novelist H.G. Wells as 'alien and uninspiring', George retorted that, 'I may be uninspiring, but I'll be damned if I'm an alien'. George VI was also described as 'bumbling'.

Yet where the mystique of royalty has gone, those interested in royal matters can contemplate a number of aspects to help answer intriguing, confusing, mysterious and entertaining questions about royalty. Royalty has had its share of accidents, rumours, scandals, misrepresentations and misconceptions. For instance, we believe now that George III suffered from porphyria and his diagnosis of 'madness' gave the nation a whole range of problems. His treatment was harsh, but it was in line with the general management of insanity in eighteenth-century Britain. Up to modern times George's condition remained mysterious and misunderstood.

Today it is thought that his madness could have been caused, or triggered, by arsenic poisoning. At least that is what scientists thought in 2003 when a sample of his hair (from the Wellcome Collection), on display at London's Science Museum, was examined. Therein the hair contained more than a hundred times the background level of arsenic expected. Could the build-up of arsenic (from cosmetic preparations and medicines) have led to the fevers noted and psychiatric changes? Or was porphyria the real cause? So, there still remains a mystery attached to George III's condition.

Many an English and Scottish monarch have made blunders, played on by detractors. Edward II learned nothing from his affair with Piers Gaveston for instance; Elizabeth I made a terrible mistake in executing Mary, Queen of Scots, who in turn had brought death closer through her diplomatic blunders; James IV of Scotland took his army to destruction at the Battle of Flodden in 1513 by taking on his brother-in-law Henry VIII; by forcing the future Edward VII into a strict educational mould for which he was not suited, Queen Victoria and Prince Albert made their son a self-indulgent roué. The list is endless.

Even so monarchs have emerged from history as 'heroes'. King Alfred, who unified the country, was the only English monarch with the suffix 'Great'; Edward I also promoted the unity of Britain; in Scotland, Robert I, The Bruce, caused the nation to be accepted as an independent country; Edward III has been singled out as 'the greatest warrior of his age'; while Henry VIII put an end to medieval England and set in motion a social, economic and religious reformation, on which his daughter Elizabeth I honed a new backbone for England internationally. All these monarchs and more, individually and directly, made the nation what it was to become.

The pomp and ceremony of monarchy can be judged from coronations, royal weddings and state occasions. Human nature delights in things that go wrong. One guest at Edward I's coronation in 1272 was Alexander III of Scotland, who on hearing that there was an abundance of fine food, rode in with 100 Scottish knights. When the knights dismounted to pay honour to Edward I, people in the crowd stole their horses. Many royal weddings also had farcical aspects. It is often said that the current Royal Family is dysfunctional; their ancestors also showed the same traits. When Frederick Louis, Prince of Wales, was married in 1736, his father George II, who loathed him, decided to humiliate him and his new bride Augusta, daughter of the Duke of Saxe-Coburg. While the rest of the family enjoyed the wedding dinner the couple were banished to the royal nursery.

This book covers a number of royal conundrums from Queen Victoria's 'relationship' with Highland Servant John Brown, to Elizabeth I's supposed collusion with murder. It looks at legendary monarchs like King Arthur, along with their colourful courtiers. No one need go very far into royal history to come across the quaint and quirky, with a dash of rumour, scandal, plots and assassinations. All have provided more column inches in newspapers than any other topic. Even in the twenty-first century newspapers fill columns with 'new revelations'. For instance, in 2006 an accountant started a High Court battle to prove he was the 'secret son' of the late Princess Margaret, Countess of Snowdon.

Answers to royal questions can be sought in a number of ways. By reading – a guide to some general reading is on offer in this book's Bibliography; by researching in royal archives; by reconnoitring castles, abbeys, battlefields, historical sites, churches, colleges, and stately homes. All in all the story of the monarchs of Britain is the story of the nation itself. Their lives, fads, fallacies, victories, defeats, enemies, strengths and weaknesses are all threads from which British history is woven. This book sets out to give a taster of many of these aspects to underline how the public fascination with royalty never dims.

ROYAL CONUNDRUMS

♦ How fat was Henry VIII?

> Fat Henry sat upon the throne
> And cast his eye on ham sir.
> No, no, Sir cook, I do propone
> I think I'll have the lamb sir.
>
> *Nineteenth-century nursery rhyme.*

The biographer of the sixteenth-century historian and philosopher, Edward, 1st Baron Herbert of Cherbury, pointed out to the world that Henry VIII 'laboured under the burden of extreme fat and [an] unwieldy body'. Luckily the king was dead at the time of the pronouncement, or the scribbler would have felt the edge of the axe that had decapitated two of Henry's wives.

King Henry VIII's reign from 1509 to 1547 stood at the centre of a cultural revolution in England, in which food preparation was to play a prominent part at court as the country renewed itself in an age of Renaissance and Reformation. For six years a team of experimental archaeologists have studied the workings of the Tudor kitchens at Hampton Court, the palace on the River Thames which Henry acquired from his doomed Lord Chancellor Thomas Wolsey in 1528. Hampton Court's kitchens formed a complex of 55 rooms, worked by a staff of around 200, serving twice-daily meals for a court of 600 people. Records show that in one year Henry's courtiers consumed 1240 oxen, 8200 sheep, 2330 deer, 760 calves, 1870 pigs, 53 wild boar, a multitude of fish species from cod to whale, a plenitude of fowl, from swans to peacocks, washed down with 600,000 gallons of ale. Food played an important part in Henry's profile as a sumptuous Renaissance prince and in the impressing of foreign diplomats and visitors. Henry VIII as a gargantuan trencherman exhibited a personal assertion of national independence in Catholic Europe and a front for Tudor state power. It is likely, too, that Henry increased his 'comfort eating' on the death of Jane Seymour, his third wife and love of his life, on 24 October 1536, twelve days after the birth of her son.

Physically Henry VIII was 6ft 2in tall and his well-built frame became massively fat as he grew older. As a youth – he was eighteen when he came to the throne – he was a pale-skinned, blue-eyed, auburn-haired charmer of 'fair countenance'; one Venetian visitor remarked 'His Majesty is the handsomest potentate I ever set eyes on' and a vigorous player of tennis, rider of horses and a skilled wrestler. And the Spanish ambassador noted that Henry's 'limbs were of gigantic size'. A study of his suits of armour in the Tower of London and elsewhere show that by 1512 the king had a 32in waist, which increased in the early 1520s to 35in, thence 54in in 1545. His portraits too show his swelling to fatness wherein Cornelys Matsys's 1544 portrait of him shows Henry with cheeks sagging pendulously with fat, and his eyes and mouth mere slits within bulbous swellings.

From the 1540s Henry suffered from increasing periods of ill health. He endured ulcers for many years, eventually in both legs. Commentators have supposed these were a result of syphilis, but no evidence for the diagnosis has ever been offered. Certainly the records of his chief apothecaries, Richard Babham, Cuthbert Blackeden and Thomas Alson, show no administrations of the then treatment mercury. None of his wives or known mistresses had the disease and his children showed no evidence of congenital syphilis. Yet, ulceration could have come about through varicose veins, or damage through jousting accidents or at the hunt. Henry had periods of remission, then agonising swelling and discharge; he also became depressed and the pain added to his scary, unpredictable temper. Henry's biographer Edward Hall also pointed out that by 1528 Henry suffered from bladder trouble and water retention. In all this exercise was made more difficult and Henry put on weight rapidly. By 1546 he could hardly walk; he was carried inside and out in a set of wooden, velvet and gold-decorated specially-constructed chairs called 'trams', probably like the later sedan chairs. He had to be winched onto his horse and his armour was cut open to accommodate his swollen legs. Leg bandages oozing stinking pus from his ulcers caused courtiers to always remember their scented pomanders.

Henry VIII's diet not for everyone

Neatstung Pie: A Favourite Recipe of Henry VIII

Seeth your Neats [any cattle] tung very tender and slice it in diamond slices, wash it with vergious [sour fruit juice], season it with Pepper and salt, cinamon and ginger, then lay it in your coffin [dish] with Corance [raisins], whole Mace, Onions being very small minced with marrow or else very sweet butter, some Sugar & some dates being very small minced and put therein some vergious.

A.W., *A Book of Cookrye Very necessary for all such as delight therein* (1588)

While Henry VIII's courtiers were feasting on pheasant and vension, the staple diet of his subjects was bread and cheese. Even the bread quality reflected status. Most folk ate Carter's bread, a cheap dough made of wheat and rye; while those of the yeomanry class – that is, small farmers and those ranking below gentlemen – ate Ravel bread made from wholemeal. On Henry's table would be Manchet, fine bread of costly white wheat flour.

To drink, all levels of society consumed hopless beer while Henry's guests drank fine French wines. Water was not drunk as most sources were contaminated. Fruit juices were not common as soft drinks. Cherries, strawberries and apples were plentiful in season, but citrus fruit could only be found at Henry's court, or at the houses of the nobility. Nevertheless, the *Boke of Kervynge* of 1508 warned royal cooks: 'Beware of green sallattes & raw fruytes for they wyl make your sovereyne seke.' The sale of fruit was banned during the times of Plague.

All over Henry's realm animals were slaughtered in November, with meat dried, smoked or salted; thus, meat was seldom fresh. While Henry's table groaned with the best quality cuts, lesser folk mostly ate bacon. It was illegal to poach from a landowner's tracts, with severe penalties for those caught, but pigeons and rabbits in the wild were fair game. Wild-fowlers supplied the best for Henry's kitchens, and those who lived on the coast had an ample supply of fish. Generally courtiers avoided sea fish as fresh fish did not transport well on poor roads. This caused some problems for aristocratic Roman Catholics who perforce had to eat fish on Fridays if they had no access to river fish. Salted herring and dried cod were too 'common' for fine folk to eat.

Henry died at Whitehall Palace at around 2 o'clock on the morning of Friday 28 January 1547 at the age of 55. The king's cadaver lay in its anthropoid lead coffin within a 6ft 10in elm chest in the Privy Chamber prior to its lowering into the vault in St George's Chapel at Windsor; it took sixteen Yeomen of the Guard 'of exceptional height and strength' to manoeuvre the coffin. It is recorded that during a funeral service at the Bridgettine monastery of Syon Abbey, Isleworth, Middlesex, en route for Windsor, Henry's coffin burst open spreading 'offensive matter', and filling the chapel with 'a most obnoxious odour'. Dogs were discovered soon after licking up the monarch's remains. In 1813 the vault was opened at Windsor and Henry's coffin was seen to have 'gaped open' to reveal his 'awesome skeleton'. It seems that the king's heart and viscera, removed during the process of embalming, remained in London, to be buried in the chapel of Whitehall Palace.

If a death certificate had been issued for the psychotic, paranoid bully that was Henry VIII, modern medical historians would suggest that entries could include amyloid disease, Cushing's syndrome (i.e. abnormality of the adrenal glands), chronic nephritis with uraemia and gravitational ulcer of the leg. It is estimated that Henry had a BMI of 35 and probably weighed between 25–30 stones. Thus today, Henry would be described as being morbidly obese; its cause a matter of learned opinion.

◆ Did King Canute harness the waves?

> Thou, too, art subject to my command, as the land on which I am seated is mine; and no one has ever resisted my commands with impunity. I command you, then, not to flow over my land, nor presume to wet the feet and robe of your lord.
>
> *Henry of Huntingdon,* History of the English.

Canute, known to modern historians as Cnut, erstwhile Viking king of Denmark and of Norway, was crowned King of England at Old St Pauls on 6 January 1017. He was the first Dane to be crowned King of England although his father Swegen 'Forkbeard' had conquered the land in 1013 and was elected king. Canute was married twice; first to Elfgifu of Northampton, daughter of Alfhelm, ealdorman (i.e. district governor) of Northampton, then to Emma of Normandy, widow of Athelred II 'The Unready', King of the English. Canute married Emma ostensibly to strengthen his right to the English throne; this he did while married to Elfgifu, who remained his 'handfast' wife (i.e. common-law wife) in accord with Scandinavian law.

Documents about Canute's early reign are few and although the skalds of the Scandinavian world portrayed him as a great warrior, several chroniclers are prejudiced against him. He is portrayed as tyrannical, systematically murdering or banishing the prominent nobles of Saxon England. Nevertheless, he kept several Saxon nobles on his side who he elevated, such as Godwin, Earl of Wessex, to a powerful position. He also cultivated Wulfstan, Archbishop of York and Lyfing, Archbishop of Canterbury, and with the former he issued law codes based on those already promulgated by the Saxon kings.

Canute enters British folklore with the story of him sitting on his throne on the beach and commanding the tide to turn. The popular legend suggests that Canute wanted to show his people, enemies and continental neighbours that he had authority over the waves; the implications being that he controlled the northern waters of Europe. After all, he had commanded the Danish fleet in his father's time. This would certainly be the slant given by those who wished to make him out as an arrogant, harsh ruler who wanted to rule and repress. Yet there was another and more plausible side to the story.

By the 1020s, Canute had mellowed his former rule and had swung towards piety. His interest in church music caused him to compose a song for the Benedictine monks to sing as he and his knights rowed past their priory on the Isle of Ely:

> Merrily sung the monks in Ely,
> When Cnut the king rowed thereby;
> Rowed knights near the land,
> And hear we these monks sing.

He gave considerable donations to the church – particularly Christchurch (Canterbury) in the hope of buying salvation for his soul. Thus in trying to command the waves he was piously indicating that he did not have power over nature. More than this too, he was showing obsequious courtiers, who had suggested that even the waves would recede at his command, of his mortality. According to

Henry of Huntingdon (*c.* 1084–1155), in his *Historia Anglorum*, as the waves soaked Canute's feet, he rose from his throne and addressed his assembled companions thus: 'Let all men know how empty and worthless is the power of kings, for there is none worthy of the name, but He whom heaven, earth and sea obey by eternal laws.' Thereafter, noted the biographer Goscelin (fl. 1099), he discarded his gold crown, as a sign of humility, and placed it on the figure of Christ crucified at Winchester Minster.

Where these events were supposed to take place is a matter of dispute. Traditionally they are sited at Bosham on England's south coast. Yet a much earlier account by the Norman author of *Lestorie des Engles* Geoffrey Gaimar (fl. 1140) – who does not refer to Canute sitting on a throne – sets the events in the estuary of the Thames.

Canute died aged around 50 of a terminal illness at Shaftesbury, Dorset, on 12 November 1035 to be buried at the Old Minster, Winchester. His bones today are in one of the painted wooden chests at Winchester cathedral on top of the choir screen in the presbytry, mingled with those of Saxon and Danish kings. As a monarch who conquered, established and ruled one of the most powerful of all Scandinavian empires, Canute showed himself to be one of the most important rulers of the day whose potent sovereignty was universally recognised. So the story of the waves may have had an element of truth when chroniclers wished to portray the background to Canute's authority. Today the story is cited as an instance of futility and ignorant arrogance.

♦ Why did Charles II hide in an oak tree?

A TALL DARK MAN ABOVE TWO YARDS HIGH
Rump Parliament poster appeal for the capture of Charles II after the Battle of Worcester, 1651.

Boscobel House, Shropshire, lies where the old Forest of Brewood covered the area, 9 miles north-west of Wolverhampton. It was built around 1630 by John Giffard as a hunting lodge and its name derives from the Italian bosco bello (beautiful wood). The family of Giffard was Roman Catholic at a time when non-attendance of Church of England services fell foul of heavy fines and Roman priests were in danger of execution if caught. Indeed a member of the Giffard family had acted as a double-agent in the Babington Conspiracy (1586), which intended the murder of Elizabeth I and the installation in her place of the Scotto-French Mary, Queen of Scots. The plotters were duly punished and Mary, Queen of Scots was executed in 1587. At the time of Charles II's flight from the Battle of Worcester, Boscobel House was rented to a Roman Catholic family of farmers, the Penderels, so Boscobel's owner Charles Giffard – one of the king's fleeing party – suggested they make for the isolated Giffard 'safe house' of Whiteladies further on. By Kidderminster and Stourbridge the fleeing royal party arrived at (now ruined) Whiteladies at dawn, 4 September 1651.

The king was disguised as one 'Will Jones', a woodman, in a 'green jerkin, grey cloth breeches, leather doublet and greasy soft hat'; his 'royal clothes' were disposed of. As Cromwellian troops were in the vicinity looking for fugitives from the battle, Charles hid in woodland, his aristocratic retainers having now dispersed. The king would be safest travelling with few retainers, one of which was Richard Penderel. By 9 September Cromwell had placed a price of £1,000 on the king's capture. No one ever claimed the prize. As they made their way from Whiteladies in the direction of the Severn, Charles and Penderel dodged troopers and, frugally fed by trusted Penderel tenants, they decided that there were too many hazards in their path and they must make for Boscobel House and the comparative safety of the Penderel household.

What were the events that brought Charles II to Boscobel House? Charles Stuart was the eldest surviving son of Charles I and his queen Henrietta Maria, daughter of Henry IV of France. He was born at St James's Palace, London, on 29 May 1630. After a safe childhood in the magnificence of his father's palaces, Charles was 12 when the Civil War broke out. Quickly he became proficient in military activities and at the age of 14 he was in command of Royalist troops in the West Country. The tide of war swung against the Royalists and, following the loss of Hereford and Chester in 1645, Charles heeded his father's advice and fled to France via the Scilly and Channel Islands to reach his exiled mother in Paris. By 1648 he was in Holland, where his sister Mary, the Princess Royal had married William, Prince of Orange. Here Charles had a dalliance with Lucy Walter (d.1658), who bore him a son James in 1649; the child went on to be Duke of Monmouth. While in the Hague, Charles heard of his father's execution at Whitehall Palace on 30 January 1649.

On 16 February 1649, the month before the new (republican) parliament abolished the monarchy, Charles was proclaimed king in Jersey, and a short while later the Scottish parliament proclaimed him monarch (if he was prepared to recognise the Scottish Covenant of 1638). Ever a man to bend with the wind, Charles agreed an ambiguous treaty with the Scots and despite Cromwellian occupation of Scotland he was crowned King of Scotland at Scone Abbey on 1 January 1651.

While Oliver Cromwell went on to show the Scots he meant business, in July 1651 Charles led an army into England. On 3 September they were at Worcester; nearly 17,000 Royalists under Charles, with James, the 1st Duke of Hamilton and David Leslie, Baron Newark faced 28,000 Roundheads led by Cromwell, Charles Fleetwood, Col Thomas Harrison and Col John Lambert. Fierce fighting took place at Powick Bridge, south of Worcester. Battle raged for 5 hours, but Charles was driven back into Worcester city. He tried to rally his straggling, defeated troops. At length Charles was persuaded to escape by way of St Martin's Gate. The Royalist cause was destroyed, but it remained to save the person of the king.

Charles II own version of the melodramatic escape from the Battle of Worcester was recounted to diarist Samuel Pepys twice; the first time was aboard the RY *Royal Charles* on 23 May 1660 en route to his triumphal restoration, then again at Newmarket races in October 1680. Although Sir Walter Scott enthralled his readers in a fictional version of the escape in his novel *Woodstock* (1820), the main facts of the events are these: On 3 Sept 1651 Charles vanished into the darkness north of Worcester with a small group of Royalists including George Villiers, 2nd Duke of Buckingham, James Stanley, 7th Earl of Derby and John Maitland, 2nd Earl (later Duke) of Lauderdale. They were heading for the sanctuary of Brewood Forest and then – recommended by Lauderdale and Derby – the 'loyal house' of Boscobel. So this is what brought Charles to the Boscobel policies.

Safe for a while Charles caught up with news of the aftermath of the battle and heard that Royalist Major William Carlis was hiding in the nearby wood. Carlis now joined Charles and the pair perched themselves in a thick foliated pollard oak from where they could observe the environs of the house. Later Charles recounted to Samuel

Pepys: 'While we were in the tree we [saw] soldiers going up and down … searching for persons escaped.' The king was able to sleep for a while in the tree; although a cushion had been provided by the Penderels, the king's 6ft 2in frame was uncomfortably contorted. That evening (6 Sept), the king and Major Carlis descended from the oak and took refuge in Boscobel House. That night Charles rested in a priest's hiding place at the top of the building but next day Cromwell's troopers were deemed far enough away for the king to walk in the garden.

This was just the beginning of Charles's tortuous escape plans: from lawyer Thomas Whitgreave's house, Mosely Old Hall, where troopers searched the house while the king hid in a secret room, to Col John Lane's home at Bently Hall near Walsall and then on to the Cromwellian-held Bristol. Dogged by bad luck no passage was available for Charles at Bristol and it was not until 15 October at 4 o'clock in the morning that Charles embarked at Shoreham for the Continent. Subsequent biographical details of Charles II are well known. He was restored to the throne in 1660 and crowned at Westminister Abbey on 23 April 1661. Charles ruled until his death at Whitehall Palace, 6 February 1685, aged 54.

Today a descendant of the original tree marks the spot of the dramatic affairs. A spin-off for these events was once celebrated as Oak Apple Day. Until the middle of the nineteenth century it was celebrated as a public holiday on 29 May, Charles II's birthday and the day of his restoration in 1660. Some fervent Royalists even wore oak leaves in hats and lapels, while others decorated house doorways with oak boughs. Charles also contemplated founding a new order to be called Knight of the Royal Oak, but plans were never set in motion. The tree too, was an inspiration for the 'Royal Oak' inn signs.

♦ What was the real relationship between Queen Victoria and her Highland servant John Brown?

He has been taken and I feel again very desolate, and forlorn … for what, my dear faithfull Brown … for he was in my service for 34 years and for 18 never left me for a single day … did for me, no one else can. The comfort of my daily life gone … the void is terrible … the loss is irreparable! The most affectionate children, no lady or gentleman can do what he did.

Queen Victoria to Alfred, Lord Tennyson, Osborne, 14 August 1883.

One morning in September 1866 the British Minister Plenipotentiary, the Hon. E.A.J. Harris, based at Berne, Switzerland, opened his copy of the Gazette de Lausanne and was horrified to read the following:

On dit [They say] ... that with Brown and by him she consoles herself for Prince Albert, and they go even further. They add that she is in an interesting condition, and that if she was not present for the Volunteers Review, and at the inauguration of the monument to Prince Albert, it was only in order to hide her pregnancy. I hasten to add that the Queen has been morganatically married to her attendant for a long time, which diminishes the gravity of the thing.

Queen Victoria pregnant by her Highland Servant! Harris nearly succumbed to apoplexy. Without consulting the Foreign Secretary, Lord Edward Henry Stanley (later 15th Lord Derby), Harris made an official complaint to the Swiss Federal Council concerning the paper's allegations. The Swiss authorities did nothing. The Foreign Office was somewhat embarrassed at Harris's intervention and officially withdrew the complaint through the Swiss ambassador to the Court of St James. Nevertheless, Harris had given the scurrilous nonsense the oxygen of publicity it would not otherwise have achieved. Back in Britain, not even the socialist radical weekly *Reynolds's Newspaper* – certainly no supporter of Queen Victoria and the Royal Family – followed up the story. Where the allegations had come from is unclear. Some say they originated in Paris to be imported to Britain in French pornography, yet from such gossip branched a whole tree of slander and innuendo; its echoes still reverberating today.

Who was this Scotsman who earned the hatred of so many, including Queen Victoria's eldest son the Prince of Wales? Why did Brown play such a prominent role at Queen Victoria's court? John Brown was born at Crathienaird, Crathie parish, Aberdeenshire, on 8 December 1826, second of the eleven children of tenant farmer John Brown and his wife Margaret Leys. He was educated at the local Gaelic-speaking school at Crathie and at home, and from 1839 worked as a farm labourer at local farms and as an ostler's assistant at

Pannanich Wells. He became a stable boy at Sir Robert Gordon's estate at Balmoral and was on the staff when Queen Victoria, Prince Albert and the Royal family visited Balmoral for the first time on 8 September 1848.

John Brown is first mentioned in Queen Victoria's journal on 11 September 1849 during the Royal Family's visit to Dhu Loch, the year he was promoted to gillie at Balmoral. By 1851 Brown had taken on the permanent role of leader of Queen Victoria's pony on Prince Albert's instigation. In 1852 the Royal family bought Balmoral and a new castle was designed by Prince Albert, to be completed in 1855. In 1858 John Brown became personal gillie to Prince Albert. Until the prince's death on 14 December 1861, John Brown was a prominent attendant when the Royal Family were at Balmoral, particularly on the 'Great Expeditions' Queen Victoria and her entourage made to various locations in Scotland.

The mental decline into which Queen Victoria slipped for several years on the death of Prince Albert is well chronicled and in 1864 the queen's second daughter and third child Princess Alice, the Keeper of the Privy Purse Sir Charles Phipps and Royal Physician Dr William Jenner, met to discuss Queen Victoria's sustained depression and reluctance to appear in public. From this it was suggested that John Brown be brought from Balmoral to help remind the queen of 'happier times' on vacation in Scotland and to encourage the queen to go horse riding again. Thus, in December 1864 John Brown arrived at Osborne House as groom.

In this way began John Brown's elevated career at court. Slowly his brusque, no-nonsense manner increasingly appealed to the queen and a pattern of daily horse rides began. When the queen became too rheumatic to sit on a horse Brown took her out in a pony cart. She loved the way he fussed and cosseted her, as E.E.P. Tisdale remarked:

> He came to take her for daily drives, morning and afternoon. He pushed aside bowing lackeys in gaudy finery. He was brusque with the ladies who fluttered like frightened chickens in his way. The carriage was his preserve. It was his task to see that the Queen was settled amongst her cushions, his horny fingers which must ensure that her jacket was buttoned against the wind, his hands which must spread the shawl about her shoulders. Others had tended her as their Queen and mistress. John Brown protected her as she was, a poor, broken-hearted bairn who wanted looking after and taking out of herself.

It was not in John Brown's nature to be subservient and his tactless, mischief-making and blunt overbearing manner soon got to the wrong side of many of the Royal Household, from the Prince of Wales's courtiers to the secretariat under Sir Charles Grey. Brown had his own idiosyncratic way of conveying the queen's instructions to her courtiers, often twisting her words from diplomacy to rudeness. Many were appalled too at the seemingly familiar way in which he treated the queen and was downright impertinent to the queen's family. Whenever they or her staff complained she would find some excuse to exonerate Brown.

By 1865 Queen Victoria decided to keep John Brown 'permanently' on her immediate staff and he was given the title 'The Queen's Highland Servant' at a salary that rose from £150 per annum to £400 by 1872. He was also awarded the 'Faithful Servant Medal' and the 'Devoted Servant Medal'. Over the years gossip, both written and spoken about Queen Victoria's relationship with John Brown, increased and it focused on four main topics: The queen had married John Brown; she had given birth to John Brown's child; she had gone mad and John Brown was her keeper; John Brown was Queen Victoria's spiritualistic medium.

The nonsensical assertion that John Brown was married 'morganatically' to Queen Victoria was first given the light of day by the socialist republican nationalist Alexander Robertson. He produced the pamphlet *John Brown: A Correspondence with the Lord Chancellor, Regarding a Charge of Fraud and Embezzlement Preferred Against His Grace the Duke of Athole K.T. of 1873.*

Robertson had a running dispute with the 6th Duke of Atholl regarding the payment of a toll to cross the seven-arched bridge across the River Tay at Dunkeld, Perthshire. The bridge had been built by the 5th Duke and folks complained that they had to pay the halfpenny return toll even when they went to church. Queen Victoria was a firm friend of George Murray, 6th Duke of Atholl and his Duchess Anne. Robertson assumed that the queen was a supporter of their 'banditry' with regard to the toll and was therefore ripe for exposure.

Addressed to the Lord Chancellor, the 1st Lord Selborne, the pamphlet detailed several accusations against the queen and John Brown. Identifying one Charles Christie, 'House Steward to the Dowager Duchess of Athole at Dunkeld House', as the source of his information, Robertson stated that John Brown obtained regular 'admittance' to Queen Victoria's bedroom when 'the house was quiet'. Robertson also stated that he was told that the queen had married John Brown at Lausanne, Switzerland, in 1868 with Duchess Anne as witness. On publication the duchess was quizzed about the allegation and poured scorn on Robertson's assertion. Even more fanciful, Robertson stated that Queen Victoria had given birth to John Brown's child. This time he said his source was one John McGregor, Chief Wood Manager on the Atholl estates, who had told him that Brown and the queen had a love nest near Loch Ordie and there conception had taken place. The child, said Robertson, was born in Switzerland with Duchess Anne as midwife and the child was given away to be brought up by a 'Calvinist pastor' in the Canton of Vaud.

Robertson's assertions were officially noted. He was never prosecuted for his libel, although the Lord Chancellor and Foreign Secretary, George Leveson-Gower, 2nd Earl of Granville discussed the implications of the pamphlet.

Not only her courtiers but the queen herself believed that she had inherited from her Hanoverian ancestors a proclivity to madness. The mental instability of her grandfather George III in his later life was readily quoted. The queen did suffer from what the 4th Earl of Clarendon called her 'morbid melancholy', and would sometimes display a certain agitation and hysteria when beset with problems. Consequently government ministers and members of her Household would be easily blackmailed into doing what she wanted to avoid upset. John Brown understood this and his determined interference in her life was a help to tackle her moods. Thus to some this was interpreted that the queen was mad and that Brown was her 'keeper'.

With Brown being a Highlander it was presumed that he had the phenomenon known as *taibhseadaireachd* the 'Second Sight' with all its psychic attributes. As Queen Victoria was obsessed with the morbid memory of Prince Albert it was easy for gossips to conclude that the 'psychic' John Brown was her spiritualistic medium. All of these elements of gossip had deep roots and there were many willing to exploit them.

The gossip about Queen Victoria and her Highland servant did not just circulate among the nation's lower classes. Republicanism was given a boost by Queen Victoria's period of seclusion following the death of Prince Albert in 1861, and her consequent neglect of royal duty. Again there was an anti-royal prejudice that lurked in the bowels of the Liberal Party given credence by the likes of the radical MP Sir Charles Wentworth Dilke and pamphleteer Goldwin Smith. At court factions muttered against the queen and those around Albert Edward, Prince of Wales resented the supposed influence John Brown had over Queen Victoria. Furthermore, John Brown's presence at court stirred up the anti-Scottish feelings in the Royal Household that had been present since the eighteenth century. Both Queen Victoria and her prime minister, the 14th Earl of Derby, believed that certain courtiers had leaked anti-Brown and anti-Victoria comments to such journals as *Punch* and *Tomahawk*, and Derby identified such gossips to include George Villiers, 4th Earl of Clarendon (Foreign Secretary 1865–6) and court painter Sir Edwin Landseer. All the leftist clubs and the likes of the (Irish) Fenian Brotherhood feasted on and promoted anti-royalist feelings.

Although much of the gossip about John Brown and Queen Victoria was seen as ridiculous steps were taken to suppress information. For instance, when Queen Victoria died her daughter Princess Beatrice removed pages from the queen's journal 'that might cause pain' (ostensibly regarding John Brown); again on the queen's death any papers and letters regarding John Brown and the queen were destroyed on the orders of the new king Edward VII. Queen Victoria often peppered her letters with such words as 'darling one' and 'love', all used in a naive way; but these could easily be misinterpreted by anyone wishing to make trouble.

It is clear, despite public gossip and 'those horrid publications whose object is to promulgate scandal and calumny [about herself and John Brown] which they invent themselves', wrote Queen Victoria to Lord Tennyson in 1883, the year of Brown's death, that there was nothing immoral in Queen Victoria's relationship with John Brown. Queen Victoria would never have contemplated sex with a servant. Furthermore, she was never alone to carry out an affair having court ladies always within shouting distance. The significance of Queen Victoria's attraction to John Brown was that he made a career out of her. He never married, had few holidays and devoted his life to the queen, and he was a walking encyclopaedia of her likes, dislikes, moods and needs. As a downright selfish person this greatly appealed to the queen. Brown was a true and faithful friend to Victoria and despite his idiosyncratic attitude to his work and his drunkenness (to which she turned a blind eye), he was totally loyal to her. She liked him because she needed to be fussed, cosseted and spoiled. He told her the truth, spoke boldly to her and importantly too; unlike her family and senior courtiers, he was not afraid of her. Above all, when Prince Albert died Queen Victoria needed a male friend – she never really made close friendships with women – and someone to lean on. John Brown supplied all that.

♦ Why did the Jacobites toast the health of moles after King William III's death?

> Such Folks as these can never be,
> Compar'd to Royal Jamey,
> Who is our true and lawful King,
> I hope ere long he'll see me.
> *Song of a Jacobite visitor at the court in exile.*

Just before 10 o'clock on Friday 6 February 1685, James Stuart, Duke of York and Albany, Lord High Admiral, approached the bed of his brother King Charles II, now in a coma at Whitehall Palace. As the duke knelt by the canopied bed, 2 hours later, his brother died of a stroke. At 52 James now became the second of that name to be King of England and the seventh of Scotland. His second wife Mary Beatrice Eleanor, only daughter of Alfonso IV (d'Este), Duke of Modena, was crowned along with him by William Sancroft, Archbishop of Canterbury on 23 April 1685. To the disgust of some they had been crowned at Whitehall the previous day with Roman Catholic rites. Although brought up a strict member of the Anglican Church, James was admitted by his own volition to the Roman Communion in 1668; his Catholicism was to bring him nothing by worldly disaster.

Even though James II/VII lived for another sixteen years, dying at St Germains-en-Laye, Paris, 16 September 1701, he was monarch of Britain for barely more than three years after his coronation. It is true that several Stuart monarchs had captivating personalities, but James was not one of them, although he had at least seven illegitimate children by two mistresses and twenty legitimate ones by two wives.

A largely genuine and scrupulous person, James could be charmless, cruel and obstinate, and a popular squib of the day said 'the king ne'er forgets an enemy and seldom remembers a friend'.

On James's accession to the throne it became evident that he intended to restore the 'Old Religion' to his realm. He introduced a Declaration of Indulgence in 1687 restoring rights to Roman Catholics, with protestation liable to imprisonment. Thus, even though it was against the law, he appointed Roman Catholics as army officers, a Catholic was promoted Admiral and others were given prominent roles in government and academia. Yet freedom of worship was granted to all. The moves to promote Roman Catholics disheartened and alarmed most people. Was James intending to be an absolute monarch? After all he had made these moves without the consent of parliament – he had prorogued parliament at the commencement of his reign.

The Earl of Arran (son of William, 2nd Duke of Hamilton) summed up the problem of James for many: 'I must distinguish between his Popery and his Person: I dislike the one, but have sworn and do owe allegiance to the other.' Nevertheless people put up with things because James's heir was Mary, who was a Protestant, a child of James's first wife Anne Hyde. Furthermore, Mary was married in 1677 to her Protestant first cousin William Henry, Prince of and Head of the illustrious House of Orange. James's second wife, Mary of Modena, gave birth on 10 June 1688 to James Francis Edward Stuart, who at once became heir apparent and thus born to succeed as king instead of his half-sister Mary. The boy would be brought up a Roman Catholic and this, people feared, would promote a Catholic monarchy in a Protestant land.

Steps had to be taken to stop this and a group of important people including Edward Russell, the Earl of Shrewsbury and Henry Compton, Bishop of London wrote to William of Orange, then in Holland, to come to Britain to help. The rest of the events are well known. William and an army landed first at Brixham, Devon, and marched on London. James meanwhile sent his family to safety in France. James himself left to take up residence at the Château of Saint-Germains, near Paris. This court in exile became the focus of support for James especially among Irish Catholics and Scottish followers. A pro-James rebellion in Ireland was crushed at the Battle of the Boyne, 1 July 1690. When James died in 1701 his son James

Francis Edward, known to history as 'The Old Pretender', was declared 'true King of Britain' as James III of England and VIII of Scotland by his followers, known as Jacobites (from Jacobus the Latin word for James). These Jacobites were thus opposed to William of Orange as king and in the long term were responsible for Jacobite rebellions in Britain in 1688, 1708, 1715, 1719 and 1745. In the latter the Old Pretender's son, Prince Charles Edward Stuart – 'The Young Pretender' – attempted to win the throne for his father. This last attempt foundered on the battlefield of Culloden, 16 April 1746, when Prince Charles's army was defeated by his cousin Prince William Augustus, Duke of Cumberland's Hanoverian forces.

William of Orange was thus invited to rule Britain as William III, conjointly with his wife Mary II until her death from smallpox at Kensington Palace, 28 December 1694 aged 32. Although not a popular king it was during William's reign that parliamentary government began to emerge in Britain, and his death was duly hailed by the Jacobites.

During the winter of 1701/2 William's health suffered somewhat but in February 1702 he was well enough to go riding in Richmond Park towards Hampton Court. On 21 February his horse Sorrel stumbled on a mole hill; William fell off and broke his right collarbone. He insisted on being conveyed by carriage to Kensington Palace, a move which exacerbated his condition. Although he seemed to recover well, by 7 March he had a fever and was in great pain. Compos mentis, he had insight that he was dying; pneumonia with pleurisy was diagnosed by his doctors Bidloo and Fleming. William handed over his personal affairs to his aide Arnold Joost van Keppel, Earl of Albemarle, and prepared for death, dying shortly after 8 o'clock the same day at Kensington Palace. His post-mortem showed his lungs to be shrivelled with disease. News of all these happenings were relayed through the network of Jacobite spies to the Stuart court in exile. In the streets of London one informer said, 'there were several expressions of joy publicly spoke' at William's demise.

There was to be no delight for the Jacobites in the succession; William was succeeded by his sister-in-law Anne, second daughter of James II/VII by Anne Hyde. Queen Anne pointedly proclaimed herself 'entirely English' and the people rejoiced in having one of their own nation on the throne who was not a Roman Catholic. William was buried at Westminster Abbey, 'almost furtively', sneered the Jacobites.

At Jacobite and Roman Catholic dinner tables in Britain and on the Continent, toasts were made to 'The little gentleman in the velvet coat' (i.e. the mole) who had precipitated their enemy William's death.

◆ Who is said to have been the most 'evil influence' over Queen Victoria?

> I wish to observe with respect to Abdul that he has changed very much and though his manner may be grave and dignified he is very friendly and cheerful with the Queen's maids … he is very handy and intelligent and obliging and useful for his great knowledge of his own language and of course I am now quite accustomed and at home with him.
>
> *Queen Victoria to her physician-in-ordinary, Sir James Reid.*

Queen Victoria's attitude to servants was a continuing annoyance to her children. In particular, Arthur Edward, Prince of Wales, was blisteringly offended that his mother should consider a servant (i.e. John Brown) to have finer qualities than himself. From the early days of her reign Queen Victoria considered her personal servants as 'belonging to her family'. Consequently she expected servants to be treated 'kindly' and those among her children who did not so conform received a stringent reprimand. On one occasion Prince Arthur, Duke of Connaught and Strathern, her favourite son, who rose to be a field marshal, earned this rebuke from his mother: '[he must not] treat servants etc. like many do, as soldiers, which does great harm and which especially in the queen's home is totally out of place and she will not tolerate it.'

Queen Victoria showed great interest in the lives of her closest servants, and her confidential servants – her dressers for instance – were given positions of trust and responsibility. They were carefully chosen, too, from Queen Victoria's network of households including her connections with European monarchs. Servant-nepotism was thus rife. For instance, Marianne Skerret, her 'personal dresser', who also served as a kind of personal secretary, was a niece of Queen Charlotte's (Queen Victoria's grandmother's) sub-treasurer Mr Mathias; and Mary Ann Andrews, a 'wardrobe mistress' had been recommended from his own staff by Queen Victoria's uncle King Leopold of the Belgians. In return for her devotion and turning a blind eye to their faults, Queen Victoria expected absolute loyalty and discretion from her servants.

Over her long reign of fifty-four years, several of Queen Victoria's servants were charged with feathering their own nests; accusations which held some truth. Others like Captain Sir John Conroy, Queen Victoria's mother, the Duchess of Kent's Controller of the Household, tried to manipulate Victoria when she was young. His influence was considered 'malign' but another future household member would be considered by many to be 'evil'.

On 20 June 1887 Queen Victoria wrote this in her journal: 'The day has come and I am alone, though surrounded by many dear children … 50 years today since I came to the Throne!' The next day a Thanksgiving service took place at Westminster Abbey and the queen settled down to a round of Golden Jubilee celebrations, and during 23 June two new servants entered her service.

On May Day 1876, during the second Conservative administration of Benjamin Disraeli, Queen Victoria had been declared Empress of India. Ever since she had been interested in India, a place she would never visit largely because of her age, and had a wish to have Indian servants. So entering her service in 1887 came 'the slim good-looking' Abdul Karim and 'the plump and cheerful' Mahomet Buksh. From the first they made a great impression on Queen Victoria, as she said, they 'kissed my feet on arrival'. They were Muslims and khitmagars (table servants) and in their Indian dress gave a certain imperial dash to service and the royal table. The pair were the first of a group of Indians recruited for royal service by the efforts of Sir John Tyler, Governor of the North-west Province of India.

Abdul Karim, in particular, was quite different from John Brown and does not enter royal history much, yet his presence and influence was significant. Today the bulk of our knowledge about Abdul Karim comes from the memoirs of her private secretary (Sir) Frederick Ponsonby, 1st Lord Syonsby, who was to clock up forty years of royal service, and from the papers of Sir James Reid, Queen Victoria's physician-in-ordinary.

Queen Victoria was led to believe by Abdul Karim that his father 'Dr' Sheik Mohammed Waziruddin was a medical practitioner in Agra and a 'noted Surgeon-General in the army'. She was impressed

by his absorbing of her household routines, and even engaged a tutor
in English for him. It was a two-way tutoring for the queen; she
wrote in her journal on 3 August 1887: 'I am learning a few words
of Hindustani to speak to my servants. It is a great interest to me for
both the language and people, I have naturally never come into real
contact before.' Abdul Karim also introduced the queen to curries
and his attentions to her comfort stirred memories of the now dead
John Brown.

Abdul Karim complained to any who would listen that serving
at table was an ignominy for him. After all in Agra, he said, he was a
Munshi (clerk) not a menial. Ever sensitive to human dignity, when
she felt like it, the queen promoted him to Queen's Munshi in 1889;
his title in the Court Circular being 'The Munshi Hafiz Abdul
Karim, Her Majesty's Indian Secretary'. Now he took on roles that
had been John Brown's; blotting the queen's letters, and even helping
her compose comments on affairs concerning India. Whenever
Abdul Karim went on leave the queen considered it 'inconvenient'.
In 1890 Abdul Karim was painted by the Hungarian-born painter of
subjects and portraits, Heinrich von Angeli. Showing Abdul Karim
in a head and shoulders pose, wearing a turban, the portrait was hung
at Frogmore Cottage where he lived. Abdul Karim was also painted
by Laurents Regner Tuxen in 1887 and twice by the Viennese artist
Rudolph Swoboda in 1888 and 1889. His egotism knew no bounds.

Soon after his appointment Abdul Karim's prominent presence
began to annoy her family; like John Brown he became 'too big for
his boots', and his favours at court made him insufferable. At the
Braemar Gathering of September 1890, Arthur, Duke of Connaught,
complained to the Queen's Secretary, Sir Henry Ponsonby that
Karim had actually been seen 'among the gentry'. His complaint was
not relayed to the queen. In time Karim was accommodated in three
homes: Karim Cottage, Balmoral; Arthur Cottage, Osborne; and
Frogmore Cottage, Windsor. He also used John Brown's old room at
Balmoral. An incident, however, was to show his detractors that the
queen was ready to take his part.

After tea one day the queen discovered that a favourite brooch
was missing from her shawl. Her dresser Mrs Tuck confirmed that
the brooch had been in place at the beginning of tea. The footman
on duty, Rankin, suspected that it had been stolen by Hournet Ali,
Abdul Karim's brother-in-law. At length the brooch turned up at

Wagland's, the Windsor jeweller's shop. Mr Wagland confirmed that 'an Indian' had sold it for 6/- (30p). The brooch was retrieved and given back to Queen Victoria. Mrs Tuck informed the queen of Hourmet Ali's involvement, only to be confronted with her anger: 'That's what you British call justice', she shouted. For a moment the queen had slipped into her German ancestry. Although Karim's enemies were exultant, they saw again that the queen was deaf to any criticism of her favourites. In 1892, however, a more serious accusation was levelled against Karim.

Towards the end of the nineteenth century several young Indians came to Britain to further their education. One such was Rafiuddin Ahmed (b.1865). He studied at King's College, London and became a member of the Middle Temple. Of political mind Ahmed was a co-founder of the Muslim League and was an associate of insurgent elements which were forming against British Rule in India. Ahmed came to the notice of police intelligence around the time that he sought to stand for the British Parliament, and around this time too he met Abdul Karim. What worried the authorities was that Ahmed was suspected of being an agent of the Amir of Afghanistan and that Karim was passing information to Ahmed who forwarded it to the Kabul Court. Consequently, Sir Ernest Bradford, Chief of the Metropolitan Police had surveillance carried out on Karim and Ahmed. In the December 1892 issue of *Strand Magazine* an article appeared by Ahmed on Queen Victoria which reproduced a page from her Hindustani Diary. It was clear that Abdul Karim had passed this to Ahmed. Yet the authorities could not pin a charge of espionage on either Karim or Ahmed, who at the queen's prompting was given several unofficial diplomatic missions, notably to the Turkish Sultan in Constantinople. All that could be levelled against Karim and his dealings with Ahmed was opportunism.

Abdul Karim's star never waned in Queen Victoria's court firmament: as well as his residences and favours the queen elevated him into the establishment by making him a Member of the Royal Victorian Order (MVO) and a Companion of the Order of the Indian Empire (CIE). In 1893, following leave in India, he brought back with him a wife and a group of Indian women. Courtiers had long suspected that Karim was promiscuous; whether this was prejudice or not is a matter of opinion. Certainly the queen's doctor Sir James Reid treated him for gonorrhoea, and when Reid told the queen of this 'H.M. was greatly taken aback'. This did not alter the queen's attitude to him and Abdul Karim continued to accompany her suite on her jaunts at home and abroad.

When Queen Victoria died in January 1901 the new king Edward VII got rid of Karim as soon as possible. He ordered the destruction of Karim's papers at Frogmore Cottage in the presence of Queen Alexandra and his sister, Princess Beatrice. Karim lived on at Karim Lodge, Agra, until his death in 1909 aged 46. Again Edward VII made efforts to obtain any remaining papers and letters from Queen Victoria to Karim, so afraid was he that they could be used for blackmail (as had John Brown's purported papers) or embarrass the throne. The Viceroy of India, Gilbert Elliot-Murray-Kynynmound, 4th Earl of Minto, was instructed to make 'discrete investigations', and known letters were returned. None it appears would have rocked the throne.

It remains a mystery why 'so shrewd a judge of character' as Queen Victoria should think so highly of the ostensibly arrogant and devious Abdul Karim. One biographer, Giles St Aubyn, suggests: 'To some extent he aroused her maternal instincts, and she could not help feeling responsible for him.' As with John Brown she overlooked faults and failings. Her support of him too was a part, notes St Aubyn, of 'her lifelong campaign against racial prejudice'. Her deep interest in Indian affairs helped cast a rosy glow over her Indian servants. Her senior courtiers like secretaries Colonel (later Sir) Arthur Bigge and Sir Henry Ponsonby, as well as politicians, were suspicious of her bias in favour of Muslims in the face of dangerous Hindu–Muslim riots. Others like Sir James Reid were snobbish, racially prejudiced and anxious to protect the queen from Abdul Karim's perceived 'evil character and his pernicious influence upon the Sovereign'. From their point of view Abdul Karim was the most 'evil influence' over the queen.

♦ Did an Englishman compose Scotland's most famous 'royal song'?

> Speed bonnie boat like a bird on the wing,
> Onward the sailors cry;
> Carry the lad that's born to be king
> Over the sea to Skye.

Loud the winds howl, loud the waves roar,
Thunder-claps rend the air;
Baffled our foes stand by the shore,
Follow they will not dare.

Speed bonnie boat ...

Though the waves leap, soft shall ye sleep,
Ocean's a royal bed.
Rocked in the deep Flora will keep
Watch by your weary head

Speed bonnie boat ...

Many's the lad fought on that day
Well the claymore could wield,
When the night came silently lay
Dead on Culloden's field.

Speed bonnie boat ...

Burned are our homes, exile and death
Scatter the loyal men;
Yet ere the sword cool in the sheath
Charlie will come again.

Speed bonnie boat ...

The Skye Boat Song.

Of all Scotland's 'royal songs' *The Skye Boat Song* is perhaps the most evocatively haunting. Its inspiration is the story of the escape of pretender to the British throne Prince Charles Edward Stuart, legend's Bonnie Prince Charlie, following his defeat at the battle of Culloden on 16 April 1746.

Charles had been on the run from Hanoverian government troops when he made his way to the island of Benbecula on 27 April 1746, thence to the neighbouring island of South Uist. Hidden by loyal Highlanders, while others turned a blind eye to his presence, Charles seemed certain to be captured, as by 19 June 1746 South Uist was full of government soldiers. It was necessary for Charles to move on, but where? It was suggested that the prince be smuggled across the Sea of the Hebrides to Skye. The suggestion came from Hugh MacDonald, son of Somerled Macdonald of Kingsburgh House, Skye. The plan was to smuggle the prince to Skye in disguise and his guide would be Macdonald's stepdaughter Flora, then aged 24. So it was on Saturday 28 June 1746 that they set out from Rossinish, Benbecula, the prince's 5ft 10in frame clad in specially made clothes to present him as an Irish servant maid of Flora's called Betty Burke. At the risk of a hanging, for a reward of £30,000 had been put on the head of Prince Charles, four Macdonald boatmen rowed the stormy crossing to Skye. Successfully they dodged government troops and patrolling British Navy warships to land at Mugstot (now Monkstadt), and a safe lodging at Kingsburgh House. The prince's sojourn on Skye was brief, but he escaped to France and exile from Loch nan Uamh on 20 September aboard the French ship *L'Heureux*. Flora, by the by, was later arrested for her pains, but was released by the amnesty of July 1747. She died aged 68 on 4 March 1790, two years after Prince Charles.

The two elements of the song, the lyrics and music, came together from separate roots. The music was an 'air' collected by the renowned Highland singer and composer Annie Macleod (Lady Wilson) some time in the 1870s. Where she found the 'air' is a matter of disagreement among musicologists, but recent opinion says this: On an excursion to the Isle of Skye, Annie MacLeod was rowed over Loch Coruisk, known in Gaelic as *Coire Uisg* (Cauldron of the Waters), by oarsmen who broke into the Gaelic rowing song *Cuachag nan Craobh* (The Cuckoo in the Grove). This was to be the basis of her melody for *The Skye Boat Song*.

The lyrics of the song were set down by Sir Harold Edwin Boulton (1859–1935), a businessman and philanthropist, who later became director of the Royal Academy of Music. Boulton met Annie Macleod at a house party given at Roshven House, the home of the Blackburns on Loch Ailort. Here they discussed plans for their projected collection of folk songs.

Boulton left a memory of that meeting and the subsequent inspiration for the song in a piece to the editor of the *Oban Times*. His intention, he said, was to dispel 'the growth of very curious myths' which had grown around the song, the popularity of which had made the compilation and song sheets bestsellers. Boulton wrote thus:

> I . . . took the steamer to Corpach, and went by the post cart, which started in the evening, through Glenfinnan and down to Loch Ailort, where I arrived in the very early morning. I then walked the remaining four miles to Roshven. I arrived in time for breakfast, and later the whole party went out picnicking . . .
>
> While I was being rowed back in the evening down Loch Ailort to catch the mail cart, the party were humming a scrap of shanty which Miss Macleod had picked up along the coast. I did not learn till later that the original shanty had been added to, and, so to speak, fettled up, but the words we sang as we rowed the Loch were:
>
> > Row us along, Ronald and John
> > Over the sea to Roshven . . .
>
> Having driven to Corpach and again thence by steamer to Oban, and thence by train to London, I arrived at my Hertfordshire home the following day in the course of the morning, there to learn that my father and I had to start off on a business trip to Cologne the same evening.
>
> Having crossed the Channel at night, we proceeded on a tedious railway journey, and though I had now been four nights without sleeping in a bed, I could not get to sleep in the train because of the lilt of the *Highland Boat Song*, and, rattling over the very noisy German lines which were then laid on sleepers made of iron and not of wood, the words of the *Skye Boat Song* were forced upon me and fastened themselves on to the all-compelling tune. They had in the meantime taken upon themselves a Jacobite flavour, and introducing the familiar figure of Prince Charles and Flora Macdonald, and *Over the sea to Roshven* became *Over the sea to Skye*.

The composition of the song, however, added to its own mystery and Boulton further commented:

> I remember very well that when I sent the words of the *Skye Boat Song* on to Miss Macleod and to our musical colleague Malcolm Lawson, we agreed, to use a phrase of Miss Macleod's, to wrap the matter up as far as possible 'in the mists of an antiquity'.

The whole song was first published in *Songs of the North* in 1884. The 'mystery' surrounding the authorship of the song grew apace. From bothy to schoolroom, folk began to 'remember' how they had heard the song 'years ago' in the Gaelic. A variant of the piece even appeared written by Robert Louis Stevenson, so by the time the song was published it had acquired a 'history'. Yet the song remains the work of an Englishman who contributed to the Scottish romantic nationalism encouraged in its genre by misty-eyed supporters, who took the anecdotal events of the famous escape and built them into a legend.

For more than two centuries Britain's National Anthem has contained a verse that has caused some anger north of the border. It goes like this:

> Lord grant that Marshal Wade
> May by thy mighty aid
> Victory bring.
> May he sedition hush
> And like a torrent rush,
> Rebellious Scots to crush.
> God save the Queen!

Among musicologists there is some dubiety as to the origins of the tune used for the National Anthem. Nevertheless it is widely believed by historians that the verses were composed by Henry Carey (d.1743), the Yorkshire-born writer of burlesques, farces and songs. The anthem dates from around 1740 and was composed to celebrate the victory over the Spanish at Porto Bello in the War of Jenkin's Ear. Some five years later General Sir John Cope was defeated at the Battle of Prestonpans by the Jacobite army of Prince Charles Edward Stuart. When news of the defeat reached London, this sixth verse was said to have been added by an unknown musician. The marshal referred to was George Wade (d.1748), who at the time of the Jacobite Rising of 1745 was commander-in-chief of George II's forces in England, who failed to engage the Jacobite army (he was replaced by the Duke of Cumberland who completed the job). From the official records the sixth verse has never been removed.

♦ Was Elizabeth I a 'virgin' queen?

> I would rather be a beggar and single than a queen and married.
> *Queen Elizabeth I to the ambassador, the Duke of Wurtemburg.*

Elizabeth Tudor scarcely knew her mother Anne Boleyn, who was executed when Elizabeth was 32 months old. Born at Greenwich Palace, 7 September 1533, the second surviving child of Henry VIII, Elizabeth was dispatched to Hatfield Palace, Hertfordshire, when but an infant. Her young life was a series of bitter rejections and manipulations. Her elder half-sister, who ruled as Mary I of England, disowned her, and although declared illegitimate when the marriage of Henry VIII and second wife Anne Boleyn was declared void, she was later dubbed legitimate and 'heiress of a kingdom' when her father used her as a barter piece towards a political alliance through marriage. Her aversion to being a pawn may have led her to view marriage with distaste.

Intelligent, precocious and very well educated for a woman of her era, Elizabeth lived through various vicissitudes in the reigns of her half-siblings Edward VI and Mary I, to be confined in the Tower of London, then Woodstock, near Oxford, when Mary took the notion that Elizabeth was plotting against her. Yet on Mary's death at St James's Palace, 17 November 1558, Elizabeth became monarch to general rejoicing in the land.

Elizabeth's reign to her death at Richmond Palace at 3 p.m. on 24 March 1603, aged 69, has become known as 'England's Golden Age'. Yet her reasons not to marry remain a matter of conjecture and her purported lifelong virginity survives as a mystery. For Elizabeth, it seems, the marriage issue developed as a clear choice; who should she *possibly* marry as opposed to *actually* marry. As an astute ruler, Elizabeth knew that a political marriage was necessary for two reasons; to produce a legitimate heir, and to strengthen England's role in Europe. As the most eligible woman in Europe, suitors came and went from her former brother-in-law, Philip II of Spain to Charles, Archduke of Austria and even the bisexual transvestite Henri, duc d'Anjou, whose brother Charles IX, King of France had also been a possibility. The more she aged and the more she refused to identify an heir the more her government became nervous. They feared that if she died without declaring a successor, as a great-granddaughter of Henry VII, Mary, Queen of Scots would claim the rights of succession and plunge England into another bout of Roman Catholic oppression. In 1559 in particular parliament pressed Elizabeth to marry. The antiquary and historian William Camden – who was commissioned by James I/VI to write his cousin Elizabeth's biography – recorded her reply: 'I have already joyned myself in marriage to a Husband, namely, the Kingdom Of England.'

Delighting in flaunting her 'virginity', Elizabeth encouraged all to refer to her as the 'Virgin Queen', to the extent that Walter Raleigh named territory in North America in 1584 as Virginia in her honour. In all this Elizabeth flouted the opinions of the day. Shakespeare spoke for his generation when he wrote: '[Virgins compare to] one of our French wither'd pears – it looks ill, it eats dryly.' Since the Reformation virginity had lost its repute. The Protestant divine Thomas Becon, erstwhile chaplain to Protector Somerset, preached that virginity was inferior to marriage, noting that the old traditions of celebacy and virginity were 'Romish'. Publicly, at least, Elizabeth followed the ideas of Bishop John Jewel of Salisbury, that chastity was a 'gift', and that her virginal state set her apart as a kind of 'elect'. Nevertheless people asked: How could a daughter of lusty Henry Tudor be a virgin?

Victorian historians, novelists and film producers in particular have identified who they considered the most probable contender for the queen's bed, namely, Robert Dudley, Earl of Leicester (1532–88). Others too, like Robert Devereux, 2nd Earl of Essex (1566–1601), have provoked scandalous speculation, but Dudley engendered the most. His roller-coaster career as MP, supporter of Lady Jane Grey (see chapter 2), master of the ordnance and privy councillor, brought him to Elizabeth's court and his role of 'favourite'. When Dudley's wife, Amy Robsart, died in 1650, following a purported fall down some stairs, court gossips promoted the suggestion that she had been murdered to make Dudley free to marry the queen. Gossips claimed also that Elizabeth had borne Dudley a child. Was there any truth in this? To recount such stories was treason, so courtiers caught retailing them ran the risk of tongues and ears removed or the ultimate penalty of death. Elizabeth was an incorrigible flirt; during one ceremony in which she invested Dudley with his collar as earl, the foreign envoys were shocked to see her playfully tickle his neck.

Dudley's name was entwined with Elizabeth's once more in a curious tale set out by those wishing to prove that Elizabeth was not the virgin she purported to be. During June 1587, when King Philip of Spain was having an *Armada Grande* prepared for the invasion of England, a vessel bound for France was intercepted off the fortified Basque fishing port of San Sebastian. Among those on board was an Englishmen in his mid-twenties who told his interceptors that he had been visiting the Shrine of Our Lady of Montserrat in the rugged mountains near Barcelona. He was now making his way spiritually refreshed to France. Suspected of being a spy he was shipped to Madrid and imprisoned. Strangely for a person in his position his request to see Sir Francis Englefield of Englefield House, Berkshire, was granted. Sir Francis was a Roman Catholic exile from Elizabethan England at Valladolid, and had been Master of the Wards in the reign of Mary I. The young man told Sir Francis a curious story that he was the illegitimate son of Robert Dudley, Earl of Leicester and Queen Elizabeth. In time the story was relayed by an English agent in Spain to London and officially dismissed as Roman Catholic propaganda aiming to destabilise the Protestant monarchy. Yet there were those who gave it substance.

Arthur Dudley told Sir Francis that he had been brought up by one Robert Southern, servant to Katherine Ashley, then retired governess to Elizabeth. When he was about 5 years old, Dudley said that he entered the care of John Ashley, Katherine's husband, to be educated. It seems, despite official opposition, Dudley enlisted around 1580 as a volunteer to fight in the Netherlands.

In 1583 Arthur Dudley was called back to England as his 'father' Robert Southern was mortally ill. Arriving at Southern's lodgings at Evesham, he was told that Robert Southern was not his father. Southern went on to say that he had been instructed by Katherine Ashley to go to Hampton Court where one of Queen Elizabeth's ladies in waiting, Lady Harington, gave him a new-born baby to care for in his household. The infant was said to have been the illegitimate son of an unmarried court lady, who would have been dismissed if the queen had found out about it. The infant was to be brought up as Robert Southern's son and paid for from a source unknown to Southern. Sworn to secrecy on the pain of death Southern knew that he was almost out of reach of execution by mortal hands and his dying legacy to Arthur Dudley was the truth that his parents were the Earl of Leicester and Queen Elizabeth.

Arthur Dudley went on to describe his life to Sir Francis in great detail. If what he said was true it would hand the Roman Catholic opposition of Elizabeth a trump card. Dudley further told Sir Francis that since he had learned of his real parentage he feared for his life and sought exile abroad. Sir Francis understandably had certain doubts about the truth of what he had heard and devised a set of questions that would test Dudley on the relevant events of his life in England, details of the Ashley home and position, and on the main characters mentioned in the story. Dudley replied to all the questions with plausibility. Nevertheless, Sir Francis feared that Arthur Dudley was a credible spy and made an official report to King Philip.

They discussed the possibility that Arthur Dudley's story was a ruse perpetrated by Queen Elizabeth herself to recognise Arthur Dudley as her son to thwart Philip's claim to the English throne. The political ramifications were clear. Philip, too, had instructed his ambassadors to Queen Elizabeth's court to pay particular attention to her health. He monitored her smallpox scare of 1562 when, desperately ill, she commanded her councillors to appoint Robert Dudley Lord Protector should she die. His servant was also given a generous pension of £500; was this to buy his silence as 'doorkeeper' while Dudley and Elizabeth were intimate in her chambers? Diplomatic dispatches arrived regularly in Madrid on the queen's gastro-enteritis, varicose ulcers, various neuroses and migraines. Philip remembered that the Spanish ambassador reported that he had seen the queen to have 'a swollen belly'. It was put about that this was the consequence of ascites (abdominal dropsy) wherein an accumulation of fluid builds up in the belly. What if, mused Philip, this had been a cover-up for pregnancy?

The king now advised that the best course of action was to hold Arthur Dudley in secure quarters in a monastery pending further investigation. State papers in Spain have only confirmed that this is what happened to Dudley, who seems to have been kept in some comfort. From this point the trail goes cold for historians; was Arthur Dudley kept there for the rest of his life? Did he ever return to England? No one knows, so the Arthur Dudley story can add nothing to the examination of Elizabeth's claim of virginity.

The Burghley State Papers have offered historians a glimpse of what some deduce as a threat to Elizabeth's virginity when she was 15. The noted perpetrator was ambitious malcontent the Lord Admiral Thomas Seymour, Baron Seymour of Sudeley (*c.* 1508–49). He secretly married Queen Dowager Catherine Parr in April 1547, the sixth wife of Henry VIII. Seymour, it should be said, was discontented that his elder brother Edward Seymour, 1st Earl of Hertford and Duke of Somerset had not been more generous towards him. Somerset was Governor and Lord Protector during the boyhood of King Edward VI and had great power in the land. As marrying Mary or Elizabeth was out of the question Seymour saw advantage in marrying Catherine Parr. Now Elizabeth's step-father, Seymour visited the house in Chelsea where Elizabeth lived with Catherine Parr, and the governess Katherine Ashley, pained by the recollections drawn out of her, recalled:

> Quite often, Seymour would barge into [Elizabeth's] room of a morning before she was ready, and sometimes before she did rise, and if she were up he would bid her good morning and ask how she did, and strike her upon the back or buttocks familiarly ... and sometimes go through to the maidens and play with them, and so forth. And if [Elizabeth] were in her bed he would put open the curtains and bid her good morrow and make as though he would come at her, and she would go further in the bed so that he could not come at her.

Catherine Parr died on 5 September 1548 of puerpal fever and Seymour made attempts to marry Elizabeth; in time Seymour was arrested for treason and imprisoned in the Tower of London in 1549, found guilty and executed.

Reviewing contemporary papers, particularly a dossier prepared during Seymour's treason procedures in which governess Katherine Ashley and Sir Thomas Parry, erstwhile treasurer in Elizabeth's household, were interviewed, modern historians have suggested that Elizabeth may have been sexually abused by Seymour. Projecting a modern analysis on what they see as Seymour's abuse they say that Elizabeth fell in love with Seymour, after all he was something of a court stud; yet that love, they aver, was based on guilt and self-loathing. Psychologically scarred, they go on to say that in adulthood Elizabeth became an abuser, denying (sexual) fulfilment to those she had influence over, from her favourites to her ladies-in-waiting on whom she forced celibacy. Certainly she was hard on any who lapsed.

When her maids of honour, Mary Fitton and Anne Vavasour, fell pregnant out of wedlock, for instance, she had the fathers imprisoned and the girls banished from court. Again, when Henry Wriothesley, 3rd Earl of Southampton, secretly married maid of honour Elizabeth Vernon, the queen had them placed in the Fleet prison because her permission had not been sought.

It is well attested that Seymour 'snatched kisses' from Elizabeth, and 'stole embraces' from her while his wife looked on. There was even suggestion of flirtatious horse-play in the bedroom and garden with Catherine Parr present, occasions on which governess Katherine Ashley remonstrated with them. In reply to Ashley's indignation about his dealings with Elizabeth, sometimes dressed only in his nightgown, Seymour said pompously: 'I will tell my Lord Protector [his brother Somerset] how I am slandered; and I will not leave off, for I mean no evil.'

Why Catherine Parr condoned her husband's cavorting with Elizabeth – at times dressed only in his nightshirt – is a matter of speculation. Catherine was a pious woman, whose radical religious writings were admired; eventually she removed Elizabeth to the care of Sir Anthony Denny, MP and counsellor to Edward VI, and his wife Joan, at Cheshunt, Hertfordshire. Before she left Catherine lectured Elizabeth on being careful not to harm her reputation through her conduct. Elizabeth was to admit that (uncharacteristically) she 'answered little' to the reproof. Had the forbidden fruit of sex been tasted? Historian and Elizabeth I biographer Dr David Starkey, writing in 2000, said: 'I think there is good reason to believe that the affair with Seymour was sexual.'

For those who dismiss the theory that Elizabeth lost her virginity to Thomas Seymour, or anyone else, there are always the suppositions concerning Elizabeth's gynaecological history.

As the years of her reign went by, with Elizabeth maintaining her decision not to marry, gossip grew that she had some sexual deficit that made marital relations and reproduction impossible. After her death Elizabeth's godson the wit, author and High Sheriff of Somerset, Sir John Harrington, suggested that she had 'in body some indisposition to the act of marriage'. Dramatist and poet Ben Jonson further gossiped that the queen 'had a membrana on her, which made her incapable of men, though for her delight she tried many'. Again, Elizabeth Talbot, Countess of Shrewsbury, once a lady-in-waiting to

Elizabeth, remarked to Mary, Queen of Scots, who was in the care of her husband George, the 6th Earl, at Tutbury, that Elizabeth was 'not like other women' suggesting that she had no periods.

The treatment of the queen's cadaver at death remains uncertain; she left instructions that she should not be embalmed. Medical historians suggest that her death certificate might have included that she died of an infected parotid gland, bronchopneumonia, cancer of the stomach and thyroid failure. It seems that her heart was removed and was purported to be seen in a casket (along with that of her sister Mary) in the vault of George Monck, Duke of Albemarle, who was interred in the Henry VII Chapel, Westminster Abbey, in 1670 the year of Monck's death.

So despite learned opinion there is no watertight proof that Elizabeth I was not a biological virgin all her life. And for all time she will be known as the 'Virgin Queen'.

♦ Did James IV of Scotland escape death at the Battle of Flodden?

> Dule and wae for the order sent our lads to the Border!
> The English, for ance, by guile won the day;
> The Flowers of the Forest, that focht aye the foremost,
> The prime o'our land, are cauld in the clay ...
> The Flowers of the Forest are a' wede away ...*
>
> *'The Flowers of the Forest', Jean Elder (d. 1805).*

'The king did not die in battle ... He was spirited away ... I saw the Scots king alive and well ...' Comments like these and many more were circulating after the fateful Battle of Flodden, as the Scots came to terms with the awful outcome of the conflict. That day 10,000 Scots were slaughtered including the young natural son of James IV, Alexander Stewart, Archbishop of St Andrews, two bishops, two abbots, nine earls, fourteen lords and over three hundred knights – almost the whole of Scotland's nobility, gentry and administrative class.

---

* *dule*: grief; *wae*: woe; *ance*: once; *focht*: fought; *aye*: always; *cauld*: cold; *a' wede away*: all carried off (by death)

Of all the Stuart monarchs, James Stewart, born 14 March 1473, and crowned King of Scots at Scone Abbey at the age of 15, was perhaps the most accomplished. Chivalrous, enquiring and devout, he married at Holyrood Abbey in 1503, Margaret Tudor, daughter of Henry VII of England. Historically James is marked out as a great leader and remains a transitional character as Scotland emerged from the Middle Ages into the Renaissance. Nevertheless, he was to make one fatal error that devastated his nation.

Throughout his reign James tried to maintain peace with England, but was always stymied by events. Until 1512 Scotland had a technical peace with England – except for the years 1495–7 when James supported Perkin Warbeck against Henry VII.

Still, Henry had sought to secure his northern flank by marrying his daughter Margaret to James, but despite this union an undeclared naval war existed between the neighbours during 1504–12. James was plunged into a further dilemma when Henry VII prepared to do battle with France, for Scotland had had a long-standing treaty with the French dubbed in Scottish history as 'The Auld Alliance'.

Trouble brewed in this way. In 1511 the Roman Franciscan Giuliano della Rovere, who ruled as Pope Julius II during 1503–13, formed what was laughingly called the Holy League with Venice, Austria and Spain for the defence of the papacy. Henry VIII joined the League later in the year. Part of the League's intent was to support a holy war against Islam, yet the Pope's machinations caused him to declare war on Louis XII of France. The Pope considered Louis a 'schismatic' because he questioned the Pope's actions. In his defence Louis invoked the Auld Alliance and Scotland was once more on the opposite side to England. Louis invited James to draw off English troops on England's northern Borderland and the scene was thus set for disaster.

In September 1513 James IV crossed from Scotland into Northumberland with an army of some 40,000. 'No Scottish army had ever taken to the field so well equipped', wrote one historian. Facing him was the gouty septuagenarian Thomas Howard, Earl of Surrey (later 2nd Duke of Norfolk) with a force of some 26,000 which included a large number of archers. Surrey's men at arms sported short bills and halberds, whereas the Scots had 15ft French pikes. That day James IV with Matthew Stewart, Earl of Lennox and Archibald Campbell, 2nd Earl of Argyll on his right, and with

Alexander, 3rd Lord Home, Alexander Gordon, 3rd Earl of Huntly, William Hay, 3rd Earl of Errol, David Lindsay, 5th Earl of Crawford (Duke of Montrose) on his left formed his battle line. Facing him Surrey massed his son, Lord Admiral Sir Thomas Howard and Sir Edward Stanley (on James's right flank) with Thomas Lord Dacre's cavalry proceeding from behind nearby Branxton village. For the battle the Scots were in a strong position on what is called Flodden Edge. On 9 September Surrey manoeuvred his army to place himself between the Scots and their homeland. The two armies now ranged themselves on the slopes of Branxton Hill.

The battle lasted 3 to 4 hours and many assessments have been made down the centuries as to why the Scots were so routed. Modern historians suggest that the defeat arose out of James IV's 'misgovernance' of his men, the terrain and the artillery of the day. Although the Scots army had perhaps the best war technology of the period, James did not know how to use it effectively. Yet, what did happen to James that day?

Thomas Ruthal, Prince-Bishop of Durham, whose castle of Norham lay but a few miles from the battlefield, wrote to the English royal armourer Thomas Wolsey, some ten days after the battle, that James IV 'fell near his banner'. He went on: '[Surrey's army] did not trouble themselves with prisoners, but slew and stripped King, bishop, lords and nobles, and left them naked on the field.' Ruthal emphasised 'among which number [of fallen men] was the King of Scots's body found, having many wounds and naked'.

For many years afterwards rumours of James IV's survival of the battle were circulated, some given credence by Scots historians like Robert Lindsay Pitscottie (d. *c.* 1565), George Buchanan (d.1582) and John Lesley, Bishop of Ross (d.1596). The substance of what they reported was set out in three suppositions: a substitute cadaver had been dressed in James's coat-of-arms; James was seen riding hell-for-leather towards Berwick-upon-Tweed as his army was routed; James had later gone on penitential pilgrimage to Jerusalem and had never returned. But for some there was an even more convincing clincher. James IV is said to have worn 'ane belt of irone' next to the skin 'to keep green the guilty memory of his father's death' (James III appears to have been murdered after the battle of Sauchieburn, 11 June 1488). No such belt was deemed to have been discovered on the cadaver said to be that of the king. Despite all this the rumours were sufficient enough, it seems, for James's widow Margaret to divorce her second husband Archibald Douglas, 6th Earl of Angus, whom she married secretly on 6 August 1514, on the grounds that James was still alive when the marriage took place at Kinnoul, near Perth.

What was the most plausible fate of James's body? It seems that so mangled was James's body by repeated blows from billhooks that the English had difficulty in identifying him. Nevertheless, Thomas, Lord Dacre, Warden of the English March (i.e. the English side of the Anglo-Scottish border), as ambassador, knew James by sight and identified the body. First it was taken to Berwick castle where it was embalmed and encased in lead, thence transported to Richmond Palace and on to the Cathusian abbey of Sheen, Surrey, which Henry V had founded in 1414–15. Henry VIII had a mind to give his dead brother-in-law a proper burial, but there was a snag. James had been excommunicated by Pope Alexander VI and so was barred from burial in holy ground. James, therefore, remained unburied for some time. The chronicler John Stow (d.1605) noted that at the Dissolution of the Monasteries from 1536, James's body was discarded in a lumber room but his head was severed; it was described as giving off 'a sweet savour' and 'dried of all moisture, and yet the form remaining, with the hair of the head and beard red'. The head was then said to be buried in the twelfth-century church of St Michael, Wood Street, London; the church was rebuilt by Sir Christopher Wren in 1670–5 after the Great Fire of London, but was demolished in 1894 under the Union of City Benefices. At the demolition no head was found as excavations were carried out. The remains of whatever tomb James IV had at Sheen were finally eliminated when George III ordered the demolition of the site for pasturage.

♦ Who were the birthright monarchs who never reigned?

All human things are subject to decay,
And, when fate summons, monarchs must obey.
John Dryden (1631–1701), 'Mac Flecknoe' (1682).

At one time, the Celtic peoples occupied the largest part of what is now the British Isles. Their tradition of choosing a king was known as tanistry, whereby the king was elected from those nominated as successors – usually members of what was considered the royal line. Thus almost anyone who was related to the Royal Family could claim nomination to a vacant throne. This system led to many rival kings. Sometimes territories had to be divided between brothers to solve disputes. Then from the eleventh century tanistry was replaced by patrilinear succession. In this the eldest son (and occasionally daughter) succeeded to the throne. Thus, well-defined family connections occur from the reign of William I, The Conqueror (r. 1066–87) in England, and Malcolm III, Canmore – 'Bighead' – (r. 1058–93) in Scotland. Yet in the case of seventeen heirs to the English, Scottish and the united Anglo-Scottish thrones, the monarchical birthright was thwarted by fate.

ENGLAND

The House of Normandy

THE PRINCE OF THE FAT LEGS – Robert, Duke of Normandy (b. *c.* 1054).

On his death at St Gervais, Rouen, 9 September 1087, William I, The Conqueror, was succeeded by his third and favourite son who ruled as William II, Rufus. The eldest of William I's sons, with his wife Matilda of Flanders, was Robert 'Curthose', so called because of his short stature; his father nicknamed him, among other put-downs, brevis-ocrea (short boot) or gambaron (fat legs). Throughout his life Robert was disaffected. He rebelled against his father in 1077 and 1079, but was recognised as heir to the duchy of Normandy which he inherited on William's death. He was journeying home from crusade in Palestine on the death of William II thereby missing the opportunity again to succeed to the English throne. His younger brother Henry I became king and Robert went into conflict with him. Henry's army defeated Robert at the Battle of Tinchebrai (1106) and Robert was imprisoned for the rest of his life first in the Tower of London, and then in the castles of Devises and Cardiff. Robert died at Cardiff in 1134. His fine tomb is to be found in Gloucester Cathedral set before the high altar.

DROWNED IN THE ENGLISH CHANNEL – William, Duke of Normandy (b. 1102).

Dubbed 'the Atheling' (heir apparent), William was the eldest legitimate son of Henry I (r. 1100–35), Beauclerc and his first wife Matilda (formerly Edith), daughter of Malcolm III of Scotland. In November 1120 William and his half-brother Richard were travelling from Normandy to England when the 50-oar snecca *Blanche Nef* (The White Ship), mismanaged by a drunken pilot, foundered off Barfleur; they were both drowned. Although Henry was left without a male heir, his eldest illegitimate son, Robert, Earl of Gloucester (d. 1147) by Sybilla Corbet of Alcester cast an (unsuccessful) eye to the throne. Henry was married again in 1121 to Adeliza, daughter of Geoffrey VII, Count of Louvain; he had no more legitimate male heirs. The throne was claimed by Stephen, grandson of William I.

THE NEGATED NOBLEMAN – Eustace, Count of Boulogne (b. *c.* 1126), son of Stephen (r. 1135–41; deposed; restored 1141–54) and Matilda of Boulogne.

Stephen attempted to have Eustace crowned king during his lifetime to secure the succession. To do this he needed the approval of Theobald, Archbishop of Canterbury, who refused. Stephen declared his son king in 1152, but this was never acknowledged by the church. Eustace died in August 1153 at Bury St Edmunds and was buried at Faversham Abbey, Kent, a Cluniac house founded by Stephen in 1147 as a burial place for his family; the abbey was demolished in 1539.

The House of Anjou

THE REBELLIOUS PRINCE – Henry, (b. 1155), second surviving son of Henry II, Curtmantle (r. 1154–89) and Eleanor, daughter of William X, Duke of Aquitaine (she divorced Louis VII, King of France).

To designate him as heir to the throne, Henry was crowned King of England in June 1170; at the age of 5 he was married to Margaret of France. After the coronation at Winchester he was known as 'The Young King'. Encouraged by his mother, young Henry rose up against his father causing conflicts with his brothers; his mother was imprisoned. Ten years of sibling rivalry followed, but Henry did not survive to inherit the throne; he died of dysentery at Martel Castle, Turenne, on 11 June 1183 and was buried at Rouen cathedral. Henry's eldest brother, William, Count of Poitiers, had died in 1156 aged 3.

HEIR WITH THE SPANISH NAME – Alfonso, Earl of Chester (b. 1273), eldest son of Edward I, Longshanks (r. 1272–1307) and his first wife Eleanor, daughter of Ferdinand III, King of Castile.

His unusual name in British royal genealogy comes from being named in honour of his half-uncle and godfather Alfonso X, King of Castile. Alfonso died at the age of 10 at Windsor Castle. His heart was buried at the Dominican Church, London, and his cadaver at Westminster Abbey.

THE BLACK PRINCE – Edward, Prince of Wales and Aquitaine (b. 1330), was the son of Edward III (r. 1327–77) and his queen Philippa of Hainault.

Born at Woodstock, Oxfordshire, Edward was created Prince of Wales in 1343 and became the first person to have the knightly honour of the Most Noble Order of the Garter conferred upon him, which his father established in 1348. This and his achievements in such memorable battles as Crécy (1346), Poitiers (1350) and Najera (1367) made him one of the legendary figures of English history as well as a model of chivalry and courtesy. In 1361 he married his second cousin once removed, the widowed Joan, Countess of Kent, and their second son Richard of Bordeaux, (b. 1367), became Richard II (his elder brother Edward of Anjoulême died in 1372). Edward, known in history as 'The Black Prince' died in 1376 and Joan in 1385.

Why was he called The Black Prince, when he was also known as Edward of Woodstock? It was the sixteenth-century chronicler John Leland, in his *Collectanea*, who first used the nickname 'the blake prince' and in Latin as *Nigri*. Several historians have stated that the name came from the colour of his armour. His more recent biographer Richard Barber noted: 'I would suggest that [the nickname's] true origin may be in pageantry, in that a tradition had grown up of representing the prince in black armour'. Edward was buried at Canterbury, where he had founded two chantries in 1362, in the Lady Chapel crypt, but the tomb was later moved to the Trinity Chapel, to the right of the tomb of St Thomas Becket.

JOAN'S GARTER FOUNDED A ROYAL ORDER OF CHIVALRY

No other British Royal Order has been argued over by historians, as to its actual reasons for founding, than the Order of the Garter. Most, however, agree the date of foundation as 1348, and its founder as Edward III. His reason for so doing was to have twenty-four knights close to him upon whom he could rely to help him in his ongoing struggles with France. The basic idea of recruiting the flower of knighthood seems to have come from the concept of King Arthur and the Knights of the Round Table, with its tradition of courtly ceremony, jousting and chivalry. But where did the garter come from?

There is a long-held tradition that the twelfth-century castle (now badly ruined) of Wark-on-Tweed, on the Anglo-Scottish border, was the location for the garter inspiration. In 1342 David II, King of Scots, invaded England and rampaged through the northern lands as far as Durham. On his return home with carts loaded with plunder they passed close to Wark, then held by William Montague, Earl of Salisbury (then in France). The governor of Wark was the earl's nephew, Sir Edward Monatgue, who determined to deny the Scots their booty and made to attack the wagon-train as it attempted to cross the Tweed. The Scots turned upon Wark and besieged it unsuccessfully. Just to the south Edward III's army was moving towards the Anglo-Scottish border; Sir Edward managed to breach the Scots lines under the cloak of darkness and apprised King Edward of the situation. Scots flankers observing the progress of the English army warned their commanders and the Scots army withdrew to Scotland. Edward III thus arrived at Wark Castle.

At the castle was the Earl of Salisbury's wife, Joan of Kent, who later, as a widow, became Edward III's daughter-in-law when she married the Black Prince. Edward III stayed at Wark a while and one night, as he danced with the countess, one of her garters became undone and fell onto the floor. Edward picked it up, and as titters of laughter spread through the assembled company, he held it up and uttered the historic words: *Honi soit qui mal y pense* (Shame on he who thinks ill of it). Thus the garter episode led to the motto of the Royal Order.

Historians believe that Edward III first gathered his twenty-four founder knights at Windsor in 1348. Although it was founded as a male order, Edward III appointed his wife Queen Philippa and his daughters to the order giving them relevant robes and garters which they wore on their left arm. Between 1358 and 1488 around sixty-four women were appointed to the order, with Edward VII reviving the custom of so honouring women by appointing Queen Alexandra to the order in 1901 by special statute.

THE SUCCESSFUL FAILURE – Edmund De Mortimer, 5th Earl of March, 3rd Earl of Ulster, Lieutenant of Ireland (b. 1391), son of Roger de Mortimer and his wife Eleanor.

As the great-great grandson of Edward III (r. 1327–77), his dynastic claim to the throne of England was stronger than that of the first Lancastrian king Henry IV (r. 1399–1413), who usurped the throne on the deposition and murder of Richard II (r. 1377–99); Edmund was Richard's heir presumptive. Imprisoned by Henry IV and released by Henry V, Edmund achieved an important position; he accompanied Henry V to France in the Hundred Years War, played a leading role in Ireland and was a member of the Council of Regency for Henry VI. Edmund died of plague, 18 January 1425.

THE VIRGIN HEIR – Arthur Tudor, Prince of Wales, Duke of Cornwall, Earl of Chester (b. 1486), the eldest son of Henry VII (r. 1485–1509) and Elizabeth of York, daughter of Edward IV.

In 1497, aged 11, Arthur was betrothed to the Infanta Catherine of Aragon and their marriage was solemnised at St Paul's Cathedral in 1501. Arthur died on 2 April 1502, probably of tuberculosis. It is very likely that the marriage was not consummated; historians believe that Arthur was underdeveloped and sexually immature. This would prove a vital factor when his brother Henry VIII, who also married Catherine of Aragon, sought an annulment of the marriage. Arthur was interred in the cathedral at Worcester.

SCOTLAND

The House of Atholl

SCOTTISH HEIR; ENGLISH LANDOWNER – Henry, Earl of Huntingdon and Earl of Northumberland (b. *c.* 1115), eldest surviving son of David I, King of Scots (r. 1124–53) and Matilda of Huntingdon.

Their first born son, Malcolm, was murdered in infancy. The honour of Huntingdon came into the hands of the Scottish royal family on David's marriage to Matilda. This made David feudal vassal for these lands to the English king. Henry married Ada de Warren in 1139. He became a favourite of King Stephen and founded the

Cistercian abbey of Holmcultren, Cumberland, in 1150. He died on 11 June 1152 and was buried at Kelso Abbey.

The House of Stewart

ADULTERY AND MURDER – David, Duke of Rothesay, Lieutenant of Scotland (b.1378), eldest son of Robert III (r.1390–1406) and Annabella Drummond.

David married Marjorie, sister of the 4th Earl of Douglas, but he earned the hatred of the Douglases by his infidelity to his wife. When Henry IV invaded Scotland in 1400, David was arrested and imprisoned in Falkland Palace. He died of dysentery on 26 March 1402 and was buried at the Tironesian abbey of Lindores, Fife. There has always been a strong suspicion that David was murdered; the Scots Council thought it necessary later in 1402 to issue this official declaration: '[Rothesay] departed this life through the divine Dispensation and not otherwise.' Sir Walter Scott made the murder incident a feature in his novel *The Fair Maid of Perth* (1828).

ANGLO-SCOTTISH DYNASTY

The House of Stuart

BORN BY THE LION'S DEN – Henry Frederick, Prince of Wales, Duke of Rothesay (b.1594), eldest son of James I/VI (r.1603–1625) and Anne of Denmark.

Henry was born at Stirling Castle in the royal apartments by the quadrangle known as 'the lion's den' where King James kept his pet lion. At birth Henry became Steward of Scotland and had a household staff by his teenage years of 500 persons. When his father succeeded to the throne of England on the death of Elizabeth I in 1603, Henry became Duke of Cornwall. A studious boy he matriculated at Magdalene College, Oxford, in 1605. His cultivated personality clashed with that of his father who was coarse and slovenly. Supported by his mother, a marriage was talked of for Henry with the Infanta Anna, daughter of King Philip II of Spain; despite the fundamental hatred in England for the Spanish because of the armada threat. Any prospects of such a union were blighted when the Spanish insisted that Henry should become a Roman Catholic and be educated in Spain.

During the late summer of 1612 Henry's delicate health deteriorated. He was tended by his mother's personal physician Dr Theodore Turguet de Mayere, who diagnosed 'a tertian fever' through swimming in the Thames. Henry was dosed with the weird concoctions of the day which included 'Sir Walter Raleigh's Mixture' with its base of animal intestines and herbs. Henry died of typhoid at St James's Palace on 12 November 1612, whereupon his brother Charles (later Charles I) became heir apparent. It has been suggested that Henry may have inherited the 'royal malady' of porphyria. He was buried in Henry VII's chapel in Westminister Abbey beside his executed grandmother Mary, Queen of Scots. Courtiers whispered that King James, jealous of his son's popularity, had had Henry poisoned, while others like writer John Chamberlain said that Henry had been 'killed by bad medical practice'.

A popular figure, Henry, had he lived, could have been the monarch the dual kingdom needed. As biographer Ethel Carleton Williams noted, 'He would have introduced order into his father's debased, disorderly court and placed the finances of the country on a sound basis'. His public acclaim would have 'rallied the nation to the Crown' and perhaps averted the Civil Wars of 1642–8 and the execution of his brother Charles I.

CONSIGNED TO THE ROYAL SLAUGHTERHOUSE – James Scott, Duke of Monmouth (b. 1649), illegitimate son of Charles II and Lucy Walter of Haverfordwest.

Monmouth always claimed that he was the legal heir to the British throne as his parents were in fact married. He married Anne Scott of Buccleuch and his descendants are the Dukes of Buccleuch and Queensberry. Although Charles II did acknowledge Monmouth as his son, some historians believe that his real father was Robert Sydney, 2nd Earl of Leicester. Monmouth advanced in great favour at his father's court with a clutch of titles including the Garter. After serving in the Royal Navy under his uncle the Duke of York he joined the 1st Life Guards. A Privy Councillor for both England and Scotland he was sent on embassies to Europe and served in the French campaigns against the Dutch, and for a while was engaged in a plethora of appointments from Lord High Chamberlain of Scotland to Master of the Horse.

In 1678 the seeds of his destruction were sown. Bogus claims abounded of a supposed Roman Catholic plan to massacre Protestants and to overthrow the Protestant monarchy. A movement followed to establish a true Protestant succession with Monmouth as legitimate heir. Charles II proclaimed that he had had only one wife in Catherine of Braganza whom he married in 1661. Despite success in Scotland against the Covenanters, Monmouth greatly displeased his father because of his claims to legitimacy. He was sent into exile in Holland but returned without leave in 1679 to be received with great public popularity. Stripped of most of his positions, Monmouth was ordered to go abroad again; he refused and instead set out on a tour of the West Country ostensibly to gauge support for his cause.

Attempts at reconciliation with his father failed and Monmouth was arrested and brought to London from his tour of the Midlands; he was released on bail. Monmouth became the tool of Anthony Ashley Cooper, 1st Earl of Shaftesbury (d.1683), who deviously implicated him in the Rye House Plot of Whig extremists and old Cromwellians to assassinate Charles II and his brother the Duke of York. Monmouth fled and in absentia he was found guilty of High Treason. By agreeing to inform on his confederates he was granted pardon, but was expelled from the court and made his way to Holland.

On the death of Charles II at Whitehall Palace, 6 February 1685, Monmouth was still in Holland and made no delay in promoting his right to the throne. To this end he planned an invasion of England and Scotland to take place simultaneously. After landing at Lyme Regis on 11 June 1685 he was proclaimed king by his followers, but his army was routed at the Battle of Sedgemoor on 5 July. Escaping the battlefield, where he left his supporters to their fate, Monmouth was captured three days later, disguised as a labourer and hiding in a ditch.

Attainted for treason, Monmouth attempted a grovelling apology to the new king James II. His pleas were unsuccessful and he was imprisoned in the Tower of London. Monmouth was executed by beheading on Tower Hill, 15 July 1685. He was buried, head with severed body 'under the communion table', wrote Lord Macaulay, in the Chapel of St Peter ad Vincula in the Tower. His widow Anne Scott married again in 1688 and died a widow once more in 1732.

REBEL OF THE HEAVY COUNTENANCE – James Francis Edward Stuart (b.1688), the only surviving legitimate son of James II/VII (r.1685–88, although he remained King of Ireland until 1690) and his second wife Mary, daughter of Alfonso d'Este, Duke of Modena. James Francis Edward has come down in history as the 'Old Pretender'. On the flight of James II/VII he preceded his father into French exile where he was brought up and accepted as successor to the throne of Great Britain on his father's death in 1701. The problem with his legitimate succession was his Catholicism.

James II/VII had converted to Roman Catholicism and on his accession to the throne in 1685 trouble began because neither the populace of England nor Scotland wanted a Roman Catholic sovereign. James, however, was determined to restore Roman Catholicism to his joint kingdom and in April 1687 introduced a Declaration of Indulgence restoring the rights of Roman Catholics; opposition to the Declaration would lead to imprisonment. James's disregard for parliament, his intention to disestablish the Church of England, his cruel vindictiveness and the birth of a Roman Catholic heir in James Francis Edward, drove his nation to invite his Protestant son-in-law William of Orange to become monarch (jointly with James's daughter Mary); they were so crowned in 1689.

Supported by his followers, known as Jacobites, James Francis Edward was declared James III of England and VIII of Scotland. An abortive attempt was made to land an army in Scotland in order to overthrow James's half-sister Anne who had succeeded to the throne in 1702. Again on 26 August 1715 a rebellion broke out in Scotland under John Erskine, Earl of Mar to secure the throne for the 'Old Pretender' who joined the forces from France. Although the Jacobites succeeded in capturing Perth and Stirling, disaster occurred in the only battle of the rebellion at Sheriffmuir, near Dunblane. James returned to France in February 1716. Writing after the debacle in 1716, an anonymous 'rebel' remembered:

When we saw the man whom they called our king, we found ourselves not at all animated by his presence; if he was disappointed in us, we were tenfold more in him. We saw nothing in him that looked like spirit. He never appeared with cheerfulness and vigour to animate us. Our men began to despise him; some asked if he could speak. His countenance looked extremely heavy.

Another attempt was made to restore James Francis Edward, and this time with the help of Roman Catholic Spain, but this too ended in disaster at the Battle of Glenshiel.

James was to remain in exile in Europe for the rest of his life, taking up ultimate residence in Rome. He contracted what was to be an unhappy marriage with Maria Clementina Sobieski in 1719 but alienated his followers by neglecting her. Again the Jacobites rose in rebellion in 1745 under James's son Prince Charles Edward Stuart, 'Bonnie Prince Charlie', to confront disaster once more at Culloden in April 1746. James died in Rome on 1 January 1766 to be buried at St Peter's Basilica at the Vatican.

PRINCE WITH A PRICE ON HIS HEAD – Charles Edward Stuart (b.1720), son of James Francis Edward Stuart and Maria Sobieski. Known in history as 'Bonnie Prince Charlie'.

On 12 August 1745 he was proclaimed Prince Regent by the Jacobites and attempted to gain his grandfather's throne for his father but was defeated at Culloden, 16 April 1746 – the last battle fought on British soil. His escape from the battlefield to exile in Europe is the stuff of Scottish romantic legend in which Flora Macdonald featured and the 'loyal clansmen' who did not betray him, despite the £30,000 price put on his head by the Hanoverian government for his capture.

During his campaign in Scotland he met Clementina Walkinshaw (d.1802), the daughter of a Scottish Roman Catholic Jacobite; she followed Charles into exile as his mistress and travelled with him as his 'wife'. They had a daughter, Charlotte Stuart (d.1789), who was legitimised in 1784 and given the title Duchess of Albany. Clementina left Charles in 1790 because of his cruelty and lived for the rest of her life in Switzerland as the Comtesse d'Albestroff.

On the death of his father Charles styled himself King Charles III and in 1772 he married Louise, daughter of Gustavus Adolphus, Prince of Stolberg-Gedern; they had no offspring. Charles died in Rome on 1 January 1788 a sad drunk. He was buried in the Stuart vault at St Peter's Basilica at the Vatican.

INHERITOR WITH THE FACE OF A SHEEP – Henry Benedict Stuart (b.1725), second son of James Francis Edward Stuart and Maria Sobieski. Jacobite Duke of York.

Unlike his brother Charles Edward Stuart, Henry never pursued a claim to the British throne, although after Charles's death in 1788 he, and the Jacobite followers, styled him Henry IX. He took holy orders becoming cardinal in 1747 and bishop of Ostia, Velletro and Frascati in 1761. George III granted Henry a pension of £4,000 in 1800 after Henry had lost his fortune during the Napoleonic occupation of Italy in 1799. Henry died on 13 July 1807 and was buried in St Peter's Basilica, the Vatican. On the death of Henry the line of James II/VII came to an end, but the Stuart claimant to the British throne on the death of Henry was Charles Emmanuel IV of Italy, as heir to Charles I via his daughter Henrietta who married Philip, Duc d'Orleans. The theoretical Stuart claimant of modern times, Duke Albrecht of Bavaria, died in 1996; he was the head of the Royal House of Wittelsbach and European Jacobite fringe groups referred to him as King Albert I of England. He was succeeded by Hereditary Prince Franz, Duke of Bavaria (b. 1933).

SNATCHED BY THE GRIM REAPER – William Henry, Duke of Gloucester (b. 1689), the only surviving child of the nineteen offspring of Queen Anne (r. 1702–14) and George, son of Frederick III, King of Denmark. Perpetually sickly William died of hydrocephalus on 30 July 1700. The Bath MSS at Longleat contains this doggerel about William:

> For Gloucester's death, which sadly we deplore,
> Tho' Fate's accus'd, we should commend the more,
> Lest he with Burnet's faith should be imbu'd
> And learn of Churchill truth and gratitude;
> Lest two such masters should their rules instil
> And his young soul with pois'nous precepts fill.
> Untimely force Heav'n kindly did employ
> And to preserve the man destroy'd the boy.

The two purported bad influences the anonymous hand identified were Gilbert Burnet, Bishop of Salisbury and John Churchill, 1st Duke of Marlborough, both governors of Prince William Henry.

The House of Hanover

'MY DEAR FIRST BORN IS THE GREATEST ASS' – Frederick Louis (b.1707), Prince of Wales(1729), Duke of Gloucester(1717), eldest son of George II and his queen Caroline of Ansbach, who so described her son as above.

He married Augusta of Saxe-Gotha in 1736. It is clear that his 'unprepossessive personal appearance' – Frederick had sallow, heavy Hanoverian features – did not endear him to his parents, and despite their lack of interest in his education he grew up to be a fluent linguist. When his grandfather George I ascended the throne of Great Britain in 1714, Frederick was left behind in Hanover. He did not see his parents for fourteen years, until his father became king as George II in 1727. He was eagerly swept into London society as a dandy: 'Mein Gott,' said his mother, 'popularity always makes me sick, but Fritz's popularity makes me vomit.' Things got worse. Given nothing to do by his father Frederick became a wild leader of a bunch of young aristocrats, who found amusement in such things as smashing the windows of the townhouses of the wealthy; this he combined with heavy drinking, betting and vigorous fornication. In 1730 Frederick borrowed money to buy the White House (Kew House) near Richmond lodge, which became his favoured residence.

Frederick took up with one of his mother's maids-of-honour, the Hon. Anne Vane, eldest daughter of Baron Barnard; she was dubbed by one contemporary as 'a fat and ill-shaped dwarf'. Frederick acknowledged her two illegitimate children, Cornwall FitzFrederick and Anne FitzFrederick, but neither survived infancy; court gossips said they were more likely to be the bastards of John, Baron Hervey of Ickworth – Queen Caroline's two-faced Vice-Chamberlain – and William Stanhope, 1st Earl of Harrington.

After his marriage to Princess Augusta of Saxe-Gotha, and despite continuous dalliances, Frederick seems to have been a devoted husband and father to his nine legitimate children. His public popularity never diminished to George II's disappointment. A keen sportsman Frederick excelled at cricket and rounders, but politically he delighted in opposing whoever was in government.

In early 1751 Frederick's health began to fail, and during the evening of 20 March he died suddenly after a family supper. His doctors diagnosed a ruptured aneurysm. George II was immediately informed of his heir's death while playing cards with his mistress Amalie Wallmoden, Countess of Yarmouth. The king did not stop playing and later remarked: 'I have lost my eldest son, but I am glad.' Frederick was buried in the royal vault at Westminster Abbey, and today he is probably best remembered in this anonymous lampoon epitaph:

> Here lies poor Fred
> Who was alive and is dead:
> Had it been his father,
> I had much rather;
> Had it been his brother,
> Still better than another;
> Had it been his sister,
> No one would have missed her;
> Had it been the whole generation,
> Still better for the nation;
> But since 'tis only Fred
> Who was alive and is dead
> There's no more to be said.

THE NATION'S TRAGEDY – Charlotte Augusta of Wales (b.1796), the only daughter of George, Prince of Wales (later George IV), and his wife Caroline of Brunswick-Wolfenbüttel. If ever there was a 'miracle child', said court gossips, it was Princess Charlotte, as her father said he had no more than three 'bouts' of sex with his wife in their whole marriage. Charlotte's childhood was somewhat disrupted by the separation of the Prince and Princess of Wales soon after her birth, and the resultant jockeying between parents. As heir to the throne of her grandfather George III, Charlotte's young life was targeted towards getting her suitably married. Her father favoured the suit of Prince William of Orange (later William II of the Netherlands), but Charlotte would not countenance the union. Annoyed, her father dismissed her governess companion, Miss Cornelia Knight, and the rest of her ladies, and kept Charlotte under almost house arrest. The high-spirited Charlotte managed to flee to her mother's house in Connaught Place, and was only persuaded to return by friends and family including her uncles Frederick, Duke of York and Augustus, Duke of Sussex.

In 1814 Prince Leopold George Frederick of Saxe-Coburg-Saalfeld, Duke of Saxony, made a visit to England and Charlotte fell in love with him. They were married on 2 May 1816 in the Crimson State Room at Carlton House. Following a honeymoon spent at her uncle Duke of York's residence at Oatlands, Surrey, the couple set up home at Claremont House, near Esher.

During the early months of marriage Princess Charlotte miscarried twice, and a third pregnancy in 1817 progressed well. Yet on the evening of 5 November, after a labour of 50 hours, the princess was delivered of a stillborn son. Following the birth her treatment was said to have been mismanaged under the direction of the royal accoucheur Sir Richard Croft, and she died of post-partum haemorrhage and shock on 6 November 1817. Croft Subsequently shot himself in 1818 after losing a further patient in childbirth.

Princess Charlotte was buried at Royal Tomb House, St George's Chapel, Windsor, with her stillborn child at her feet. Her sepulchral monument by Matthew Wyatt in the Urswick Chantry shows the ascension of the princess and her baby, while their draped bodies lie on a catafalque.

The death of Princess Charlotte caused a crisis in the Royal Family. Her bachelor uncles were forced to seek spouses to ensure the succession. Her widower was elected the first King of the Belgians in 1831 and thus became the beloved 'Uncle Leopold' of Queen Victoria.

PRINCE OF DISSIPATION AND AMUSEMENT – Albert Victor Christian Edward, Duke of Clarence and Avondale, Earl of Athlone. The eldest son and first child of Albert Edward, Prince of Wales (who ruled as Edward VII) and his queen Alexandra of Denmark.

Known to his family as 'Prince Eddy', his premature birth at 3¾lb caused him to be 'swamped' with love by his mother, who included her second son George (later George V) in an intense cloying relationship. To them, even in adulthood she was 'Mother dear'. Queen Victoria was not so enamoured of these grandchildren noting that they were 'such ill-bred, ill-trained children' that she could not 'fancy them at all'. Lazy and backward with a hint, some medical historians say, of mild epilepsy, Eddy joined his brother George on a two-year trip in 1877 aboard HMS *Britannia*, and then a three-year cruise aboard HMS *Baccante*. Despite his apathetic attitude to life, his lack of interest in royal affairs, his dandyism and idle nature, Eddy was enrolled at Trinity College, Cambridge, received the usual royal appointments like the Garter and held several army positions.

Today Eddy's reputation is largely blackened by two events in 1888 and 1889. The first had him as a suspect in the famous Jack the Ripper murders fleshed out in book, film and documentary. The second cited Eddy as a player in the 'Cleveland Street Case', which centred on a homosexual brothel in the West End of London. Speculation on these matters continues to this day, and breathes oxygen into supposed royal cover-ups on Eddy's apparent bisexuality and seedy lifestyle.

While out shooting at Sandringham the cold that Eddy had caught, following his attendance at a funeral with his father, worsened. Royal physician Dr Manby diagnosed pneumonia, which was confirmed by the physician-in-ordinary to the Prince of Wales, Dr Laking, and specialist Dr Broadbent was called. To no avail Eddy died on 9 January 1892. He was buried in the Albert Chapel, Windsor, in a sumptuous marble and Mexican onyx tomb, the work of Sir Alfred Gilbert – better known for his statue of Eros in Piccadilly. Over the head of Eddy's sarcophagus an angel holds a crown and at his feet another angel weeps over a broken wedding wreath (he was engaged to Princess May of Teck). The 'Crown of Eternal Glory' depicted on the tomb was the only one that Eddy, and his seventeen historical colleague royal heirs, were ever destined to wear.

◆ Did King Alfred really burn the cakes?

Alfred found learning dead and he restored it
Education neglected and he revived it
The laws powerless and he gave them force
The church debased and he raised it
The land ravaged by a fearful enemy from which he delivered it
Alfred's name will live as long as mankind shall respect the past.
Inscription on the statue of King Alfred (1877) by Count Gleichen in Wantage town centre.

Alfred the Great, undoubtedly the most widely known of the West Saxons, was born around 847, the fourth son and fifth child of Ethelwulf and his wife Osburh; he was of the house of his grandfather Egbert, first of the great Wessex monarchs. Historians, following the lead of Alfred biographer and chaplain Asser, later Bishop of Sherborne, identify his place of birth as a royal villa, where Wantage now stands, in the Vale of the White Horse, Oxfordshire. Today Alfred remains a character of myth, his life venerated by chroniclers down the ages as the 'saviour of the Saxons' from the onslaughts of the Norsemen.

Alfred grew up in an atmosphere of great religious devotion and made visits to Rome. He is thought to have brought a period of prosperity to England, establishing burghs (defensive strongholds), designing a navy, and as a scholar promoting a written record of his era. The monk Florence of Worcester (d.1118), wrote this of Alfred in *Chronicon ex Chronicis*:

> Alfred the king of the Anglo-Saxons, the son of the most pious king Ethelwulf, the famous, the warlike, the victorious; the careful provider for the widow, the helpless, the orphan and the poor, the most skilled of Saxon poets, most dear of his own nation, courteous to all, most liberal, endowed with prudence, fortitude, justice and temperance; most patient in the infirmity from which he continually suffered; the most discerning investigator in executing justice, most watchful and devout in the service of god.

Some believe that Alfred actively encouraged monastic scribes to write up the annals known as *The Anglo-Saxon Chronicle*. Certainly the *Chronicle* contains an account of Alfred's battles and forms stirring propaganda for the ruling house of Wessex upon which throne Alfred sat during 871–899. It was Matthew Parris, the thirteenth-century Benedictine monk in his *Historia* who identifies Alfred as the first king to reign over all England, which in Alfred's time meant the land south and west of Roman Watling Street.

Alfred began his rule on 23 April 871 on the death of King Ethelred of battle wounds. In this year Wessex felt the full fury of the Norsemen (Danes), who pushed west up the Thames. They were defeated at the Battle of Ashdown. Nevertheless, Alfred was driven into Somerset to contemplate an effective counter-attack. Here was the scenario of the 'Alfred and the Cakes' story. The actual recorded tale goes like this: When Alfred was fleeing from the Norsemen and before he beat them at the Battle of Edington in 878, he took refuge anonymously in the house of a swineherd and his family. The swineherd's wife left a batch of loaves by the fire next to Alfred who sat sharpening arrows, preoccupied with his military problems. When the woman returned she saw her loaves were smouldering. Irate she berated Alfred: 'You wretch, you're only too fond of them when they're nicely done. Why can't you turn them when you see them burning?' A chastened Alfred meekly turned the loaves. The swineherd's wife's reaction when she discovered who she had been chastising is not recorded.

Where did the cakes story come from? Biographer Bishop Asser does not mention it, and the earliest traced version is in the anonymous twelfth-century *Life of St Neot*. The ninth-century ex-soldier cum-monk of Glastonbury Abbey, St Neot is believed to have been a kinsman of Alfred, perhaps even his half-brother, who Alfred consulted on various matters. St Neot was a powerful influence; some of his relics appeared at St Neots, Cambridgeshire, from where St Anslem gave a portion to the Abbey of Bec, Normandy. St Neot's life identifies the location of the swineherd's dwelling as Athelney 'in the remote parts of English Britain far to the west ... surrounded on all sides by vast salt marshes ...' That is the Somerset levels. It was Matthew Parker (d.1575), Queen Elizabeth I's Archbishop of Canterbury, in editing Asser's biography of Alfred, who gave future life to the 'cakes' story.

In 868 Alfred married Ealhswith (d.902), granddaughter of the King of Mercia, and had five children. Three of Alfred's granddaughters became wives of European monarchs, placing Alfred firmly in 'the genealogy of the royal houses of Europe'. By 896 the sinister shadows of the Norsemen had been lifted and Alfred's kingdom entered a period of peace. Alfred probably died at Winchester, 26 October 899, and modern medical historians believe that he suffered from Crohn's Disease, in part an illness of the intestinal tract. Alfred was buried in the Old Minster at Winchester, to be later interred before the high altar of the New Minster; again his cadaver was moved to the royal tombs at Hyde Abbey, a site much despoiled in later years.

The story of Alfred and the cakes has a certain plausibility about it; yet, was it a piece of pro-Alfred propaganda? Perhaps it was to show how Arthur, the great warrior, could show the spirit of meekness so prized by his devout court. Who knows, but the famous story has probably done more to keep Alfred's memory in the general public eye than his historical activities.

♦ Which monarchs were said to have healing hands?

> There was so great a concourse of people with their children to be touched for the Evil [by King Charles II], that six or seven were crushed to death by pressing at the chirurgeon's door for tickets.
>
> *John Evelyn (1620–1706), diary under the date 1684.*

The belief that the touch of a sovereign's hands could cure a variety of diseases, including ecrouelles (scrofula-tuberculosis adenitis – especially of the lymphatic glands), known as the 'King's Evil', was widespread in Europe. If we are to believe the French cleric Pierre de Blois, 'touching' for the King's Evil began in England as a ceremony at the court of Henry II (r.1154–89). Why would people believe that disease could be cured by the miraculous intervention of the sovereign's touch? Pierre de Blois explained why:

> I would have you know that to attend upon the king is [for a cleric] something sacred, for the king himself is holy; he is the Anointed of the Lord; it is not in vain that he has received the sacrament of royal unction, whose efficacy – if someone should chance to be ignorant of it or doubt it – would be amply proved by the disappearance of that plague affecting the groin and by the healing of scrofula.

Even so sources like Raphael Holinshed's (d. *c.* 1580) *Chronicles* indicated that the first English-based monarch to cure by miraculous powers was Edward, The Confessor (r.1042–66). Shakespeare, dipping into Holinshed, notes the fact in *Macbeth*. In the play we see Malcolm and Macduff fleeing from Macbeth to take refuge at the court of Edward. Here Malcolm witnesses 'the miracle':

> . . . strangely visited people,
> All sworn and ulcerous, pitiful to the eye,
> The mere despair of surgery, [King Edward] cures.
> Hanging a gold stamp about their necks,
> Put on with holy prayers; and 'tis spoken

> To the succeeding royalty he leaves
> The healing benediction.

William of Malmesbury in his *Gesta Regum Anglorum* declares that
Edward could also heal by transference. He quotes how Edward
cured a 'young woman suffereing from an appaling disease':

> The king sent for a vase of water, dipped his fingers in it, then
> touched the affected parts, signing them several times with the cross.
> Immediately blood and pus came out under the pressure of the royal
> hand, and the disease appeared to abate. The patient was kept at court,
> but the treatment does not seem to have been repeated.

The woman also seems to have been cured of sterility at the same
time. When reading of miraculous cures it is well to note that scrofula
is one of the diseases that 'can easily give the illusion of having been
cured' by perfectly non-miraculous means.

Monarchs of the House of Normandy appropriated the healing
by touch and by the reign of Edward I (r. 1272–1307), and thereafter,
those healed by 'touch' received a penny as a further mark of favour
as an update of Edward the Confessor's 'gold stamp'. In Edward II's
time (r. 1307–27) too, coins that were specially blessed were melted
down to make *anuli medicinales*; these rings were then given out as
healing talismans. As they were supposed to cure muscular pains they
were called 'cramp rings'.

A whole succession of monarchs in England and Scotland
'touched' for cures, including Mary, Queen of Scots and her
son James I/VI. However, during the Wars of the Roses period,
supporters of the House of Lancaster, which was deposed in 1471,
refused to admit that the monarchy of the House of York possessed
the miraculous gift. Charles II was 'very uncertain' about the ritual,
but James II/VII carried on the ritual even to his exile in France.
His son Prince James Francis Edward Stuart (James III/VIII to
the Jacobites) touched for the King's Evil at Glamis castle in 1716
when he visited with the Earl of Mar during the abortive attempt
to seize the throne. Hosted by Thomas, 8th Earl of Strathmore,
then aged 16, Prince James gave out silver touch-pieces to the
'patients'. These became much collected items; on the obverse St
Michael and a dragon appear with the inscription SOLI DEO

GLORIA (Glory to God alone) and on the reverse a three-masted man-of-war with JACO.III.D.G.M.B-FR ET HIB REX (James by the grace of God, King of Great Britain, France and Ireland). The last British-linked royal personage to carry out the ritual was Prince Henry Benedict, Cardinal Duke of York – younger son of Prince James Francis Edward Stuart – deemed King Henry IX by Jacobites.

William of Orange, brought to the throne by the revolution of 1688, considered 'touching' to be a complete superstition, but when Queen Anne came to the throne in 1702 she was persuaded to reinstate the ritual. Dr Samuel Johnson was 'touched' by Queen Anne in 1712 as a baby of some 30 months old. Johnson's biographer James Boswell noted: '[Johnson's] disfigured … countenance [was] naturally well-formed and hurt his visual nerves so much that he did not see at all with one of his eyes'. Queen Anne's 'healing hands' had little effect on Johnson.

Nevertheless, Anne was an enthusiastic 'toucher'; in April 1703 she touched 100 persons and in May of the same year another 200 in St James's Palace courtyard. The office remained in the English Prayer book until 1719. Even illegitimate 'royals' were deemed to have curative powers. Charles II, bastard son the Duke of Monmouth, was one; a buckle of his found after the Battle of Sedgemoor of 1685 was considered capable of affecting cures. Curiously the social anthropologist Sir James George Frazer (1854–1941), in his *The Golden Bough* (1890), pointed out that 'scrofula received its name of the King's Evil from the belief that it was caused as well as cured by contact with a king', showing how politics and denominational religion can purge the dark side of a superstition for advantage.

♦ Was King James II/VII's baby son a changeling?

Changeling: A child substituted for another.

Chambers 20th Century Dictionary.

James had caught the first glimpse of a hope which delighted and elated him. The Queen was with child.

Thomas Babington, Baron Macaulay (1800–59), History *(1848).*

In the early days of 1688, gossip began to flow through the corridors of court to the coffee houses of London that King James II/VII's second wife, Queen Mary of Modena, now married fourteen years, was absenting herself from public ceremonies. The excuse was indisposition. Few were fooled. Her Catholic ladies were hanging sacred relics around her bed for a safe pregnancy with the added prayer that the child be a son. The nation listened to the gossip with a mixture of sarcasm and apprehension.

What was extraordinary about this? Nothing. Although the monarch was 54, his wife was 29 and in full health. Although it was five years since her last pregnancy, she had borne four children, although they had all died young. Many in the nation believed that there would never be an heir to the throne from King James's loins, and considered the gossip to be the beginnings of a Jesuit plot.

King James had turned Roman Catholic in 1668 and his wife Mary was an ardent upholder of the faith. James's Declaration of Indulgence of April 1687, restoring rights to Roman Catholics to service in any administrative position, and the king's determination to overthrow the Church of England, engendered a huge anti-Catholic surge among his largely Protestant subjects. This was made worse when the pregnancy rumours were rife for triumphant Roman Catholics at the prospect of a male Catholic heir stuck in the nation's craw. As Lord Macaulay wrote in his *History*: 'The Roman Catholics would have acted more wisely if they had spoken of the pregnancy as a natural event, and if they had borne with moderation their unexpected good fortune'.

On the morning of Sunday 10 June 1688, Prince James Francis Edward Stuart was born at St James's Palace. Detractors believed that Mary had been moved from Whitehall at dead of night to the less commodious accommodation of St James's to suit nefarious Catholic purposes. For many Protestants, St James's Palace was riddled with Roman Catholic priests 'running disreputable errands along secret passages'. This birthday, though, would be kept sacred by Roman Catholics, but it set in motion another curious rumour. The gossips said that the child had been born dead and that a changeling had been smuggled into the Queen's room in a warming pan to conceal a stillbirth; and that the whole was a Roman Catholic plot. One of the promoters and believers of such a plot was Gilbert Burnet, Bishop of Salisbury, who made much of it in his *History of his own Times* published eight years after his death in 1715.

The ridiculousness of this gossip is self-evident. Purely for political purposes, such a royal birth was a public event in which many courtiers would be present. Estimates show that there were sixty-seven witnesses in the queen's bedchamber, of which eighteen were privy councillors; thus, too many persons to be privy to a conspiracy. Yet, the warming pan story was so disquieting that King James called two extraordinary sessions of his Privy Council to hear testimony that the new Prince of Wales was the son of Queen Mary by him.

Within a few months of Prince James's birth and the public announcement that he would be brought up a Roman Catholic, the coup of Whig aristocrats named the Glorious Revolution erupted, and eventually James II/VII fled his kingdom to permanent exile. The baby would enter history as the 'Old Pretender' giving birth to the movement of the Jacobites and the romance of their activities that lives on today.

◆ If Edward VIII had not abdicated who would be monarch today – and why did the abdication cause a 'royal feud'?

> Hark the Herald Angels sing,
> Mrs Simpson pinched our King.
> *Street doggerel at the Abdication, 1936.*

On the death of George V on 20 January 1936, his eldest son Edward Albert Christian George Andrew Patrick David, Prince of Wales, born at White Lodge, Richmond Park, Surrey, 23 June 1894, ascended the throne of Great Britain as HM King Edward VIII. Eleven months later at Windsor Castle he uttered these famous words in a broadcast to the nation: '… you must believe me when I tell you that I have found it impossible to carry out the heavy burden of responsibility and to discharge my duties as King as I would wish to do without the help and support of the woman I love'.

A few minutes after 2 p.m., on Saturday 12 December 1936, two days after signing the Instrument of Abdication, the king left England aboard HMS *Fury* bound for France. He was now HRH the Duke of Windsor. On 3 June 1937 the Duke of Windsor married the 41-year-old twice-divorced American, Mrs Wallis Warfield Simpson, at the house lent by Charles Bedaux, the Château de Candé in Touraine, France. A civil ceremony had been conducted by the Mayor of Monts, docteur Mercier, followed by a religious service celebrated by the Revd Robert Anderson Jardine, vicar of St Paul's Church, Darlington (who had volunteered to marry the royal couple in defiance of his bishop's order not to). Thereafter, the Duke and Duchess of Windsor entered exile until the duke's death on 28 May 1972.

When Edward VIII had become king, his brother Prince Albert, Duke of York became heir presumptive. He was not heir apparent because there was no reason why the 42-year-old king would not have children on marriage. If Edward had still been on the throne in 1952, when his brother Prince Albert (who became King George VI on Edward's abdication) died, and if Edward had had no children, then Princess Elizabeth (the present Queen Elizabeth II), Prince Albert's elder daughter would have become heir presumptive. What of Edward's other brothers? The bisexual Prince George, Duke of Kent, had died in 1942, and the next male brother after Prince Albert, Prince Henry, Duke of Gloucester, would not have become heir presumptive unless Princess Elizabeth and Princess Margaret had predeceased him. So Princess Elizabeth would have become Queen Elizabeth II on Edward's death in 1972 instead of ascending the throne in 1952.

The abdication had several other consequences for the Royal Family. On the one hand the entry of Wallis Simpson, as one historian put it, 'was to act as a catalyst in the removal of a disastrously unsuitable monarch from the British throne'; and on the other it produced an on-going 'royal feud' between the Duchess of Windsor and the new queen who eventually became Queen Elizabeth, the Queen Mother. The use of the term 'feud' in this connection seems to have originated with the Duchess of Windsor. For some thirty years the two women never met but when George VI died at the age of only 56, psychologically worn out by the stress of monarchy, the widowed Queen Mother referred to the Duchess of Windsor as 'the woman who killed my husband'. History records that the Duchess of Windsor's description of the Queen Mother ranged from the 'Dowdy Duchess' to 'the Monster of Glamis'.

Out of all of Edward VIII's sisters-in-law, Queen Elizabeth, then Duchess of York, was the closest and most supportive. All that changed when Wallis Simpson arrived in his life in 1931. Apart from his devastated mother, and his puzzled sister the Princess Royal, Elizabeth had many reasons to regret the abdication. In the first place a huge lifelong burden would pass to her shy, stuttering husband who had not been trained like his brother for monarchy; there would be stress for herself too, as now a whole new complexity entered the royal equation. Elizabeth genuinely admired Edward VIII, sustained him when he was having difficulties with his father George V, and often sought to raise his spirits.

Edward VIll – dubbed Duke of Windsor after the abdication – believed that after he sojourned in Europe for a while and after his marriage to Wallis Simpson, he could return to Britain, live at his beloved Fort Belvedere, and reinvent a role for himself (on his own terms), with his new wife at his side; a wife accepted, of course, by the Royal Family as 'Her Royal Highness'. None of this happened. It is still widely believed that the Duchess of Windsor was denied the HRH title because of Queen Elizabeth's influence over her husband.

It was said too, that driven by hatred of the Duchess of Windsor, Queen Elizabeth was completely hostile to the Windsors. Historians feel that this is an unjust view. What Queen Elizabeth resented was what the Windsors were doing to her husband. For some considerable time the Duke of Windsor showered his brother George VI with unwelcome advice, demands, complaints about perceived snubs to himself and his wife, and bullying. Wherever they went in Europe they were an embarrassment to the Royal Family back home (see chapter 9). All of which, in particular, made Queen Elizabeth nervous about their future effect on her husband. Should the Windsors come back to Britain, Elizabeth was afraid they would upstage the Royal Family in social circles. The Windsors did return to Britain in September 1939 as guests of Maj Edward and Lady Alexandra Metcalfe, but the duchess was not received by the Royal Family, and the duke only saw the king. In Columbia University, New York, in an archive of papers of Prince Paul of Yugoslavia, there is a letter dated 2 October 1939 which makes Queen Elizabeth's views on the Windsors quite clear:

I had taken the precaution to send [the Duchess of Windsor] a message before they came [as the Metcalfe's guests] saying that I was sorry that I could not receive her. I thought it more honest to make things quite clear. So she kept away, & nobody saw her. What a curse black sheep are in a family.

Wallis Simpson, the duchess, had met Elizabeth for the first time at Buckingham Palace on 27 November 1934. Commenting in 1974, the Dowager Lady Hardinge of Penhurst remembered this of the encounter:

I am afraid Mrs Simpson went down badly with [Elizabeth] from the word go. It may have been rather ostentatious dress, or the fact that she allowed the Prince of Wales to push her forward in what seemed an inappropriate manner. The Duchess of York was never discourteous in my experience, but those of us who knew her well could always tell when she did not care for something or someone, and it was very apparent to me that she did not care for Mrs Simpson at all.

Later Wallis Simpson mimicked Elizabeth's 'voice, mannerisms and facial expressions' during a party at Fort Belvedere. Elizabeth walked in as Mrs Simpson was giving her performance and one guest, Ella Hogg, noted: 'from the moment of overhearing, the Duchess of York became her implacable enemy. Mrs Simpson said she had no sense of humour'.

Queen Elizabeth certainly disliked the Duchess of Windsor's 'indiscretions' as she saw it, and her 'proprietory manner with Edward VIII'. Perhaps the Duchess of Windsor's bitterness at the perceived ill-treatment of her husband by his family outweighed any feelings she had for Queen Elizabeth. Overall both women were strong, determined characters, vital, energetic and fun loving; and both dominated their husbands; as well as being 'cheerfully fond of alcohol'. The Duchess of Windsor was once asked: 'Why the feud?' She replied that she believed Queen Elizabeth was jealous of her for marrying Edward VIII instead of him marrying her.

PRETENDERS AND USURPERS

♦ Was Empress Matilda an early promoter of
women's rights?

> On bier lay King Henry
> On bier beyond the sea.
> And no man might rightly know
> Who his heir should be.
>
> *Piers of Langtoft (1135).*

She was known as *Domina Anglorum*, 'Lady of the English', and was
born at Winchester around 1102, the only legitimate daughter of
Henry I of England and his first wife Matilda, elder daughter of
Malcolm III, King of Scots. At first she was called Alice (Aethelic),
but was renamed for her mother when, as a child, at Wilton nunnery,
she was betrothed to Heinrich V, Holy Roman Emperor and King of
Germany. The marriage ceremony took place at Mainz on 7 January
1114, and the same day Matilda – Maud to the Saxons – was crowned
Empress by the Archbishop of Cologne. Her marriage, inspired by
the politics of the day, was not happy.

Twenty years her senior, Heinrich died in 1125 leaving Matilda
a childless widow. She returned to England where the death of her
remaining brother William in the *Blanche Nef* sea disaster in 1120 had
left her heir presumptive to her father. In a wish to make his fiesty
daughter a female king (there were no queens regnant in twelfth-
century christendom), Henry I insisted that his barons swear an oath
of fealty (loyalty) to Matilda at Christmas 1126. Several Norman
barons, privately for their own safety, resented Matilda's position
of influence, considering her 'haughty and superior' like her father.
Furthermore, they did not wish to submit to the rule of a woman.
This included her cousin Stephen, Count of Mortain and Boulogne.

In 1127 Henry I arranged a second marriage for the reluctant Matilda. This time it was to Geoffrey V, Plantagenet (Angevin), Count of Anjou and Maine. Ten years older than her groom Matilda submitted to the marriage at Le Mans on 22 May 1127. To the Norman barons this was another bone of contention in Matilda's disfavour as the Angevins were hereditary enemies; the thought of a Count of Anjou as a co-ruler of England was anathema. During the marriage, however, Matilda had three sons: Henry II, King of England, Geoffrey VI, Count of Nantes and William.

King Henry I died during December 1135 and Matilda's cousin Stephen, a grandson of William I, the Conqueror, usurped her throne, to be crowned on St Stephen's Day, 26 December 1135, by William de Corbeil, Archbishop of Canterbury. Matilda made the most vigorous protest, but Stephen's usurpation was recognised by Pope Innocent II. His brother Henry of Blois, Papal Legate and Bishop of Winchester secured the treasury which Stephen now used to bribe his opponents including David I, King of Scots, his wife's uncle.

Matilda set about raising military support and landed at Arundel, Sussex, on 30 September 1139. She gathered to her several powerful barons including her half-brother, Robert, Earl of Gloucester, who defected from Stephen's court. Civil war erupted and lasted for eight years. As the *Anglo Saxon Chronicle* put it 'Christ and His Saints slept' while rape, pillage and death stalked the land. Stephen was eventually captured at Lincoln in February 1141 and was imprisoned at Gloucester's castle at Bristol. His brother Henry now turned against him and at a Legatine Council of the English at Winchester, usurper Stephen was deposed and Matilda was proclaimed 'Lady of the English', on 7 April 1141. She was never crowned, but sometimes styled herself as Queen, or more often Empress. She ruled England in her uncrowned state for less than a year, the first woman to do so for All England.

Stephen's usurpation had fired Matilda to pursue her own course. 'Fierce, proud, hard, cynical', she was the figurehead of an army to become the most prominent 'warrior queen' since Boadicea. Although arrogant, and possessor of a fiery temper, and living for politics, Matilda also showed qualities of grace and piety, particularly in making a series of pious foundations. Her independent spirit would be an inspiration for women's rights in an age when men were dismissive. The Florentine writer Petruccio Ubaldini (b. *c*. 1542) singled out Matilda as one who pursued *intervenido virilmente* (a manly role) showing that 'women can be wise, prudent and capable'. Would that her son Henry II had taken her advice against the appointment of Thomas Becket as Archbishop of Canterbury.

Stephen's supporters had not lain down their arms. The struggle continued with each side winning then losing. From time to time Matilda was in danger; once she escaped from Devises disguised as a corpse bound to a bier; again in 1142 she escaped from Oxford Castle in a white cloak to blend with the snow-covered landscape, being lowered by rope and walking unharmed over the frozen Thames. All this was recounted by Robert of Lewis, Bishop of Bath in his *Gesta Stephani* with the words '[it] was the evident sign of a miracle'. By 1144 Matilda's husband Geoffrey seized Normandy from the restored Stephen's grasp and Matilda withdrew there.

Matilda's eldest son Henry took her place in 1153 and with her old supporters continued the fight. This time the situation was resolved without more bloodshed. By the Treaty of Westminster it was agreed that Stephen would remain as king with Henry as his accepted heir. Stephen died of the consequences of appendicitis at Dover Castle on 25 October 1154, to be buried at Faversham Abbey.

Matilda thus lived to see her son set firmly on the throne of England as Henry II. She died at the Abbey of Notre Dame at Rouen on 10 September 1167, to be buried at the Convent of Bonnes Nouvelles. She was later transferred to the Abbey of Bec, to be reburied before the high altar in 1282. Her tomb became a meeting place for women of all ages seeking help and wise counsel by spiritual association. In 1847 her remains were rediscovered and reburied in Rouen cathedral. Matthew Paris in his *Chronica Majora* identified the way Matilda had shown how women could have the confidence to be influential. He said the clues were in her epitaph: '... great by birth, greater by marriage, greatest by motherhood'.

♦ Which pretender worked in the royal kitchen?

It is great pity that ye be deceived
By a false priest, that this matter began;
And that ye his child as a prince received
A boy, a lad, an organ-maker's son.

French Franciscan Friar Bernard Andre, 'Vita Henrici Septimi'.

Few entering the royal kitchens paid much attention to the young man sitting quietly in the inglenook slowly turning the spit while the king's roast spat and sizzled in the heat. Yet for a few months he had been in the cockpit of history to challenge the rights of Henry Tudor, Earl of Richmond, who now ruled England as Henry VII. The young man was Lambert Simnel and the catalyst for his rise to historical immortality took place 2 miles south of Market Bosworth.

Today the battlefield of Bosworth is set among the quiet rolling fields of Leicestershire, with modern interpretation boards to recall the events that brought an end to the thirty-year Wars of the Roses. Many still claim that Yorkist King Richard III, who died that day, was not the personification of evil as portrayed by Shakespeare. Nevertheless, Richard's seizure of the throne of England in 1483 and the imprisonment of his predecessor Edward IV's sons, Edward, Prince of Wales, and Richard, Duke of York, in the Tower of London, sparked a rebellion that brought down the House of Plantagenet. Edward, Prince of Wales was never crowned after his father's death, but he reigned for seventy-seven days as Edward V until Richard, his uncle, made himself Lord Protector and imprisoned the boys; they then vanished from public sight.

On 22 August 1485 the French-backed invasion force of some 2,500, led by Henry Tudor and his skilled tactician the Earl of Oxford, faced the 10,000-strong army of Richard III. In less than 2 hours the superior Yorkist force was negated when 4,000 men under the command of the brothers Thomas and William Stanley changed sides. Richard was unhorsed after he had killed Henry's standard-bearer William Brandon and Sir John Cheney with a war axe and died 'fighting furiously alone … in the thickest press of his enemies'. According to tradition the crown of England – probably just a diadem which had been worn by Richard over his helmet – was found hanging on a hawthorn bush. It was retrieved by a soldier and placed on Henry Tudor's head creating him Henry VII of England. Thus Henry Tudor became king by victory rather than dynastic rule. Henry had possibly the worst claim to the throne of England since William the Conqueror and it was estimated that there were at least twenty-nine people alive who had a better claim to the throne than he.

The dubious roots of his accession meant that Henry Tudor had to use considerable political guile and self-centred dedication to retain what he had won. By right of descent the person with the strongest claim to Henry's throne was 10-year-old Edward, Earl of Warwick, son and heir of the dead George, Duke of Clarence, who was therefore the nephew of Richard III. Thus Henry found reasons to have him imprisoned and later executed for treason in 1499. To strengthen his claim to the throne Henry married Elizabeth of York, the eldest daughter of Edward IV, thus uniting the houses of York and Lancaster. Richard III had declared Edward IV's children illegitimate, but Henry's Act of Parliament legitimised them again, which underlined the tenuousness of Henry's claim. Henry was beset with fears that other claimants to his throne would appear. Two significant pretenders did come forward in Lambert Simnel and Perkin Warbeck.

Lambert Simnel, the future royal kitchen boy, enters the list of pretenders when he was about 11 years of age. A child of humble origin, with a name several historians dispute, Lambert Simnel was born in Oxford in 1475, the son of a joiner, as noted by the Rolls of Parliament, although other sources say his father was an organ-maker. He was educated by an Oxford priest, Richard Simons, and Polydore Virgil says in his *Anglia Historia* that Simons 'taught the boy courtly manners'. Through Simons, Lambert Simnel came into the household of John de la Pole, Earl of Lincoln, whose uncle was Edward IV. A supporter of Richard III, de la Pole was Lord Lieutenant of Ireland and recognised as heir presumptive to the English throne. It must be remembered that during the reign of Richard III Edward IV's sons, Edward and Richard, 'The Princes in the Tower', vanished and may have still been alive when Henry VII won the throne. John de la Pole believed that he could use Lambert Simnel to further his ends.

Lambert Simnel was around the same age as claimants Edward, Earl of Warwick and the incarcerated Prince Richard of York. At first de la Pole advanced Lambert Simnel as Richard of York, then changed the pretence to Edward of Warwick. Later in 1486, ostensibly for his safety, Lambert Simnel was taken to Ireland, a haven for Yorkist supporters. Henry VII's spies reported what was going on and Henry produced the real Edward of Warwick from prison. Nevertheless, support for Lambert Simnel grew and he was duly crowned King of England in May 1487 in Christ Church cathedral, Dublin, as Edward VI.

With the support of Lambert Simnel's 'aunt' Margaret of York, Duchess of Burgundy, John de la Pole now invaded England in June

1487 with Lambert Simnel as figurehead of the army. On 16 June the invaders met Henry's forces at Stoke-on-Trent, Nottinghamshire. De la Pole was killed while Lambert Simnel was captured and imprisoned.

As he was only 12 years old, Henry pardoned Lambert Simnel and treated him kindly. He was given a job, says Polydore Virgil, as a scullion and turnspit in the royal kitchens and advanced to be the king's falconer. Simnel died around 1525. Why did the Yorkist factions go to so much trouble to promote Lambert Simnel as a claimant? On the face of it the pretence was ludicrous. Did John de la Pole, as heir presumptive, have an alternative agenda in mind, just to destabilise Henry's claim? The truth is likely never to be known.

♦ Who was the Flemish boy who would be King of England?

The little cockatrice of a king.
> *Francis Bacon,* History of the Reign of King Henry VII *(1622).*

If Henry VII thought that pretender Lambert Simnel would be the last of the impostors to threaten his throne he was disillusioned. A more serious contender appeared in the personage of one Perkin Warbeck. The tenuousness of Henry's claim to the English throne, and the uncertainty of the whereabouts or mortality of the rightful heirs, encouraged Perkin Warbeck to declare himself Richard, Duke of York, and in 1494 Richard IV, King of England. Henry feared this pretender more than anyone else in Europe.

Who was Perkin Warbeck? Modern historical research shows him to be the son of a French minor official Jehan de Werbecque and his wife Katherine de Faro. He was born in 1474 at Tournai, Flanders (now Belgium). After working as an assistant to Breton merchant Pregent Moro he was first noted in Cork, Ireland, in 1491 as a member of Moro's crew on a venture out of Portugal. Of distinctive Plantagenet looks, Warbeck spoke fluent English and had a detailed knowledge of the family and court of his supposed father Edward IV. Warbeck somewhat undermined his credibility by claiming first to be Edward, Earl of Warwick, then a natural son of Richard III, and finally Richard, Duke of York, the younger of the 'Princes in the Tower'. It seems that he was generally vague about the fate of his older 'brother' who had reigned for seventy-seven days as Edward V. Nevertheless, Warbeck managed to persuade a group of Irish, English and European noblemen of the validity of his claim to the English throne.

Warbeck was at first called from Ireland and encouraged in his claim by Charles VIII of France who wanted to use him as a figurehead in an invasion of England; Charles dumped him when he made peace with Henry VII in 1492. Warbeck's supposed 'aunt' Margaret of York, Dowager Duchess of Burgundy – sister of Edward IV – seems to have given Warbeck backing, military support and tutoring in the ways of the court. Even so, Warbeck's most important backer was Maximilian I, the German Emperor. Thus, with Maximilian's encouragement Warbeck declared himself Richard IV and in Ireland raised an invasion force.

For some twelve months Perkin Warbeck vacillated between Ireland and the Continent seeking support. Henry's agents successfully persuaded many nobles not to aid Warbeck, for by 1493 Henry was aware of the truth about Perkin Warbeck's lowly origins. Yet, Henry's northern neighbour proved an exception. James IV of Scotland received Warbeck at Stirling Castle in 1495 and decided to support him financially and militarily. The support of Warbeck fitted nicely into James's foreign policy of strengthening European alliances and the possibility of having a form of puppet king in England plus the extra prize of Berwick-upon-Tweed and other strong fortresses along the Anglo-Scottish border.

James further permitted Warbeck to marry a royal cousin, the Lady Katherine Gordon, daughter of George, 2nd Earl of Huntly, in January 1496 at Linlithgow Palace. That same year James and Warbeck crossed into England with an army of 1,400 soldiers to gather support for Warbeck's claim. Little interest was engendered and the army went no further than a handful of miles into England. The Scots army now took the excuse to settle old scores and conducted a foray of burnings, rapes and pillaging in the border region. When Richard, Lord Neville acting for Henry VII appeared with an army of 4,000 James IV scuttled back to Scotland. Sickened by the Scots pillaging, Warbeck had already made his way back to Edinburgh to make his next move.

Once back in Ireland with his new wife in July 1497 Warbeck secured support and sailed with four vessels from Wexford to England.

The Cornish had rebelled against Henry VII's taxes so Warbeck landed with his force at Whitesands Bay, near Land's End in friendly Cornwall. Leaving his wife at St Michael's Mount, Warbeck was proclaimed King Richard IV at Bodmin and made a forced march to Exeter which, in the event, was successfully defended by the Earl of Devon. Warbeck now fled with the chief officers of his court to Taunton. Lured out of sanctuary at Beaulieu Abbey, where he had escaped to avoid the advancing army led by Giles Daubeny, Warbeck threw himself on Henry VII's mercy. Appearing before the king on 5 October 1497 at the Treasurer's House at Exeter he confessed to his impostorship. Henry made him do this in front of Lady Katherine Gordon who was given every respect as a royal personage. After her husband's confession she was placed in the household of Elizabeth of York, Henry's queen. Henry was lenient, allowing Warbeck to live at court. After a madcap attempt to escape which took him as far as Sheen Abbey, where the prior begged Henry to spare Warbeck's life, he was imprisoned in the Tower of London. This was ironic in two ways; firstly, this was where the 'Princes in the Tower' – of whom he pretended to be the younger – were last seen alive, and secondly, close by was the incarcerated Earl of Warwick who he had also impersonated. In time Warbeck and Warwick, who had become somewhat simple-minded, plotted a conspiracy to escape to continue claims to the throne. This forced Henry's hand. They were both charged with treason and condemned to death; Warbeck's charge was arguably legal whereas Warwick's was murder because he was a legitimate threat to Henry's throne. Warbeck was executed by hanging, drawing and quartering at Tyburn as a common felon on 23 November 1499; he was 25.

◆ Was Lady Jane Grey a rightful queen or a child victim?

Oh, Merciful God, consider my misery, best known unto Thee; and be Thou unto me a strong tower of defence. I humbly require Thee. Suffer me not to be tempted above my power, but either be Thou a deliverer unto me out of this great misery, or else give me grace patiently to bear Thy heavy hand and sharp correction ...

Plea of Lady Jane Grey penned at the Tower of London, 11 February 1554.

Known to history as 'the Nine Days Queen', Jane Grey was the blameless sacrifice in the plots of her zealous father-in-law John Dudley, Duke of Northumberland. He endeavoured to hold the Protestant religion in sway in England following the death of the young King Edward VI in 1553, instead of the Roman Catholic dominance which would result from the crowning of Henry VIII's eldest daughter Mary. How did the 15-year-old Lady Jane Grey fall foul of England's vicious Tudor politics?

Born at Bradgate Manor, 5 miles from the market town of Leicester, on or around 12 October 1537 – the same day that Prince Edward, Henry VIII's only male heir was born – Jane Grey was the granddaughter of Princess Mary Tudor, Queen of France and Duchess of Suffolk, sister of Henry VIII; Jane was the eldest daughter of Henry and Frances Grey, later Duke and Duchess of Suffolk. Diminutive in stature yet admired for her beauty and sweetness of character, as great-niece of Henry VIII Jane was prominently placed in society and very well-educated for the day. She spent her childhood at Bradgate and the Grey's Westminster home at Dorset Place. A classics scholar with a great talent for languages and a staunch adherent of the Protestant Reformation, Jane's father's chaplain John Aylmer (d.1594), later Bishop of London, acted as her tutor. In 1546 Jane became a member of the household of Queen Catherine Parr, a close friend of her grandmother now Dowager Duchess of Suffolk. Jane's life at Queen Catherine's Chelsea Manor House, the royal court, and later the Seymour home of Sudeley Castle, Gloucestershire, when Catherine married once more, brought Jane into contact with the highest in the land. Her happy life was disrupted on the early morning of 6 September 1548, when the 36-year-old Catherine Parr died of childbirth fever, whereupon Jane became the ward of Queen Catherine's second husband Lord High Admiral, Sir Thomas Seymour, Lord Sudeley, brother of Edward, Duke of Somerset, Lord Protector of England during the minority of Edward VI.

From this point Lady Jane Grey became a political pawn. Her fate developed in this way: During his last days Edward VI signed an amendment to his late father's 1546 will – the ambiguous *Device* – setting out a new succession path for the English throne. In its hastily drafted wording Edward's half-sisters Mary and Elizabeth would not succeed him, or the descendant of his aunt Margaret, Queen of Scots. Instead the male heirs of Lady Frances (Grey), Duchess of Suffolk and niece of Henry VIII, would succeed. As there were none at this date this meant that the male heirs of Frances's surviving daughters Jane, Catherine and Mary would succeed. When the amendment was written the girls had no sons, so the Privy Council directed that the throne should go to Lady Jane Grey as heiress presumptive. There was some doubt among the Privy Councillors of the legality of the *Device* but on Edward VI's death on 6 July 1553, Jane was duly named successor and proclaimed Queen of England in London on 10 July. Jane did not want to become queen and made this disavowal: 'The Crown is not my right, and pleaseth me not. The Lady Mary is the rightful heir.' Nevertheless, she was persuaded that her ascension to the throne would help the Protestant cause. Meanwhile, Henry VIII's eldest daughter Mary, favoured successor to her half-brother, particularly by Roman Catholic interests, fled to East Anglia to muster loyal forces to her cause.

A few weeks before the succession, on 21 May 1553, Jane Grey married largely for political reasons, Lord Guildford Dudley, the 17-year-old sixth son of the 1st Duke of Northumberland at Durham House, London. The marriage was against her will and Jane was coerced into it by intimidation and violence.

The Duke of Northumberland had assumed the role of Protector of the Realm during Edward VI's reign. His scheme was to have his son declared joint-monarch with Jane. This, Jane refused to countenance, for at the beginning of her marriage she had little affection for her husband. The English nobility were unhappy with Northumberland's schemes and in the country there was growing support for Mary Tudor. Jane Grey held the title of Queen of England for nine days, 10–19 July 1553, for Northumberland's supporting army was dispersed without bloodshed and he was arrested and beheaded for treason on 22 August 1553. Jane Grey and her husband were arrested too, and imprisoned in the Tower.

At first Mary Tudor, who was crowned queen at Westminster Abbey on 1 October 1553, was prepared to be lenient to the teenage 'usurper' to her throne. But two factors brought Jane's ultimate doom nearer. Her father Henry Grey was involved in the rebellion against Queen Mary organised by Sir Thomas Wyatt and Edward Courtney, Earl of Devonshire to prevent the marriage of Mary to the Roman Catholic King Philip of Spain. Again, Jane Grey refused to recant her Protestantism.

Jane was found guilty of treason at the Guildhall, London. The sentence was death, but as Jane was of royal blood her execution had to be observed reverently. She was led to the block by Lieutenant of the Tower of London, Sir John Brydges, and accompanied by 200 Yeomen of the Guard. Witnesses said that she met her end with 'calm fortitude', yet when blindfolded she showed anxiety when she could not locate 'the block with her grasping hands'; thus aged 16 Lady Jane Grey died on Tower Green on 12 February 1554. A little earlier the same day Jane's husband was executed on the same charge at Tower Hill; a more public location. From the window of her prison Jane watched his headless body being borne away on a cart. Jane was buried without religious ceremony alongside her husband near the north wall of the chancel of the Chapel Royal of St Peter ad Vincula in the Tower, not far from the bodies of executed queens Anne Boleyn and Catherine Howard. A modern representative of Lady Jane Grey through her sister Catherine, wife of Edward Seymour, Earl of Hertford, is Beatrice Mary Grenville Morgan-Grenville, Lady Kinloss (b.1922). According to the will of Henry VIII her line has a legitimate line to the throne.

♦ Which commoner tried to push George V off the throne?

… we have a large file of correspondence about this gentleman and for some years have taken no notice of him.
George V's Private Secretary Sir Clive Wigram comments on Anthony Hall, 15 July 1931.

The arena was the Bull Ring, Birmingham. The protagonist was a former policeman who harangued the crowds saying that despite the fact that King George V had his royal posterior firmly on the throne of Great Britain, he, Anthony Hall, was the rightful heir to the throne. Hall regaled the swelling audience that he was going to 'rebuild Britain', reduce the National Debt, develop overseas trade, boost the homeland economy and nationalise the public services for the good of the nation … all when he was crowned King Anthony I. More than that, he said he had 'explosive evidence' that would topple the House of Windsor forever.

His pronouncements only raised a perfunctory eyebrow in Whitehall and Buckingham Palace, but when Hall started to make scurrilous attacks on George V, with threats to assassinate him, the authorities decided to act and he was shadowed by Special Branch. As far as the public was concerned, it was emphasised in the corridors of power that George V's anxiety about and involvement in the counter-action should remain secret.

Anthony Hall was born in 1898 at Little Dewchurch, near Hereford, and served in the Shropshire constabulary as an inspector; later he became an export trader. Hall told his listeners that he was the direct descendant of one Thomas Hall, the bastard son of Henry VIII. To strengthen his case that his forebears should have succeeded to the throne on the death of Elizabeth I in 1603, Hall assured his audience that King James I/VI was a 'changeling' who could not have been the son of Mary, Queen of Scots, because he was deformed with a head too large for his body and legs so weak that he could neither walk nor ride. He even cited one James Erskine, who as a baby had taken King James's place. He went on: 'Now we know that [James I/VI] was an impostor and I will therefore call him the missing link. ... In fact he is the cause of all the trouble because having proved that he was an impostor, it is obvious that all the kings who claim to be descendents of his are not entitled to their jobs ...'

On 2 February 1931 Hall fired off an open letter to George V, which was taken up by the national press, stating his claim and urging the king to surrender the 'Imperial Crown'. He challenged George V to a fight in court with the loser to be executed. Hall's public posturing was highlighted to the Labour government's Home Secretary J.R. Clynes's civil servants by Birmingham's Chief Constable. On 6 July 1931 he wrote: 'It is quite evident that this man's mind is not steadily balanced and in the ordinary course no notice would be taken of him; but his references to the King are highly offensive and it might be desirable to stop this man behaving as he is doing.' The police further noted that Hall said he 'would have no hesitation shooting [George V] as he would a dog. The King [is] German and has no right to rule our country.'

The king's private secretary Sir Clive Wigram (d.1960), became involved because George V had been fully informed of the events in his red boxes; he asked if Hall's 'effusions' could not be stopped? Wigram wrote to the Home Office on 13 July 1931 from Buckingham Palace: 'His Majesty quite agrees that a stop should be put to his effusions but feels that it might not look very well for a man who is obviously demented to get 6 months imprisonment. Would it not be possible to keep him under observation with a view to his final detention in an Institution, without actually putting him in prison?'

Documents released for public consumption at the National Archives, Kew, in 2006 show that Hall was summonsed. Despite Special Branch monitoring that Hall had left the Shropshire Police in 1919 in disgrace, and that he had been gassed during the First World War and was clearly barmy, they took the threats seriously. After making further 'scurrilous attacks' on George V on 24–5 July 1931 Hall was arrested. On George V's insistence he was interviewed by two doctors, Walter Jordan and Hamblin Smith, but neither felt that they could certify Hall as insane. Hall was found guilty in court and fined £25 for a breach of the peace.

On 12 August 1931 Hall gave a further public haranguing at the Bull Ring, boasting the authorities had failed to find him insane or send him to prison. He made a public farewell and disappeared from view. Hall died in 1947 leaving no male heir. His brother, based in the United States, did not follow up the Hall claim and the House of Windsor received no further dynastic threats from this source.

◆ Who was England's 'Lost Queen'?

How do I thank thee, Death, and bless thy power
That I have passed the guard and 'scaped the Tower!
And now my pardon is my epitaph
And a small coffin my poor carcase hath;
For at thy charge both soul and body were
Enlarged at last, secure from hope and fear
That among saints, this among kings is laid,
And what my birth did claim my death has paid.
Lines by the Bishop of Norwich at the death of Lady Arbella Stuart.

Look down the family tree of Lady Arbella Stuart and her name appears boldly among the dynasties of the Tudors and Stuarts.

See how the spider's web of branches trace her back to her great-great-grandfather Henry VII of England, down through her great-grandmother Margaret, Queen of Scots, her grandmother Margaret, wife of Matthew Stuart, 4th Earl of Lennox, to her father Charles Stuart, 6th Earl of Lennox (d.1576) and mother Elizabeth Cavendish (d.1581), brother and sister-in-law of Henry Stuart, Lord Darnley, second husband of Mary, Queen of Scots. There Arbella's name sits alongside her husband William Seymour, who in time became Duke of Somerset, who could also trace his lineage back through Mary, daughter of Henry VII. Together they made a dangerous dynastic threat to others seeking the throne.

Arbella Stuart (Latinised: Arabella) was born around 10 November 1575 at the Hackney house of her paternal grandmother Margaret, Lady Lennox, and christened at the parish church of Chatsworth. Charles Stuart, her father, died when Arbella was 18 months old, leaving her mother Elizabeth in strained financial circumstances. Elizabeth died when Arbella was 6 and the child was now in the charge of her grandmother, four times married Elizabeth Talbot, Countess of Shrewsbury, known to history as the redoubtable, ambitious 'Bess of Hardwick'. Well-educated, and because of her background, Arbella knew well the courts of Elizabeth I – who thought her pushy and arrogant – and James I/VI. To James she was an unsettling figure; she was after all James's first cousin and to many Arbella had a more legitimate right to the throne than James on the death of Queen Elizabeth in 1603. James was the senior descendant of Henry VII, but had not Henry VIII's will declared that all 'aliens' be excluded from the succession? Born in Scotland in 1566 James was considered by some as an 'alien', but Arbella being English-born was not an alien in these terms. Thus, to James's supporters Arbella was a dynastic threat.

In the early months of his reign James ignored the tortuous rumours that linked Arbella with alleged plotting against him by such men as Henry Brook, 8th Lord Cobham and Sir Walter Raleigh. Their scheme was to depose James and put Arbella on the throne; their machinations earned them a capital sentence which James countermanded in his own idiosyncratic way at the last minute. Until 1609 James then treated Arbella with kindness yet parsimony. He kept her at court where he could keep an eye on her. But alas, her marriage caused her to descend into disaster.

Over the years Arbella's name was linked for future matrimony 'with every single prince in Christendom'. Yet her romance with William Seymour is somewhat lacking in historic detail. By 2 February 1610 they were betrothed and married on 21 June. Arbella's marriage to Seymour was provocative to King James; it had been in secret and without the permission of her royal cousin. This act of 'virtual treason' to a man twelve years her junior had sent King James into a frenzied fit. Not only was a royal prerogative slighted, but Seymour was a dynastic threat, for he was a grandson of Lady Catherine Grey who was of the line descending from Margaret Tudor. So for her secret marriage James put William Seymour in the Tower and Arbella under house arrest at Lambeth with plans to move her out of harms way to the north of England under the supervision of the Bishop of Durham. En route for Durham, Arbella fell ill (or pretended to be so), and the party lodged at a 'sorry inn'. From here, on 3 June 1611, dressed as a man, she slipped away from her captors, for both she and her husband had planned a double yet separate escape. William effected a successful escape but was delayed by a rapid hue-and-cry from making rendezvous with Arbella. Incandescent with rage King James ordered the Lord High Admiral, the Earl of Nottingham, to organise a pursuit as the escapees made their separate ways to France. The pursuit was carried out by Admiral Sir William Monson. Arbella's party was able to join Captain Corvé's French barque to take them to France, however, just off Calais Arbella was caught by Captain Griffen Cockett's pinnace *Adventure* and she was returned to England. William Seymour successfully escaped to Ostend. In time he made his peace with James and received the Garter and the dukedom of Somerset in the year of his death, 1660.

After capture James incarcerated Arbella in the Tower as a 'close prisoner' under the Lieutenant of the Tower Sir William Waad (or Wade). Although in close confinement she was allowed servants. Her health declined and she was reported to be 'dangerously sick of convulsions' to which was added that she 'continues crakt in her brain'. Plots flowed round her for her escape but they came to nothing. At length she died on 25 September 1615; some said she had been poisoned, but she is more likely to have died from malnutrition. In death she had a little more honour, although King James ordered that there be no court mourning for his royal cousin. James further ordered that her coffin be laid inside the tomb which he had constructed for his mother Mary, Queen of Scots, whose cadaver was moved from Peterborough Cathedral to Westminster Abbey. This is a strange quirk of fate: When Mary Stuart fled to England after her deposition, one of her successive custodians was Bess of Hardwick at the Shrewsbury family country houses of Sheffield Castle, Sheffield Lodge and Chatsworth. There Arbella, Mary Stuart's niece-in-law, had been her child companion.

There is some doubt among historians whether or not Arbella had any pretensions to the throne of England and Scotland, despite the possible brainwashing to this end by her maternal grandmother Bess of Hardwick. So Arbella Stuart has lain in Westminster Abbey scarcely noticed yet had she been male, she might have succeeded to the throne after all.

♦ Which rival queen disturbed Elizabeth I's peace of mind?

Never did any human creature meet death more bravely; yet, in the midst of the admiration and pity which cannot be refused her, it is not to be forgotten that she was leaving the world with a lie upon her lips [i.e. that she never in word, thought or deed conspired to the death of Elizabeth I]. She was a bad woman, disguised in the livery of a martyr.
James Anthony Froude (1818–94), assessment of Mary, Queen of Scots.

The hubbub of 300 voices fell silent as the tall woman in black satin entered the great hall of Fotheringay Castle. She clutched a crucifix and prayer book in her hand as she walked with dignity, though stooped with illness, through the silent ranks of Elizabeth I's loyal subjects. As she reached the centre of the great hall she saw for the first time a wooden stage, hung with black. By two stools stood the Earls of Kent and Shrewsbury who had accompanied the warrant signed by Elizabeth I ordering the event on this day of Wednesday 8 February 1587. Near to the earls was placed a cushioned stool and glinting on the floor adjacent was a great axe by a beheading block.

The lady was handed up onto the stage and listened without emotion as the commission for her execution was read out. She ignored Richard Fletcher, Dean of Peterborough, as he intoned Protestant prayers; almost as a duet she read aloud from a Latin psalter prayers of her own faith. When she had finished the executioner, Bull, who was to be paid £10 for his duty, knelt before her to ask for forgiveness. She granted it. As she disrobed her outer dress, helped by her attendants Jane Kennedy and Elizabeth Curie, the crowd gasped to see the dark red petticoat. Was this the final insult to the Protestant nobles assembled? Did the lady flaunt the liturgical colour of martyrdom of the Roman Catholics?

A white cloth embroidered with gold was tied round the lady's eyes and head. She knelt on a cushion in front of the block. The silence was broken only by the lady's clear voice: '*In te Domino confido, non confundar in aeternum.*' (In you Lord is my trust, let me never be confounded.)

She laid her head on the block and stretching out her arms she said: '*In manus tuas Domine, confide spiritum meum.*' (Into your hands O Lord I commend my spirit.)

As the clocks of the castle rang the hour of 10 a.m., the axe fell twice to sever the lady's head. 'So perish all the Queen's enemies', shouted the Dean of Peterborough. The 'enemy' was Mary, Queen of Scots, and on that day she was 44 years old and had been in English captivity for nineteen years, but all her life she had been a rival for the throne of England and a particular thorn in the flesh of Elizabeth I.

At her accession on 17 November 1558 Elizabeth Tudor had certain difficulties. Her Catholic subjects desired to be united fully with Rome and have their position restored in the establishment. They tended to uphold Mary Stuart's claim and were inclined, too, to support Catholic Spain whose ruler Philip II wished to marry his sister-in-law Elizabeth Tudor as a dynastic political move. However, the greatest disturbance to Elizabeth's peace of mind was a Roman Catholic challenge from Mary Stuart.

Mary Stuart became Queen of Scots at the age of 6 days old when her father James V died in shame and disgrace at Falkland Palace after his rout by the English at Solway Moss in 1542. At the age of 16 Mary became Queen of France as the consort of Francis II and boldly claimed the throne of England through her grandmother Margaret Tudor, Queen of James IV of Scots and sister of Henry VIII. In Roman Catholic eyes Mary's case was strengthened by the fact that they did not recognise Henry VIII's divorce from Catherine of Aragon, thus rendering Elizabeth Tudor a bastard. Again, in 1570 Pope Pius V issued a bull of 'excommunication and deposition' against Elizabeth making toleration of Roman Catholicism in England no longer possible; this also hardened Roman Catholic opposition to her among her subjects.

When Francis II died in 1560 Mary, Queen of Scots, returned to Scotland to rule a land riven with intrigue as the Protestant nobles, 'The Lords of the Congregation', jockeyed for position and feathered their nests from the dismantling of the medieval church's property following the Reformation. They feared, too, an annexation to Catholic France with the coming of Mary. Mary's life was now filled with plot, counterplot, murder and martial conflict. In 1566 her Italian secretary was murdered; in 1567 her second husband Henry Stuart, Lord Darnley was murdered and her third husband, James Hepburn, Earl of Bothwell, was generally regarded as one of Darnley's murderers; consequently Mary was considered to have turned a blind eye to the murder. The same year as Darnley's death Mary's loyal troops were defeated at Carberry Hill and again in 1568 at Langside. She escaped to England and throwing herself on the mercy of Elizabeth I was incarcerated for her pains. Mary now became the focus of plots to assassinate Elizabeth I and put Mary on the throne of England. The Ridolfi Plot (1571), the Throgmorton Plot (1583) and the Babington Plot (1586), all to this end, failed. The result was Mary's execution in which justification was set out of the interests of England's subjects and the ideas of the time. Whether or not Mary was a party to the assassination plots is a matter of conjecture, but she did encourage rebellion and while she lived she was a source of danger to Elizabeth. Mary paid the price, yet to execute a crowned monarch in exile was unjust. Elizabeth showed further meanness and cowardice in trying to avoid all responsibility for Mary's death, punishing her loyal servants William Davidson, her second secretary, and William Cecil, Lord Burghley, Chief Minister, for carrying out her orders.

It has been disputed that Mary was a pretender to the English throne at all. Mary never proclaimed herself as an heir superior to Elizabeth. Her objective seems to have been recognition as the rightful heir to the throne on Elizabeth's passing. After all, it was the Pope and the King of France who promoted Mary as a pretender, the latter making Mary quarter the arms of England on her escutcheon and allowing herself to be called Queen of Scotland, England and Ireland. A constant problem too was that Elizabeth showed no desire to nominate an heir, saying that to do so 'set a winding sheet before my eyes'.

THE PLOTS AGAINST QUEEN ELIZABETH I INVOLVING MARY, QUEEN OF SCOTS

The Ridolfi Plot, 1571

Roberto Ridolfi was a Florentine banker and papal agent in London who channelled Vatican money into England to assist Roman Catholic interests. Even so he was a double agent. He played a role in distributing the 1569 Papal Bull of Pius V excommunicating Elizabeth I and denying her legitimacy to the English throne. The plot's intention was to enlist a Spanish army of invasion to support a parallel English Roman Catholic uprising, under the leadership of Thomas Howard, 4th Duke of Norfolk, and place Mary on the throne. Denied of her liberty Mary was only too willing to encourage 'madcap and dangerous schemes from her escape'. Ridolfi set out for the Low Countries to meet Philip II of Spain's military commander the Duke of Alva. The duke was lukewarm about the scheme, but in Rome Ridolfi gained more support and in Madrid Philip was enthusiastic. Sir Francis Walsingham's intelligence network – aided by Ridolfi's double-dealing – apprehended letters and ciphers concerning the plot, backed up by confessions under torture. Mary was instantly and incontrovertibly implicated, particularly by her envoy, John Lesley, Bishop of Ross, who crumpled under the threat of torture. Norfolk went to the block on 2 June 1572 and Elizabeth refused her House of Commons pleas to arraign Mary for treason. Confronted with her complicity Mary remained defiant and self-righteous. Elizabeth realised that Mary was prepared to have her assassinated, thus any 'sisterly solidarity' between them was at an end.

The Throgmorton Plot, 1583

From the late 1570s Roman Catholic priests began to appear in England and Pope Gregory XIII issued a new Papal Bull of excommunication against Elizabeth. In 1581 anti-Roman Catholic Statutes were passed to stem the dissemination and practice of the faith on political rather than spiritual grounds. Mary Stuart gave tacit encouragement to any plots, schemes and intrigues that were notified to her. One significant plot discovered by Sir Francis Walsingham's agents was a plan put together by the French 3rd Duc de Guise, Philip II of Spain and Mary, with the prominent English Roman Catholic Sir Francis Throgmorton as go-between. The plan was to sponsor invasion, rescue Mary and murder Elizabeth. In November 1583 Throgmorton was arrested and under torture confessed; Mary denied complicity, but the Spanish Ambassador Bernardino de Mendoza was expelled.

The Babington Plot, 1586

From 1585 'a motley crew of English refugees, religious fanatics, double agents and romantic hotheads' planned a new rescue of Mary Stuart and Elizabeth's murder. The leader was Father John Ballard who recruited a 25-year-old Roman Catholic gentleman, Anthony Babington, 'to play the hero and rescue Mary'.

He unwisely put his plans in a letter to Mary. His letter was read by Walsingham's agents who let it pass to Mary. Would she reply and incriminate herself? She did. Unwilling to delay arrests, Elizabeth ordered them and all the conspirators were caught. Elizabeth was horrified at 'Mary's enthusiasm for her death'. At last Mary was arrested and tried for treason. On 20 September 1568 Babington was brutally executed, followed by the beheading of Mary on 8 February 1587.

♦ Which regicide was called 'Old King Noll'?

> His grandeur he deriv'd from heaven alone,
> For he was great e'er fortune made him so
> And wars like mists that rise against the sun
> Made him but greater seem, not greater grow,
>
> No borrowed bays his temple did adorn
> But to our Crown he did fresh jewels bring;
> Nor was his virtue poison'd soon as born
> With the too early thoughts of being king.
> *John Dryden (1631–99), 'Heroick Stanzas consecrated to His Highness Oliver' (1658).*

The Dutch produced a whole series of cartoons showing Oliver Cromwell (1599–1658) with the regalia of kingship, and J. Schex painted the brooding portrait of Cromwell refusing the Crown of Great Britain after the execution of Charles I in 1649. Nevertheless, Schex caught an emotion of doubt in Cromwell's face. Was 'Old Noll', as detractors sometimes called him, really tempted to have himself crowned king? A pretender manqué?

In 1657 during the first session of Cromwell's Second Parliament – for England was declared a Free Commonwealth after Charles I execution – 'The Humble Petition and Advice' offered the crown to Oliver Cromwell as part of a revised constitutional settlement. This presented Cromwell with a dilemma. Cromwell was instrumental in abolishing the monarchy, yet for six weeks he agonised over the offer. At first he was attracted by it, for it offered a certain degree of stability for the country. But the army leaders, and more so the common soldiery, were strongly hostile to the 'trappings of monarchy'. So, in a speech of 13 April 1657, Cromwell said that God's providence had spoken out against the monarchy and he continued: 'I would not seek to set up that which Providence hath destroyed and laid in the dust, and I would not build Jericho again.' He contented himself with the right to nominate his successor.

Nevertheless, Cromwell was ceremonially installed as 'Lord Protector of the Realm' at Westminster Hall, with many of the symbols and regalia of monarchy. Cromwell came into the hall clad in robes of purple velvet, lined with ermine. He processed to the Coronation Chair which had been brought from Westminster Abbey; he sat on it despite its taint of centuries of kingship. Before Cromwell, on a table, lay a Bible, and the sword and sceptre of the Commonwealth. The only person seated near him was the Speaker of the House of Commons. As soon as Cromwell had taken the oath, the fanfare of trumpets sounded and the heralds assembled proclaimed him 'Lord Protector of the Commonwealth of England, Scotland and Ireland' (this time omitting the word 'Realm'). Oliver Cromwell sat without a crown, for his republicans had destroyed the crown of kings.

Ironically, too, the office of Lord Protector had greater powers than Charles I ever had. There followed a promulgation of a written constitution known as the 'Instrument of Government' and Cromwell ruled the Commonwealth with a council of twenty-one and a parliament of 460 members; even so he was virtually a dictator. Thereafter Cromwell was often addressed as 'Your Highness' and from this date he conferred knighthoods. Although parliament had given Cromwell the palace of Hampton Court after the Battle of Worcester (1651), Cromwell and his wife Elizabeth Bourchier held court mostly at Whitehall Palace, to surround themselves with a fair degree of pomp, much to the disgust of his ascetic supporters. Elizabeth Cromwell also attracted much venom for her imperiousness. Cromwell had an 'inner court' of 'fifty soberly dressed gentlemen and [was] guarded by scarlet soldiers'. Although Westminster Palace 'was the scene of more prayer than revelry' than had been during royal times, Puritan circles were scandalised by 'dancing until dawn to the strains of forty-eight violins' when Cromwell's daughters married. Cromwell embellished Hampton Court and he extravagantly imported horses from Tripoli and Aleppo; 'the Court never had better stables than under the Protector', one biographer wrote. Republicans who had supported Cromwell in the country and in parliament felt betrayed; many pamphleteers spoke out against his 'trappings of kingship' like the Quakers James Nayler and George Fox.

Cromwell did not hold his office for long; in 1658 he was struck down by malarial fever (probably first contracted while he campaigned in Ireland in 1649) and urinary symptoms; he died at Whitehall on 3 September. Cromwell was interred in a huge vault specially constructed at the eastern end of Henry VII's chapel at Westminster Abbey. He had a funeral resplendent with state honours. Diarist John Evelyn left this record:

October 22, 1658: Saw the superb funeral of the Protector. He was carried from Somerset House in a velvet bed of state, drawn by six horses, housed with the same; the pall held by his new Lords; Oliver lying in effigy, in royal robes, and crowned with a crown, sceptre, and globe, like a king. The pendants and guidons were carried by the officers of the army; the Imperial banners, achievements, etc., by the heralds in their coats; rich caparisoned horse, embroidered all over with gold; a knight of honour, armed cap-à-pie, and, after all, his guards, soldiers, and innumerable mourners. In this equipage, they processed to Westminster; but it was the joyfullest funeral I ever saw; for there were none that cried but dogs, which the soldiers hooted away with a barbarous noise, drinking and taking tobacco in the streets as they went.

Republicans in the crowd were dismayed at the regal pomp of Cromwell's cortege when they remembered the solemnity and pathos of the burial of Charles I at St George's Chapel, Windsor, on 9 February 1649, attended by a few friends and the faithful William Luxton, Bishop of London.

Despite being succeeded by his incompetent son Richard, who resigned on 25 May 1659, Cromwell's Protectorate fell and parliament restored Charles II to the kingdom in 1660. In 1661 Cromwell's cadaver was exhumed from Westminster Abbey. It was drawn through the streets on a hurdle (a rough sledge) to Tyburn, hanged on a three-cornered gibbet for 24 hours, all on the anniversary of Charles I's execution, 30 January. Eventually his severed head was displayed on a pole outside Westminster Abbey until 1695 when it fell off during a storm. The head changed hands several times to be buried in 1960 in the grounds of Sidney Sussex College, Cromwell's Alma Mater.

ROYAL MARRIAGES
AND ROMANCES

♦ Which king expressed his love in stone
monuments?

Where 'ere my lady's holy bier did lie
King Edward built a cross where all might pray.

Anonymous Victorian verse.

Edward I, of the House of Anjou, by-named 'Longshanks',
(r. 1272–1307), was born at the Palace of Westminster on 17 June
1239, the eldest son of Henry III and Eleanor of Provence. At the
age of 15 he married at the monastery of Las Huelgas, 13-year-old
Eleanor of Castile, Countess of Ponthieu, daughter of Ferdinand III,
King of Castile and his wife Jeanne de Dammartin. It was a political
union to help protect England's last foothold in France, the southern
borders of Gascony. Eleanor was known as 'the Infanta of Castile',
and in English parlance this sounded like 'Elephant and Castle', a
title given to many taverns. Although disputed, it is said this was the
name derivation of the district of south London which has been a
confused traffic junction since the seventeenth century.

Throughout their married life Edward and Eleanor were inseparable;
she even accompanied him on crusade in 1270. The mother of
sixteen children by Edward, Eleanor died of a fever at Harby, near
Grantham, Nottinghamshire, on 24 November 1290 in the house of
one Master Weston. She was on her way north to join Edward, then
in Scotland, to advance his incursions. Edward was stricken with grief
at her death. At first her body was taken to St Catherine's Priory,
Lincoln, but on the route that her embalmed cadaver was conveyed
to London Edward ordered the erection of stone monuments at
the sites where her body rested each night. The monuments were
in the form of elaborate crosses; twelve in all. The crosses at Lincoln

(fragment in Lincoln castle), Grantham, Stamford (fragment), Stoney Stratford (destroyed in the Civil War), Woburn, Dunstable, St Albans and West Cheap (now Cheapside, fragment in the London Museum) have vanished. Three remain. At Waltham, Hertfordshire, the cross is polygonal in shape with pedestals showing decorated shields of Ponthieu, Castile, Laon and England, with accompanying statues of Eleanor. The cross at Geddington, once a royal hunting lodge, is triangular and is the best preserved. The cross at Hardingstone, outside Northampton, is set near Delapre Abbey and is the work of John of Battle and dates from 1291. All are fine examples of Gothic art and the new decorated style pioneered by Edward I's masons. Edward was probably inspired to erect his crosses by similar wayside crosses he had seen in France; certainly the passage of the bones of Saint Louis IX, on their way from Paris to burial at St Denis, were similarly marked.

Probably the best known cross is associated with Charing Cross, London, once known as King Mews, which here in Edward's day was a hamlet. The cross was the work of the king's mason Richard of Crundale, assisted perhaps by his son Roger. Of Caen stone the cross was surrounded by Corfe marble statues of Eleanor by Alexander of Abingdon. In a decayed state it was finally destroyed by the Puritans in 1647. In 1863 a replica cross, still in place, was erected at the cost of £1,800 in the forecourt of Charing Cross station. A design by A.S. Barry has statues by Thomas Earp.

Eleanor's body was entombed in the Confessor's Chapel, Westminster Abbey, at the feet of her father-in-law Henry III. Her gilt-bronze effigy still conveys something of the serenity and beauty which first captivated Edward I. Her viscera were buried at Lincoln cathedral, and although this monument was destroyed during the Civil War, a replacement was set in place in 1891. Eleanor's heart was buried at the Dominican monastery of Blackfriars, London, a house destroyed at the Dissolution of the Monasteries.

♦ Why did Henry VIII marry six times?

Choose yourself a wife you will always and only love.
Advice of John Skelton (c. 1460–1529), created poet laureate by Oxford and Cambridge universities, to pupil Prince Henry (later Henry VIII), in 'Speculum Principis', (c. 1499).

Henry VIII's marriage records read like this:

1. Catherine of Aragon (1485–1536), daughter of Ferdinand II, King of Aragon and Isabel I, Queen of Castile, married at Greyfriars Church, Greenwich, 11 June 1509. Marriage annulled, 23 May 1533. Six children; only one survived, became Queen Mary I.

2. Anne (*c.* 1500–36), daughter of Thomas Boleyn, Earl of Wiltshire and Ormonde and Lady Elizabeth Howard, married at York Place (later Whitehall Palace), 25 January 1533. Marriage declared invalid, 17 May 1536. Three children; one ruled as Elizabeth I. Executed.

3. Jane (*c.* 1508–37), daughter of Sir John Seymour and Margery Wentworth, married at Whitehall Palace, 30 May 1536. Died in childbirth. Son became King Edward VI.

4. Anne (1515–57), daughter of Johann II, Duke of Cleves and Marie of Julich and Berg, married at Greenwich Palace, 6 January 1540. Marriage annulled, 9 July 1540. No offspring.

5. Catherine (*c.* 1520–42), daughter of Lord Henry Howard and first wife Joyce Culpeper, married at Oatlands Park, Surrey, 28 July 1540. No offspring. Executed.

6. Catherine (*c.* 1512–48), daughter of Sir Thomas Parr of Kendal and Maud Green, married at Hampton Court Palace, 12 July 1543. Outlived Henry to marry again. No offspring.

Although Catherine of Aragon became Henry VIII's first queen she was first married to his brother Arthur, Prince of Wales, on 14 November 1501. Five months after the marriage, the consumptive, syphilitic Arthur died at Ludlow Castle. Had the marriage been consummated – 'last night I was in Spain', boasted Arthur – did he infect his wife with syphilis? These were to remain mysteries to be raked over later, for Catherine insisted that she came out of her first marriage *virgo intacta*.

By 1503 Catherine was proposed as a bride for Prince Henry; a papal dispensation was obtained from Pope Julius II for Henry to marry his brother's widow, yet Henry VII dithered in pressing for the marriage ceremony as he hoped for a better candidate for Henry's nuptial bed. No such candidate appeared, and on the death of Henry VII in 1509, Henry ardently in love, married Catherine at Greyfriar's Church, Greenwich on 11 June. Four children were born; three stillborn and one who lived barely eight weeks, until in

1516 Catherine gave birth to Mary Tudor. Another stillborn birth occurred in 1518, following two further miscarriages. Catherine had no more pregnancies.

Henry and Catherine ceased to co-habit in 1526 and the following year the long divorce process began. The basis of Henry's divorce suit was affinity; that is it was 'illegal' for him to marry his brother's widow despite the Pope's dispensation. Although Catherine had powerful support from her nephew, the Emperor Charles V, and in Rome, a compliant Thomas Cranmer, Archbishop of Canterbury, declared the marriage null and void on 23 May 1533 and an Act of Parliament sealed the issue.

Catherine was demoted to Dowager Princess of Wales. Throughout she refused to accept the divorce and died of cancer at Kimbolton Castle on 7 January 1536. The queen Henry had loved with a deep devotion and whose spirit was never crushed by the divorce was buried at Peterborough Cathedral.

Contemporary commentators suggest that Henry also fell in love with his second wife Anne Boleyn. Anne knew the ramifications of court life well. Her father held various diplomatic posts and she served as a court lady in the household of Henry VIII's sister Mary, Queen of France, then that of King Louis XII of France's daughter Claude, and by 1521 she was back in England as maid-of-honour to Queen Catherine of Aragon.

Anne's French court manners were considered charming by the young gentlemen at Henry VIII's court. Records show that she had a probable sexual relationship with Henry Percy, son of the Earl of Northumberland, then resident in the household of Cardinal Wolsey. It is likely too that they had some sort of betrothal agreement. Her name was also linked with the notorious adulterer Sir Thomas Wyatt, whose pursuit of Anne would later earn him a sojourn in the Tower. Henry VIII paid her increasing attention too, transferring his affection from his mistress, Anne's elder sister Mary Boleyn. For some time Anne fended off Henry's advances, but kept him interested with coquettish flirting and amorous letters. Probably she became his mistress around 1527 and in 1532 Henry made her Marchioness of Pembroke. Anne was pregnant by Henry in December 1532, and at that point a divorce from Catherine of Aragon loomed prominently in Henry's mind.

The divorce was sealed by parliament in May 1533, but Anne and Henry had been secretly married on 25 January that year; five days after the divorce Anne was crowned queen, the last queen consort ever to have a separate coronation. Anne gave birth to Princess Elizabeth on 7 September and Henry's disappointment at not having a son meant his ardour for Anne diminished. By 1534 he had taken up with one of Anne's ladies-in-waiting, Jane Seymour.

The loss of a possible male heir by miscarriage in 1536 brought Anne's fate nearer. A commission was set up to examine her conduct. In time, on no real evidence and dubious accusations extracted by torture, Anne was accused of an incestuous relationship with her brother George, Viscount Rochford, and treasonous adultery with a gentleman of the King's Chamber Henry Norris. The superstitious, too, noted that the deformity on one of her hands (a rudimentary sixth finger) indicated that she was a witch. Anne was arrested and taken to the Tower where she was interrogated about her life and relationships. On 17 May 1536 an ecclesiastical court declared the royal marriage null and void *ab initio* (from the beginning); again the pretext of affinity was quoted because of Henry's relationship with Mary Boleyn.

Anne was condemned to death and beheaded on Tower Green on 19 May 1536, to be buried at the Chapel of St Peter ad Vincula. Just before her death Anne summed up her royal progress: 'The king has been very good to me. He promoted me from a simple maid to be a marchioness. Then he raised me to be a queen. Now he will raise me to be a martyr.'

A day after the execution of Anne Boleyn, Henry announced his betrothal to Jane Seymour and they were married eleven days later. Jane Seymour was half second-cousin to Anne Boleyn so she was not out of place as maid of honour to Catherine of Aragon and Anne Boleyn, despite her somewhat humble birth as daughter of a 'simple knight', Sir John Seymour of Nettlestead, Suffolk. Jane was not considered a court beauty and her skills were not to promote any physical attributes but to entrap Henry VIII. She seduced him by posing as a simple, innocent girl. Courtiers noted that she successfully resisted Henry's carnal approaches with the inference that the road to her bed was through marriage; she was after all a conservative Roman Catholic.

When Anne Boleyn was being tried and executed Jane Seymour with discretion took up residence at the family house of Wolf Hall, near Savernake, Wiltshire. Eleven days after Anne's execution Henry and Jane were married in the Queen's Closet, York Place. The outbreak of plague in London and Jane's pregnancy, meant that plans for Jane's coronation were put off (she was never crowned). On 12 October 1537 Jane gave birth to a boy, Prince Edward, at Hampton Court. Henry was ecstatic and ordered lavish celebrations; his son's christening was attended by both his half-sisters, Mary and Elizabeth. Twelve days after the birth Jane died of puerperal fever and she was buried in St George's chapel Windsor. As herald and chronicler Charles Wriothesley (d.1562) commented, Jane 'reigned as the King's wife ... one year and a quarter'. She had given Henry what he most desired, a son, and for him she was the 'perfect wife'. How long Jane would have remained in Henry's favour after Edward's birth is a matter of speculation.

Jane Seymour was only dead a week when Lord Great Chamberlain, Thomas Cromwell, pressed Henry to seek a wife that would stress an alliance with a foreign royal house. English ambassadors to the Continental courts began their search and by 1538 the daughter of the Duke of Cleves entered the frame. After all, the duke was one of the most keen and strong supporters of the Protestant Reformation. What did she look like? Henry dispatched Hans Holbein to paint a likeness. Henry's envoys backed up the opinion that Anne of Cleves was beautiful 'as the golden sun excelleth the silver moon'.

A marriage negotiation was completed on 4 October 1539 and Dutch-speaking Anne arrived at Deal that December to make for Rochester to meet her eager fiancé. Henry was aghast at what he saw, dubbing her the 'Flanders Mare', her looks repulsing him. If he could have reneged on the marriage Henry would have gladly. He could not, and the marriage, conducted by Thomas Cranmer, Archbishop of Canterbury, went ahead. The marriage was never consummated – they are said to have played cards on their wedding night for 8 hours. A girl of limited education and no knowledge of spoken English, her personality at odds with what Henry found attractive in a woman, forced Henry to eject her from Court. Henry hurried to gather pretexts for an annulment. He had not wanted the marriage; it was not consummated; and had not Anne been pre-contracted to the son of the Duke of Lorraine? That was enough. A convocation pronounced the marriage null and void on 9 July 1540.

Anne did not object to the divorce proceedings. Henry endowed her with money and two houses. A friendship developed between them – he dubbed her 'sister' – and she remained on good terms with her step-children. So Anne became a well-provided divorcee, but some historians believe that she hankered after re-marrying Henry, especially after Catherine Howard was executed. It was not to be and Anne outlived Henry by ten years. Anne died at Chelsea on 17 July 1557. She was buried in a tomb on the south side of the altar of the Confessor's Shrine at Westminster Abbey.

Henry's fifth wife, Catherine Howard was Anne Boleyn's first cousin, mirroring her sensuality but outdoing her in promiscuity. With her grandfather, the 2nd Duke of Norfolk, Catherine was well-placed in court circles, but this highly sexed girl had a long list of physical lovers from Henry Manox her music teacher, to her cousin Thomas Culpeper. She first met Henry VIII at the London residence of Stephen Gardiner, Bishop of Winchester. Instantly attracted, Henry had Catherine promoted to maid of honour to Anne of Cleves.

Henry's repugnance for Anne of Cleves made it easier for Catherine Howard to ensnare Henry. On that day in May 1540 which marked the annulment of Henry's marriage to Anne of Cleves, the Council urged Henry to move swiftly towards a new marriage 'to the comfort of his realm'. Catherine was well placed through scheming to be prime candidate and Henry and Catherine were married on 28 July 1540.

Refreshed in vitality by his high-spirited bride, Henry rode and hunted with new vigour, and lavished property and jewellery on Catherine. Repulsed by Henry's growing girth and physical ailments, Catherine made the very unwise move of taking up again with her former lovers, particularly one of her grandmother's retainers Francis Dereham and Thomas Culpeper. During a progress that Henry and Catherine made to the northern lands of his kingdom, and with the help of her lady-in-waiting Viscountess Rochford, Catherine had Culpeper smuggled into her apartments. It was only to be expected that Henry would find out when the Council heard of the infidelities. At first Henry did not believe the accusations but, being very upset, he went off on a prolonged hunting trip.

In due time Catherine was placed under house arrest at Syon House, and her lovers along with sundry members of the Howard family were brought to trial. Dereham and Culpeper were executed. In 1542 parliament agreed a Bill of Attainder against Catherine which was given the Royal Assent through the Council (to spare Henry's tender feelings on the matter) on 11 February. Two days later Catherine and her aider and abetter Viscountess Rockford were executed at Tower Green. Catherine was buried near to her cousin Anne Boleyn in the Chapel of St Peter ad Vincula.

Courtiers noted how the infidelities aged Henry VIII further and for a while he was a broken man. At length his spirits revived and a year later he was jockeying again in the marriage stakes. Henry's sixth and last wife Catherine Parr came from a rich, influential northern family which was at the centre of court affairs. Henry VIII was in fact her third husband, she having first married Sir Edward Borough (d. *c.* 1533), and then John Neville, 3rd Baron Latimer (d. 1543). Four months after Latimer's death she married Henry at Hampton Court Palace on 12 July 1543.

This time the syphilitic, ailing Henry VIII was looking for a stepmother to his children; from her two marriages Catherine Parr had no children, except step-children from Lord Latimer's first marriage. But in his courtship Henry had a rival. It was gossiped at court that Catherine Parr was enamoured of Henry's brother-in-law Thomas Seymour. Before they could marry Henry intervened and claimed Catherine Parr for himself.

Historically the well-educated 'religious radical', Catherine Parr could be called the first Protestant Queen of England, remembering though, as with Anne of Cleves and Catherine Howard, no arrangements were ever made for her coronation. An accomplished religious debater, Catherine wrote learned papers. This would lead her into danger with the pro-Roman Catholic factions, led by Gardiner and Wriothesley; in 1546 a charge of heresy against her was prepared, although slipping into senility, Henry defended her against the caucus.

Henry's motives for marrying Catherine Parr paid off; she was a kindly, attentive step-mother bringing together Henry's three mismatched children Mary, Elizabeth and Edward, promoting their education and encouraging their intellectual talents. Catherine gave Henry a round of family life he had not had since Jane Seymour's day. When Henry departed for the war zone in France in 1544 he left Catherine to rule as Governor of the Realm and Protector, a role she carried out with assiduity and competence.

After Henry died at Whitehall, 28 January 1547, Queen Dowager Catherine married the womaniser Thomas Seymour, and became aunt to her step-son now Edward VI. At the age of 36 Catherine became pregnant and gave birth to a daughter. She died of puerperal fever on September 1548, to be buried in St Mary's Church, Sudeley Castle, Gloucestershire. (She was reburied in the Chandos vault in 1817.)

♦ Was George III a bigamist?

All descendants of George II under 25 years of age (except the issue of princesses marrying into foreign families) must obtain royal consent, otherwise the marriage is void.

Royal Marriages Act, 1772.

In the National Archives at Kew there is a curious royal marriage certificate. It enters the name of Prince George William Frederick, Prince of Wales, and a Quaker girl called Hannah Lightfoot, and their marriage as being on 17 April 1759. Officially the prince, who became George III on the death of his grandfather George II in 1760, married at St James's Palace, 8 September 1761, HSH Princess Sophia Charlotte of Mecklenburg Strelitz. So does the Kew certificate show that George III was a bigamist?

Prince George, the son of Frederick Louis, Prince of Wales (d.1751), was born at Norfolk House, London, on 24 May 1738. He was not wayward like his father and despite being obstinate he was well-educated, but among his character faults was a lack of judgement which led him to stuff a skeleton into his juvenile cupboard.

The skeleton was given a public airing in 1866 in the Court of Probate and Divorce, wherein barrister Dr Walter Smith represented one 'Princess' Lavinia, who claimed to be the 'legitimate granddaughter of Prince Henry Frederick, Duke of Cumberland', sixth child of Prince Frederick Louis and George III's brother. The claim, opposed in court by Attorney General Roundell Palmer, and before Lord Chief Justice Sir Alexander Cockburn, was that Lavinia's grandmother Olive Wilmot had secretly married the scapegrace Cumberland. Lavinia thus pursued recognition of her royal rights and titles in court. The basis of the plaintiff's case was a cache of documents left by Olive Wilmot when she died in 1834. They showed signatures of George III, William Pitt (as Earl of Chatham) and Lord Brooke (as Earl of Warwick) attesting to Olive's royal birth and affirming a clutch of monetary donations to her. In the event the claim was dismissed on a jury verdict, although Lavinia pursued the claim until her death in 1871. During his address to the court barrister Smith made the astonishing claim that before his marriage to Princess Sophia Charlotte, George III had been married to one Hannah Lightfoot. He was queried by the Lord Chief Justice as to the relevance of his statement and was admonished for his 'great indecency to make such uncouth and unverified statements about the royal family'. Yet, the public were intrigued by the assertion: Who was Hannah Lightfoot?

Records show that she was born in London on 12 October 1730, the daughter of Quaker Matthew Lightfoot (d.1733), a shoemaker of Execution Dock, Wapping-in-the-East, and his wife Mary Wheeler (d.1760). Gossip of the day recounts that Prince George first saw Hannah sitting in the window of her uncle's linen draper's shop by St James's Market (now Waterloo Place and Regent Street). Struck by the girl's beauty, he arranged for one of his mother Augusta, Princess of Wales's maids of honour, Elizabeth Chudleigh (later Countess of Bristol), to effect a meeting; this she did, added the court gossips with relish, with the assistance of a high-class pimp called Jack Emm.

When Prince George's father died in 1751 he became heir apparent and it was thought necessary by his mother and others that George's mistress be married. Thus Hannah married a grocer, one Isaac Axelford on 11 December 1753. Other versions of the story say that Prince George snatched Hannah before she could be married to Axford and married her himself in 1757 or 1759; the dates vary from version to version. The documents of the 1866 trial showed that three children were born of the union to be named as George Rex, John Mackleon and Sarah Dalton. The event of children became an accepted story in the biography *The Fair Quaker, Hannah Lightfoot* by Mary Lucy Pendreth. Again, the theme was taken up by John Lindsay in *The Lovely Quaker* who gave further details of George Rex's pedigree and his ultimate residence at the Cape of Good Hope. Professor Ian R. Christie, a historian with a special interest in George III's life and reign, researched the George Rex story with the conclusion that it was 'based on evidence which is without exception hearsay or else suspicious in origin ...' Over the years variations of the Hannah Lightfoot story have emerged, but most note that she died around 1759.

The documents produced for the 1866 trial were deemed a forgery, and today authenticity has never been proven. During the purported year of Hannah Lightfoot's death, Prince George fell in love with Lady Sarah Lennox (1745–1820), daughter of Charles, 2nd Duke of Richmond, a great-granddaughter of Charles II and his mistress Louise de Kéroüalle, Duchess of Portsmouth. The royal family and their advisers thought a marriage for Prince George with a British commoner was not acceptable and a German princess was sought. Thus historians largely agree that if Hannah Lightfoot existed at all there was no marriage between her and Prince George and consequently George III was not a bigamist. However, curious stories persist. Archaeologists working at St Peter's Church, Carmarthen, West Wales, in 2000, discovered an unmarked brick barrel vault in the centre of the chancel, before the altar. The work was precipitated by the fact that the huge church organ was sinking and the floor needed shoring up. The organ had been a personal gift, tradition has it, from George III in 1796, who had intended it for Windsor Castle. As the archaeologists worked downwards four coffins were revealed, along with this obscured gravestone:

IN THIS VAULT ARE DEPOSITED THE REMAINS OF
CHARLOTTE AUGUSTA CATHERINE DALTON, ELDEST
DAUGHTER OF JAMES DALTON ESQUIRE, FORMERLY
OF THIS TOWN AND OF BANGALORE IN THE EAST
INDIES. SHE DIED ON THE 2ND DAY OF AUGUST, 1832,
AGED 27 YEARS.
ALSO THE REMAINS OF MARGARET AUGUSTA DALTON,
SECOND DAUGHTER OF DANIEL PRYTHERCH, ESQ. OF
THIS TOWN AND OF ABERGOYLE IN THIS COUNTY, BY
CAROLINE HIS WIFE, YOUNGEST DAUGHTER OF THE
ABOVE JAMES DALTON. SHE DIED ON THE 24TH DAY OF
JANUARY 1839 IN THE NINTH YEAR OF HER AGE.

As news spread of the discovery, Dalton family historians began to associate the grave with the 'Sarah Dalton', purported daughter of George III, who married one James Dalton. Again, they asked, why did George III give an expensive organ to an obscure church in Wales? Mystery plied on mystery; was the gift to hallow the place of worship of his daughter? The jury is still out.

◆ Which 'Prince of Pleasure' sought to marry a double widow?

> Mrs Fitzherbert has, I believe, been married to the Prince. But it is a
> very hazardous undertaking, as there are two acts of Parliament against
> the validity of such an Alliance; concerning her being a subject and
> her being a Catholick. God knows how it will turn out.
>
> *Frances, Lady Jerningham, 1785,* The Jerningham Letters *(1896).*

Against the rich backdrop of eighteenth-century London society
and the heady milieu of high Tory and Whig politics, a royal romance
unfolded. Whispers of a secret and illegal royal wedding first began in
December 1785. The players were HRH George Augustus Frederick,
Prince of Wales (b.1762) and the twice-widowed Maria Anne
Fitzherbert (b.1756). Known in history as the 'Prince of Pleasure',
George developed from a spoiled child into an extravagant libertine
whose duties as Prince of Wales were marginalised to indulge a
profligacy never before seen in court circles. He was only 16 when
he had his first affair with the 'darling of the London stage' actress
Mary 'Perdita' Robinson, and leaped from bed to bed with a dozen
or so other mistresses until the day he met the young widow who
was to be the love of his life.

Born Mary Ann Smythe on 26 July 1756, to Walter Smythe of
Bambridge, Hampshire and Mary Errington of Red Rice, Maria
Fitzherbert came from a Roman Catholic county family and was
educated at a convent school in Dunkirk. In 1775 she married the
wealthy, but fifteen years older, Edward Weld of Lulworth Castle.
Some three months after the marriage Edward Weld died as the
consequence of a riding accident. Well off, Mary Weld re-entered
society and was a magnet for landed English recusant suitors. One
such was Thomas Fitzherbert of Swynnerton, whom she married
in 1778, and it was around this time that she latinised her name to
become Maria Fitzherbert. She gave birth to a baby son who died in
infancy. Maria lived the life of a lady of fashion, but by 1780 Thomas
Fitzherbert had succumbed to tuberculosis; he died in 1781 while
they were at Nice. Maria now took up residence at Richmond Hill
on an enhanced income from her second husband.

Tradition has it that the Prince of Wales met Maria Fitzherbert
at the opera in 1784; she was a guest of her cousin Lord Sefton and

joined his party in his box. As she left at the end of the performance on the arm of her uncle Henry Errington, the Prince of Wales approached them: 'Who the devil is that pretty girl you have on your arm, Henry?' They were introduced and he was instantly smitten.

As the Prince of Wales's passion for Maria Fitzherbert increased, she became a source of great interest in London society. It is clear from an early stage of the relationship that Maria refused to be his mistress. Nevertheless, he showered her with jewels and gifts and commissioned Thomas Gainsborough to paint her portrait. Probably for the first time in his life the Prince of Wales thought of marriage. But there were huge obstacles to a union with Maria. There was still much prejudice in the country against Roman Catholics, many royalists doubted their loyalty to the Crown. The Act of Settlement of 1701 excluded the heir to the throne from marrying a Roman Catholic and the Royal Marriages Act of 1772 forbade any descendant of George II from marrying without the monarch's permission. Again the 1753 Marriage Act 'required vows to be taken before a clergyman inside an Anglican church unless permission were given for the marriage to take place elsewhere. The Book of Common Prayer had to be used.' And, for good measure a marriage between the Prince of Wales and Maria Fitzherbert would be further illegal under the 1714 Act which 'outlawed anyone's doing anything to prevent the heir from succeeding to the Crown'.

Despite all this the Prince of Wales's ardour never decreased and was now taking on historic importance. Not having her for mistress or wife was sending the prince frantic. He even stabbed himself in the hope that 'a hint of death might bring about a marriage'. On visiting his sickbed where he lay bandaged from his wound, the Prince of Wales told Maria that the only thing that would 'induce him to live' was for her to agree to be his wife. Although she accepted a ring to mollify him, Maria embarked for the Continent with her friend Lady Anne Lindsay in the hope that her absence would put an end to the Prince of Wales's ardour. She was wrong.

Maria eventually returned to her house in Park Street, Mayfair. She and the prince renewed their relationship and discussed how they could marry. The prince talked wildly of changing the royal marriage laws when he was king, knowing full well that under present circumstances a legal wedding was impossible.

The Prince of Wales had difficulty in persuading a clergyman to conduct the (illegal) marriage; at length the Revd Robert Burt, one of the Prince's chaplains-in-ordinary, agreed to break the law for a fee of £500 and a promise of increased royal patronage. And so at her house at Park Street, on the evening of the 15 December 1785, Maria Fitzherbert married the Prince of Wales with Maria's brother Jack (John) Smythe and her uncle Henry Errington as witnesses. The Prince of Wales then wrote out a marriage certificate which is still in the Royal Archives. It read:

> We, the undersigned, do witness yt George Augustus Frederick, Prince of Wales, was married unto Maria Fitzherbert, this 15th of December 1785. [Signed] George P., Maria Fitzherbert, Henry Errington, John Smythe.

Assessed under English law their marriage was void, although curiously Pope Pius VI regarded the Anglican nuptuals as valid.

Increasing debts drove the prince and Maria to retire to Brighton. Although debts were written off, more amassed and the prince was forced to legally (but ecclesiastically bigamously) marry Caroline of Brunswick. The marriage turned out to be a disaster and Maria (on the clearance of the Roman church) agreed to live with the prince once more. This continued off and on until the setting up of the Regency in 1811.

Maria Fitzherbert retired to the house in Brighton, 54 The Steine, which the prince had bought, where she lived until her death on 27 March 1837. She was buried in the Roman Catholic church of St John the Baptist, Brighton. She was not entirely cut off from the Royal Family on the death of George IV in 1830. His successor and brother William IV visited her and continued her allowance of £6,000 a year. Despite continued philandering during their marriage, and with the prominence of a new mistress in Lady Hertford, George insisted: '[Maria] is the only woman I shall ever love'; at his death a miniature bearing her portrait was found round his neck.

Maria's motives in marrying the Prince of Wales have been a source of curiosity. Did she sincerely love him? Enough to ignore the illegalities and the strictures of her faith? Was she solely driven by self-importance, knowing full well that such a union was a farce?

In marrying the prince Maria embarked, as biographer James Munson wrote, '[on] one of the grandest, and most passionate, as well as most public, of the world's great love affairs'.

♦ Which royal duke married twice – illegally? And which one hated arranged marriages?

Will you allow me to come this evening? It is my only hope. Oh! Let me come, and we will send for Mr Gunn. Everything but this is hateful to me. More than forty-eight hours have passed without the slightest nourishment. Oh, let me not live so. … If Gunn will not marry me, I shall die.

HRH Prince Augustus, Duke of Sussex to The Lady Augusta Murray, 4 April 1793.

Prince Augustus Frederick, Duke of Sussex, was born at Buckingham House, St James's Park, 27 January 1773, the sixth son and ninth child of George III and Queen Charlotte. Educated at Göttingen University, along with his brothers Ernest, Duke of Cumberland and Adolphus, Duke of Cambridge, Augustus was not destined for the army like his brothers because of 'convulsive asthma'. He travelled and studied classics at Rome to become something of a scholar; he had a passion for music and books – his 50,000 volume collection included 5,000 bibles. While in Rome he fell into the matrimonial net set out by Lady Charlotte Stewart for her daughter Augusta, the second daughter Lady Charlotte had had by her husband John Murray, 4th Earl of Dunmore. Lady Augusta was five years the prince's senior, was considered 'plain' and had inherited her mother's bossiness.

Following what seems to have been a mutually celibate relationship the prince married Lady Augusta at Rome on 4 April 1793 under the Anglican rite by the Revd Gunn. They were married again at St George's, Hanover Square on 5 December. Both ceremonies were in contravention of the Royal Marriages Act of 1772.

George III was much angered by the illegal marriage and it was declared null and void by the Court of Arches on 3 August 1794. Augustus and Augusta lived together despite all this and two children were born. Sir Augustus Frederick d'Este (1794–1848) was born in Essex and became Deputy Ranger of St James's and Hyde Parks, and unsuccessfully claimed the dukedom of Sussex on his father's death. Augusta Emma d'Este

(1801–55) was born at Lower Grosvenor Street, London, and married Thomas Wilde, 1st Baron Truro, who became Lord High Chancellor from 1850–52. Neither of the children left issue.

For years the illegal union alienated Prince Augustus from George III and his Court, but by royal licence in 1806 Lady Augusta assumed the surname of de Ameland and was styled Countess. An estrangement developed between the prince and Augusta and she died at Ramsgate in 1830.

Once again, in contravention of the Royal Marriages Act, around 2 May 1831, Prince Augustus married Lady Cecilia Letitia Underwood, widow of Sir George Buggin and daughter of the 2nd Earl of Arran. Although she was twelve years younger than the prince there were no offspring from the union. Small in stature and quaint in dress, Cecilia was accepted by the Royal Family as the prince's wife, and in 1840 Queen Victoria created her Duchess of Inverness.

While his morganatic illegal wife became a personality in society, Prince Augustus was a great patron of art, science and literature. He was held in great favour by Queen Victoria, who he gave away at her wedding to Prince Albert in 1840. At the time, one wag was heard to remark: 'The Duke of Sussex is always ready to give away what does not belong to him'.

Prince Augustus died of erysipelas at Kensington Palace on 21 April 1843. In his idiosyncratic way he left instructions that he was to be buried at Kensal Green Cemetery, north of Paddington. This is certainly because he wanted, in due time, for his wife to be buried with him; her cadaver would not have been accepted for the royal vault. Lady Cecilia died at Kensington Palace on 1 August 1873.

It was Queen Victoria's wedding day, Monday 10 February 1840. Among the guests that day were the queen's uncles Prince Augustus, Duke of Sussex, who 'sobbed throughout the ceremony' and Prince Adolphus, Duke of Cambridge, who 'made, loud good humoured comments'; alongside them was Cambridge's son Prince George William Frederick Charles, who at 21 was the same age as his cousin the queen. Rumour had it that Prince George had been skulking abroad for some time in case he had been forced to marry Victoria. He commented to any who cared to hear, 'arranged marriages are doomed to failure'.

George went on to be a field marshal and commander-in-chief of the British Forces from 1856–95, but his marriage caused more scandal in court circles. Later, on the day of Queen Victoria's wedding, Prince George met Sarah – called Louisa – Fairbrother (b.1815), the fifth daughter of Robert and Mary Fairbrother, a theatrical printer family in Covent Garden. Louisa had gone on the stage in 1830 and was a well-known actress in pantomime at the Theatre Royal, Drury Lane, the Lyceum and Covent Garden. Possessed of a captivating charm she was considered a 'classical beauty' and Prince George was instantly smitten. It is likely that Prince George knew that Louisa already had an illegitimate son Charles (1839–1901), whose father was probably Charles John Manners-Sutton, 1st Viscount Canterbury, Speaker of the House of Commons. A relationship developed and marriage was discussed; a marriage that would not have been acceptable to the Royal Family. Nevertheless, and in contravention of the Royal Marriages Act, Prince George and Louisa were married at St John's Church, Clerkenwell, on 8 January 1847. Thereafter Louisa was known as 'Mrs FitzGeorge', and took up residence at 6 Queen Street, Mayfair, 'where', wrote George's biographer the Revd Edgar Shepperd, 'the Duke devoted to his wife all the hours he could spare from his public duties and private engagements'. Prince George had his official residence at Gloucester House, Piccadilly.

Three children were born of the union. George William Adolphus FitzGeorge (1843–1907), served in the army; Sir Adolphus Augustus FitzGeorge (1846–1922) became a rear admiral, and Sir Augustus Charles Frederick FitzGeorge (1847–1933) also served in the army and was his father's private secretary. Louisa had given birth too, on 22 March 1841, to a daughter Louisa Catherine; she was never openly acknowledged as Prince George's daughter but she took the name FitzGeorge and was frequently at her putative father's house; she died a childless widow in 1919.

Louisa FitzGeorge suffered a distressing two-year illness and died on Sunday 12 January 1870 to be buried in the mausoleum Prince George had erected at Kensal Green. Prince George died at Gloucester House on 17 March 1904. His morganatic illegal marriage was deemed to be a happy one and he openly mourned Louisa's death for the rest of his life. On his wedding day he was to have said this to his new bride:

You alone know love, or ought to know, how blessed and happy I feel
that this day made you my own and me yours.

◆ Who were the youngest royal child grooms and brides to inherit or be consort to the thrones of England and Scotland?

The passion of John for his queen [Isabella of Angoulême], though
it was sufficiently strong to embroil him in war, was not exclusively
enough to secure conjugal fidelity; the king tormented her with
jealousy, while on his part he was far from setting her a good example,
for he often invaded the honour of the female nobility.

Agnes Strickland (1796–1874), historian on King John, 1840.

No one had seen the like before as the great English wagon-train
trundled through France. Two hundred men-at-arms, knights, clerks,
stewards, sergeants, squires and retainers, all led by Thomas Becket,
Chancellor of England, slowly made their way through town and
village. Crowds flocked to see the five-horse wagons and packhorses
loaded with furniture, clothes, food, beer, and chests of gold and silver
plate, bound for the French Court. There King Louis VII and his second
wife Constance of Castile awaited the marriage proposals carried by
Becket from King Henry II of England. In a short time, in that year
of 1158, it was agreed that the French king's daughter Marguerite be
betrothed to Henry the Younger, eldest surviving son of Henry II
and Eleanor of Aquitaine. An early marriage was not contemplated as
Marguerite was 2 years old and young Henry 4. They were married
though when Henry was crowned King of England in his father's
lifetime (a Capetian practice) at Westminster Abbey on 24 May 1170.
Henry the Younger never succeeded his father, dying in 1182.

Had Henry the Younger reigned he would have been the youngest
monarch to marry, but ten more monarchs and consorts were to
marry in the Middle Ages before they were 13. On 24 August 1200,
John Lackland, King of England, married Isabella (d.1246), daughter
of Count Aymer Taillefer of Angoulême as his second wife. She was
just 12 and John just over 32. In his *Chronica Majora* Matthew Paris
made this comment on the royal couple:

He detested his wife and she him. She was an incestuous and depraved woman, so notoriously guilty of adultery that the king had given orders that her lovers were to be seized and throttled on her bed. He himself was envious of many of his barons and kinsfolk, and seduced their more attractive daughters and sisters.

Isabella it seems continued to lead a racy life after John's death in 1216.

Henry III (r. 1216–72), married off his sister Joan to Alexander II (r. 1214–49), King of Scots. At his marriage at York on 18 June 1221, Joan was some ten months over her tenth birthday and Alexander was not yet 23. Joan died in 1238, their marriage being childless; yet this was another political marriage which led to much diplomatic haggling between the two kingdoms. Eleanor, daughter of Count Raymond Berenger of Provence, was around 13 when she married Henry III on 14 January 1236 at Canterbury Cathedral. He was a few months over 28 years old. They were married some thirty-six years, their first child (Edward I) being born in 1239 when Eleanor was 16 and they went on to have eight more children. Another political marriage occurred between Henry III's eldest daughter Margaret (d. 1275) and Alexander III (r. 1249–86), King of Scots. Margaret was just over 11 years old at the marriage in York on 26 December 1251 and Alexander just over 10; they had three children, all of whom died within five years of their mother.

Historians have described the wedding of 13-year-old Eleanor, daughter of King Ferdinand III of Castile and 15-year-old Edward I (r. 1272–1307), at Las Huelgas, Castile, in October 1254, as 'one of the great love matches of history'. They were to have sixteen children. Another long marriage, but childless, was that of David II (r. 1329–71), King of Scots, to Joanna (d. 1262) daughter of Edward II of England at Berwick-upon Tweed on 17 July 1328. David – the heir to King Robert I, The Bruce – was just over 4 years old and Joanna 7. Another heir to the throne, like David II, was Henry Boilinbroke, when he married Mary (d. 1394) daughter of Humphrey de Bohun, Earl of Warwick, at Arundel, Sussex on 3 April 1367. She was around 11 years of age and Henry just over 13. Mary gave birth at 13 and Henry ruled as Henry IV (r. 1399–1413). One marriage never consummated was that of Richard II (r. 1377–99) to Isabella (d. 1409), daughter of Charles VI of France. Richard was then 29 and Isaballa 6 years old. The marriage was part of a peace treaty between England and France.

Scotland's kingdom was expanded when James III (r. 1460–88) married Margaret (d. 1486), daughter of Christian I of Denmark, at Holyrood Abbey on 10 July 1469, for her dowry included the islands of Orkney and Shetland. The last of the young marriages of the Middle Ages was that of Margaret Tudor, daughter of Henry VII to James IV (r. 1488–1513), King of Scots at Holyrood Abbey on 8 August 1503. Margaret was around 13 and James 30 years old. Through this marriage, one hundred years later, the thrones of England and Scotland were united under James I/VI.

♦ Were Queen Victoria and Prince Albert the 'perfect couple' of her diaries?

You have again lost your self-control unnecessarily.

Note from Prince Albert to Queen Victoria, 1861.

Queen Victoria was married to Prince Albert of Saxe-Coburg for twenty-one years until his untimely death at 11:45 p.m. on the night of 14 December 1861 in the Blue Room, Windsor Castle. She had been smitten with Albert from the first; on welcoming him and his brother Ernest to Windsor on 10 October 1839, she confided in her journal, 'It is with some emotion that I beheld Albert – who is *beautiful.*' They were married at the Chapel Royal in St James's Palace on Monday 10 February 1840; that morning Queen Victoria wrote in her journal: '. . . the last time I shall sleep alone'. Her love for Albert was at first overwhelming, but there were often vehement scenes followed by days of tension.

Albert always had a problem with Queen Victoria's fiery temper. It was well known to Albert that George III had supposedly died insane and his mental state haunted his children and grandchildren. George Villiers, the Earl of Clarendon remembered that Albert always dreaded overexciting the Queen who was prone to fits of hysteria. When he tried to placate his wife he made things worse. 'If he answered back he further opened the wound', wrote biographer Giles St Aubyn. 'If he remained silent, he was accused of having no feelings.' If he tried to back off, retreating to his study, the queen would relentlessly follow him. What Queen Victoria needed was a loving man who stood up to her, who would reduce her to tears then kiss and make up with reassurances of love. What she got was a man embarrassed at her tantrums, baffled by accusations, and what seemed to be a patronising, chilly, indifferent attitude.

Queen Victoria self-critically acknowledged that she was 'over sensitive and irritable and had an uncontrollable temper when annoyed'. Even as an old lady, when crossed, she would furiously sweep everything from her writing table onto the floor. A woman of intense emotions and violent passions, Queen Victoria's states of mind are well chronicled. She was most disturbed and unhappy during and after her nine pregnancies, a condition she hated. Her physician Sir James Clark wrote in his diary: 'I feel at times uneasy. Regarding the queen's mind, unless she is kept quiet ... the time will come when she will be in danger.'

The first major quarrel between Albert and Victoria was over Baroness Louise Lehzen, the formidable figure from Hanover who had been governess first to Princess Feodora (Queens Victoria's half-sister) then to Victoria. Soon after their marriage Albert realised that he was to be locked out of the affairs of state. He was also excluded from Victoria's personal affairs which were in the hands of Baroness Lehzen. Albert became bored with court life and was frustrated by the baroness's unbending control of Victoria's household. He saw the baroness as a schemer who supported Queen Victoria's resolve to keep her prerogatives and keep his hands off State affairs; in letters to his brother he called Lehzen *die Blaste* (old hag). George Anson, Albert's treasurer and private secretary considered Lehzen a 'danger to domestic happiness'. Albert began to pursue a vendetta against Lehzen; he became obsessed with her. In a letter to Baron Stockmar of 16 January 1842, he deemed her 'a crazy, stupid intriguer, obsessed with the thirst for power who regards herself as a demi-god, and anyone who refuses to recognise her as such is a criminal'. She would have to go. Queen Victoria considered Albert's criticisms of Lehzen to be unwarranted; she told him so and Albert stomped off deliberately avoiding his wife for several days. At length the Queen agreed that Lehzen be retired; the baroness left Buckingham Palace on 23 September 1842 with an annual pension of £800; she died at Bückeburg, Hanover, in 1870 aged 85. Queen Victoria never forgot her old governess and at heart never forgave Albert. The arrangement of her household and the bringing up of their nine children was always a minefield of dispute between Victoria and Albert.

Queen Victoria's obsession with Prince Albert's memory, and her prolonged period of mourning after his death, which kept her out of the public eye and fuelled republicanism, masks the domestic friction in their marriage. He would scold her in front of their children, criticise her before her ladies, and he would send her lengthy, boring, written recriminations if he disagreed with her, and he treated her like a child. As time passed Albert took over more and more of her duties and she became resentful of the time he had to spend away from her. Thus she felt lonely and neglected; she needed whole-hearted attention, such as her prime minister Lord Melbourne had once given her.

Although she was proud of his achievements, Victoria was jealous of Albert's absorption in subjects in which she felt excluded, from (European) politics to science and from architecture to agriculture. She was also jealous of Prince Albert's devotion to his children. In particular he favoured their eldest daughter Vicky, the Princess Royal, who with her huge intelligence best lived up to Albert's high expectations. This made Queen Victoria overly critical concerning her daughter's behaviour.

In analysing the characters and temperaments of Queen Victoria and Prince Albert, two people could not have been more different. While having a capacity for love and friendship, Queen Victoria was egotistical, possessive, emotional, hot-tempered, strong-willed, and autocratic. She was more complex than Prince Albert, the key to whose character reflected in his workaholic nature (often to the exclusion of anything else), his shyness, melancholy, and ungraciousness. Albert was a loner who hated scenes, and his self-righteousness masked generosity of spirit. Their characters produced a domestic disharmony that was at odds with the 'happy home life of our own Dear Queen', which was projected to the public by the media of the day.

◆ Was King George V married twice?

I say, May, we can't get married after all! I hear I have got a wife and three children!

George, Duke of York (later George V) to Princess May of Teck 1893.

It was called the 'Mylius Case'. Radical journalist Edward F. Mylius published in November–December 1911, in the seditious Paris-based republican paper the *Liberator*, a story that in Malta in 1890, when he was Prince George, Duke of York, he had secretly married a daughter of British Admiral Sir Michael Culme-Seymour (d.1920). The story had been circulated some years before in the newspaper the *Star* and by Queen Victoria's request had been denied in various newspapers, like the *Reynolds's Newspaper*, by such as Sir Arthur Bigge her private secretary. Officially, of course, Prince George married his dead brother the Duke of Clarence's ex-fiancée Princess May of Teck at the Chapel Royal, St James's Palace on 6 July 1893. The imputation in Mylius's article, entitled 'Sanctified Bigamy', was that George's marriage was 'a sham and shameful … [a] bigamous marriage, and an offence against the church'. And that George's children of the marriage were illegitimate. The article further stated that three children had been abandoned as well as their mother by George to satisfy the Royal Marriages Act.

This time it was decided to refute the allegations in law and Edward Mylius was arrested for criminal libel on the advice of the Solicitor-General Sir John Simon and the Attorney-General Sir Rufus Isaacs. The case was tried before Lord Chief Justice, Lord Alvestone and a select jury on 1 February 1911.

The prosecution, led by the Attorney-General, satisfied the jury that Prince George was not in Malta in 1890. He certainly was aboard HMS *Thrush* as commander in 1890, in which his vessel was required to tow a torpedo boat from Gibraltar to North America, but he never landed in Malta.

Sir Michael Culme-Seymour gave evidence that his younger daughter Laura Grace had died in 1895, unmarried, and had never spoken to Prince George, and that his elder daughter Mary Elizabeth (d.1944) never met Prince George, and married Vice-Admiral Sir Trevelyan-Napier in 1899. Part of this latter testimony was not strictly true: according to the *Hampshire Telegraph* and *Sussex Chronicle* on 21 August 1891, Mary Culme-Seymour had opened the dancing at a ball at Portsmouth Town Hall with Prince George. The fact, however, was not relevant to the bigamy accusation.

Edward Mylius refused to accept the jurisdiction of the court, as in private session Lord Alverstone had denied him the right to call the king as sole witness. Mylius was convicted and given a sentence of twelve months imprisonment. He was released on 3 December 1911 having served a shorter term. On his release from prison Mylius renewed his allegations on George V by publishing in New York a pamphlet *The Morganatic Marriage of George V.* In it he reiterated his accusations that had brought him to trial, but the pamphlet drew no legal response. In his diary for 1 February 1911 George V wrote: 'The whole story is a damnable lie and has been in existence now for over twenty years. I trust that this will settle it once and for all.'

♦ Did British monarchs use contraceptives?

A Gentleman of this House [Wills Coffee House, 1 Bow Street, London] ... observ'd by the Surgeons with much Envy; for he has invented an Engine for the Prevention of Harms by Love-Adventures and has, by great Care and Application made it an Immodesty to name his Name.

'On the inventor of the condom', Tatler Magazine, *1709.*

In the picture archives of the British Library there is a print of 1744 dubbed 'Quality control in a condom warehouse'. It shows a gentleman purchaser offering his fee while a seated woman blows into the contraceptive he is about to buy to test its capability. On a table lies a range of condoms of different sizes in production while a clergyman blesses the merchandise. On the floor a cat and dog fight over a discarded condom; above them a line of condoms are suspended of prodigious sizes. The business looks prosperous, but Britain always lagged behind other nations when it came to contraception. Condoms were known among those who felt need of them from the seventeenth century. The first recorded modern mention of them is in Gabriello Falloppio's *De Morbo Gallico* published after the author's death in 1564. Even so there was a persistent belief throughout the eighteenth century that condoms were a British invention.

Better-off men in the eighteenth century probably used condoms to protect themselves from venereal diseases when consorting with street whores. From the early 1700s condoms were available from London street sellers in St James's Park, Spring Gardens, the Play-House and the Mall. Mostly made of animal membrane, biographer James Boswell noted in his *London Journal* for Saturday 4 June 1763, that the condoms worked best if they were first dipped in the lake at St James's Park. Soldiers used them even earlier; such a condom dating from around 1650 was found in a cesspit at Dudley Castle.

There were a range of 'contraceptive potions' available from apothecaries, but they were disdained by many, as were other contraceptive techniques such as the rhythm method, *coitus interruptus* and saline douches. It was not until 1823 that contraception was given a public airing by political radical Francis Place in his handbill *To the Married of Both Sexes*. Ideas on contraception were also taken up by a printer called Richard Carlile in his journal *The Republican*, and later in 1825 in a full publication *Every Woman's Book; or, What is Love?* A boost to such publications was given by philosopher John Stuart Mill who circulated them while a junior clerk in the India Office. Socialist Robert Dale Owen in his *Moral Physiology* (1830) advocated the 'complete withdrawal method' while George Drysdale's *Elements of Social Science* (1854) offered 'five techniques of contraception'.

The high incidence of illegitimacy among British royal houses from the days of Henry I (d.1131), with his estimated twenty-five illegitimate children at least, would suggest that contraception was not high on the list of royal concerns. One popular story has it that a 'royal physician', one 'Dr Condom', invented the preventative sheath to help Charles II reduce the roll of his illegitimate children; there seems to have been a decided lack of success as the king had at least sixteen illegitimates by some eight mistresses. A pamphlet issued around 1690 entitled *Duchess of Portsmouth's Garland* has Charles II's mistress Louise Renee de Kéroüalle (Duchess of Portsmouth) using 'new fashioned sponges to clear her ... from slimy sperm'. Dr Condom – whoever he was – did not invent the sheath. The Ancient Egyptians beat him to it as a sketch of the XIX Dynasty (1350–1200 BC) shows.

Other monarchs had more diverse difficulties than Charles II. His brother James II/VII and his wife Mary of Modena took the waters of Bath to produce a male heir, and it is thought that Queen Anne visited the town for the same purpose.

By the reign of Queen Victoria, from 1837, 'a pall of prudery lay over nineteenth century England'; methods of contraception were little known, or spoken about, and were considered 'not respectable'. Although printed adverts for condoms did not appear until the early years of Edward VII's reign – whether he availed himself of them during his career of serial adultery is not known – their mention in the press always caused a public sensation. For eighteen days during November–December 1886, the nation was spellbound by the Campbell *versus* Campbell legal case. This evolved after the collapse of the marriage of Lord Colin Campbell – fifth son of George, 8th Duke of Argyll – and his wife, the former Gertrude Blood. Lord Colin accused his wife of adultery with Charles Spencer Churchill, Duke of Marlborough, General William Butler and London's fire chief Captain Eyre Massey Shaw, and others. Lady Campbell counterclaimed.

Calling before Sir Charles Parker Butt, the trial included an examination of the Campbells's sex life. Answering a question from lawyer Frank Lockwood, Lady Campbell admitted that contraceptives had been used during their sexual intercourse. This was because Lord Colin was thought to have syphilis. This gave rise to the public belief that contraception was in regular use among the upper classes in their adulterous relationships. Both the Campbells were exonerated at the trial. Lord Colin died in 1895 and Lady Campbell in 1911. Although her life had more to it than the promiscuity of earlier years – which earned her the title of Victorian 'Sex Goddess' – her court appearance added a facet or two to the history of Victorian contraception. With her brood of nine children Queen Victoria and Prince Albert seem not to have practiced contraception. Even so, Frenchman Hector France found in London's Petticoat Lane, a vendor selling condoms bearing the portrait of Queen Victoria.

Whatever advice on contraception was given to royalty by their physicians, one royal doctor's opinion was clear. While the Lambeth Conference of Bishops of 1920 condemned the use of 'artificial means of restriction', physician-extraordinary to George V, Lord Dawson of Penn, denounced the conference's opinions in these terms:

> The love envisaged by the Lambeth Conference is an invertebrate, joyless thing – not worth having. Birth control is here to stay.

The royal doctor made the headlines with his opinion of contraception, a feat not repeated since the days of Charles II.

MURDERS, PLOTS
AND ASSASSINATIONS

♦ Who shot King Harold in the eye?

> … a shower of arrows fell round King Harold, and he himself was
> pierced in the eye. A crowd of horsemen now burst in, and the King,
> already wounded, was slain.
>
> *Archdeacon Henry of Huntingdon in* Historia Anglorum *(1154).*

Look along the length of the Bayeux Tapestry and pause at section
29 and there you'll find him. *Hic dederunt Haroldo corona Regis* (Here
they give Harold the king's crown), reads the heading caption,
describing how the Witangemot (assembly of nobles) offers to
Harold Godwineson the diadem that makes him Harold II, King
of the English. Harold (b. *c.* 1022) was crowned on 6 January 1066
at Westminster Abbey, in the full knowledge that on the death of
his brother-in-law Edward the Confessor (d. 4 January 1066), said
French sources, William, Duke of Normandy would be recognised
as heir instead of Edward's grandson Edgar the Aetheling. Harold
had already paid homage to William in this connection. So Harold's
action precipitated the most famous battle on English soil at Senlac
Hill, north of Hastings, on 14 October 1066.

The 70m long Bayeux Tapestry, often known as 'Queen Matilda's
Tapestry', is purported to have been commissioned some ten years
after the battle by William the Conqueror's half-brother Odo de
Conteville, Bishop of Bayeux. Its embroidery, tradition tells us, was
carried out by Matilda, Queen of England, Duchess of Normandy,
and her ladies; its length depicting her husband William's exploits
and the events of the battle.

On 25 September 1066 at Stamford Bridge, Harold defeated
the combined forces of his traitorous exiled brother Tostig, Earl of
Northumberland and Harold Hardrada of Norway, bent on seizing

the realm. By this time William and his Norman army had landed at Pevensey and Harold prepared to confront the invaders. The details of the Battle of Hastings are well known; William won the day and the kingdom, but Harold's death is still a matter of historical contention. Section 57 of the Bayeux Tapestry bears the caption: *Hic Harold Rex interfectus est* (Here King Harold dies). The panel shows a knight pulling an arrow out of his head; next to him is a mounted soldier hacking at a falling knight. But which figure is Harold? Are they both Harold? Certainly the first figure gives rise to the famous story of Harold being killed by an arrow in the eye. If it is accepted that the Bayeux Tapestry is a piece of Norman propaganda to boost William's exploits, as the tapestry says (panel 58) *Hic Franci pugnant et ceciderunt quierant cum Haraldo* (Here the French fight and Harold's followers succumb), the arrow in the eye might be a medieval metaphor for a punishment for Harold for reneging on his oath to William. So the second figure may be Harold too being finally slain by the mounted knight. This would back up what Henry of Huntingdon wrote. Interestingly, Professor David Bernstein in Morillo's *The Battle of Hastings* notes that he saw a line of small holes in the fabric 'leading to the fallen figure's forehead …' Was there once another arrow here, removed by the embroiderers? Berstein thinks that this is proof of Harold's infamy being underlined, as blindness was the medieval metaphor for divine punishment.

♦ Was King William II, 'Rufus' murdered?

> Here stood the oak tree in which an arrow shot by Sir Walter Tyrell [sic] at a stag glanced and struck King William the Second, surnamed Rufus, on the breast of which he died instantly on the second day of August anno 1100.
>
> *Rufus Stone set up in the New Forest by Lord John Delaware, 1745.*

William II, by-named 'Rufus' because of his ruddy cheeks and red hair, son of William the Conqueror and his wife Queen Matilda of Flanders, was born in Normandy around 1057. Although his father's favourite son, William had a bad press mostly because of his heavy hand with the Church. Here's what the *Anglo Saxon Chronicle* says about him after his death:

In his days, therefore righteousness declined and evil of every kind towards God and man put up its head. He oppressed the Church of God … I may be delaying too long over all these matters, but everything that was hateful to God and to righteous men was the daily practice in this land during his reign. Therefore he was hated by almost all his people and abhorrent to God. This his end testified, for he died in the midst of his sins without repentence or any atonement for his evil deeds.

Today it is difficult to obtain an objective assessment of William Rufus. Contemporary chronicles – written by monks – were prejudiced against him. They pointed out that he was opinionated, arrogant, irascible, irreligious, and avaricious. This was the opinion, too, of historians into the nineteenth century, but more recent scholars have moderated the view of William Rufus. It is true that he had powerful enemies among his barons, family conflicts added to opposition and there were those who, because he never married, smeared him further as a homosexual. William of Malmesbury stated that William's court was effeminate with young men who 'rival women in delicacy of person, to mince their gait, to walk with loose gestures and half naked'. Nevertheless William seems to have been a competent soldier and was an able and capable king, who achieved working relationships with Malcolm III of Scots and the Welsh princes. Yet his temperament and pretensions annoyed both prelate and noble. All of this led to the speculation as to the manner of William Rufus's death.

On the first evening of August 1100 William Rufus and a party of seven, including his brother Count Henry Beauclerc, William de Breteuil, Robert FitzHamon and Walter Tirel, Lord of Poix in Normandy, slept at a hunting lodge near Brokenhurst in the New Forest. The next afternoon they set off for the chase. Assisted by huntsmen the party took up their positions in groups. William Rufus and Tirel placed themselves, waiting for the huntsmen to drive the game towards them. A deer broke cover as the sun was sinking, and William Rufus fired an arrow which wounded the beast, but not fatally. As William Rufus watched the deer's movements and the sun dazzled over the forest, another deer came into view and this time Tirel loosed an arrow, but hit the king instead. Breaking off the arrow William Rufus fell from his horse, falling onto the broken arrow shaft which penetrated deeper and hastened his end. Tirel dismounted, examined the unconscious king and then, to future historians' puzzlement, leapt on his horse and galloped away. The contemporary accounts of what actually happened are confusing. Immediately it was proclaimed an accident, with Tirel identified as the unfortunate perpetrator. But was William Rufus deliberately slain?

Historians have gathered to present theory after conspiracy theory concerning William Rufus's death. For instance, Duncan Grinnell-Milne, in his *The Killing of William Rufus* believes that the death was part of a plan by William Rufus's brother, Count Henry Beauclerc, to attain the throne; he was crowned King of England at Westminster on 6 August 1100. If this were so, Henry had to move fast. William Rufus's chosen heir, his brother Robert, Duke of Normandy, was due back from crusade with a wife and legitimate son. So Henry had a motive for murder to clear the throne before Robert's return. In the king's hunting party were men loyal to Henry and a hunt was a good opportunity to make murder look like an accident. Henry was a ruthless character who was, as biographer James Chambers commented, 'at least capable of contemplating [murder]'. On the evening of that fateful day, Henry left the New Forest at a gallop to secure the royal treasury.

It is interesting to note that Tirel was married to Alice de Clare, whose brothers Gilbert de Clare, Earl of Tunbridge, and Roger de Clare, were Henry's men and were present in the hunting party that day. It is thought that Tirel's rapid flight from the scene was assisted by the de Clares; Tirel did not know the terrain for a rapid escape and a ship was conveniently waiting to take him to France. It cannot be proved that Henry played an active part in his brother's death although he had a strong motive to be so involved. As Emma Mason has pointed out in her biography of William Rufus, Henry 'seemed well prepared for the eventuality [of his brother's death] and assured of powerful backers in his bid for the throne'. Certainly the de Clares did well out of Henry's rise, with gifts of land and prominent positions in church preferment and at court. Did Tirel sacrifice himself for the de Clares advantage? He lived in exile but his lands in England and France were never confiscated as one would have expected had he been deemed guilty of murder.

The official verdict of accidental death was never officially challenged, although Tirel did always swear that he was innocent of murder. There was no official investigation. William Rufus's body was hastily conveyed onto a charcoal-burner's cart from the New Forest to Winchester for burial. His bones were not to be given eternal rest. In 1107 the great tower of Winchester cathedral collapsed. William of Malmesbury noted that people gossiped that the tower's collapse, smashing William Rufus's tomb, was 'divine disapproval' of his character. William Rufus was reburied at more than one site in the cathedral until his bones were placed in a tomb chest above the screen on the north side of the presbytery. During the Civil War these mortuary chests were hauled down by Cromwell's troops and the bones of William Rufus, King Cnut, Queen Emma and their son King Harthacnut (and others) were used as missiles to smash the cathedral windows. Later the bones were collected up and mixed up in the mortuary chests where they remain today.

♦ Is it true that Henry II was responsible for Thomas Becket's death?

What miserable drones and traitors have I nourished and promoted in my household, who let their lord be treated with such shameful contempt by a low-born clerk.
Henry II expressing his anger at Thomas Becket as quoted by the archbishop's biographer and witness of his murder Edward Grim (fl. 1170–77).

On 29 December 1170, Thomas Becket, Archbishop of Canterbury, was murdered in his cathedral of Christ Church, Canterbury. The perpetrators were four Norman knights – close associates of King Henry II – Reginald FitzUrse, Hugh de Morville, William de Tracy and Richard le Breton.

The story of Thomas Becket's martyrdom is perhaps the most famous ecclesiastical murder of all time, the power of his personality transcending almost nine centuries. He has been the subject of countless biographies and internationally acclaimed plays by such as T.S. Eliot (*Murder in the Cathedral*, 1935) and Jean Anouilh (*Becket*, 1961). Born around 1118, the son of a Norman merchant, he was educated by the Augustinians at Merton Priory, London and Paris to become a notary and entered the service of Archbishop Theobald of Canterbury. Against a background of royal turmoil when various contenders were claiming the English throne, Thomas studied canon law at Auxerre and Bologna. In the year Henry Curtmantle was crowned Henry II, Thomas was appointed to the important archdeaconship of Canterbury in the church that was still the repository of most of the learning and much of the law that applied to Christendom in general and England in particular.

Thomas Becket's talents were impressive and in 1155 Henry II made him Chancellor of England, a role Thomas threw himself into with great vigour and enthusiasm. An extraordinary intimacy sprang up between them and Thomas pursued Henry's policies with relish. Thomas even devised taxes (which fell heavily on the church) to pay for Henry's expedition against Toulouse in 1159. In 1161 Archbishop Theobald died and Henry saw a wonderful opportunity to subjugate the church to the state. He would make his own man Thomas Becket Archbishop of Canterbury. It took Thomas a year to accept; in 1162 he became archbishop but refused to remain Chancellor. On the appointment a change came over him, and herein for historians lies the enigma of Thomas Becket.

Despite the fact that he engendered a tax that had been hard on the church in 1159 – as one chronicler put it, 'Having in his hand the sword of state, he plunged it into the bosom of the church, his mother' – as archbishop did he now feel he owed a greater loyalty to the church 'his mother' rather than the king? Or did he see himself now as more powerful than when he was Chancellor? Whatever Thomas now believed his quarrels with the King became stormy and regular. In 1163 he successfully defied the king on a point of taxation at the council at Woodstock; the first time this had ever happened in English history. Their quarrels reverberated across Europe. Thomas endeavoured to reclaim church property from the crown; he prohibited the marriage of Henry II's brother William of Anjou to the Countess de Warenne; he opposed royal jurisdiction over 'criminous clerks in holy orders' and these activities went on and on until Thomas was forced to flee to France. Even in exile he called the king's authority into question. Thus, he became a thorn in Henry II's side.

Thomas remained in exile for six years but returned on 1 December 1170 following a reconciliation with Henry, however, he had no intention of knuckling down to the royal will or to the English bishops whom he had also thwarted and excommunicated.

Henry flew into one of his rages when in France he heard of Thomas's latest rulings. Henry's fury ended with the frenzied question: Was there no one in his entourage who would protect him from this low-born priest? Four of his knights slipped away and crossed the Channel in great secrecy. The rapidity of their departure begs the question: Were they anxious to act before Henry withdrew his words? After all, it had happened many times before; Henry was free with his statements often regretting them afterwards. But even so, his words on Thomas could not normally be interpreted as a licence to murder.

So that is how Thomas Becket came to be murdered and strangely the outcome was a victory for both Thomas and Henry. On 21 February 1173 Pope Alexander III canonised Thomas, and he entered history as a Christian martyr. His shrine remained a focus for pilgrims until in 1538 Henry VIII declared that Thomas was murdered as a defender of 'his usurped authority, and a bearer of the iniquity of the clergy'. In death Thomas had secured the church's independence from the Crown under the law which remained until the Reformation.

As for Henry II he was rid of the most serious challenge to his kingship, although overall he had set in motion a political blunder. His rash words had been a catalyst for Thomas's murder and, apart from being under ecclesiastical censure, none in England pointed a finger at Henry as having ordered Thomas Becket's death. Even John of Salisbury, later Bishop of Chartres, who was with Thomas at the time of the murder, makes no mention of the king's possible culpability in his chronicles. Yet, William of Sens, also later Bishop of Chartres, said that 'the King admitted … that he had provided the cause of Thomas's death and had in effect killed him'. Somewhat tardy in his efforts at exoneration, eventually in 1174 Henry did public penance at Thomas's tomb in Canterbury cathedral, where he was scourged at the hands of the monks of Christ Church.

♦ Did Queen Isabella order the death of Edward II?

> She-wolf of France, with unrelenting fangs,
> That tear'st the bowels of thy mangled mate.
>
> *'The Bard' (1757) by Thomas Gray (1716–71).*

Set out on the chess board the queen is a formidable piece; no more trenchant queen of England ever played in the game of medieval chess between England and France than the beautiful 'she-wolf' Isabella, daughter of the Capetian Philip IV – Philippe Le Bel – of France and his wife Johanna I of Navarre. On 25 January 1308 at the cathedral church of Notre Dame at Boulogne, the 12-year-old Isabella married by papal dispensation Edward II (b.1284), King of England for six months since the death of his father Edward I, 'Longshanks'. As Elizabeth Longford noted, she 'is probably the most vilified of England's queens'.

Edward II's reign has received scathing analysis, for instance, T.F. Tout in *Edward I* (1890) identified him as 'a coward and a trifler'. Edward spent the bulk of his reign opposing his barons not on great issues, but to defend his favourites the Gascon Piers Gaveston, with whom he had fallen in love as a teenager, and Hugh le Despencer.

Although Edward seemed captivated by his new wife, from her landing at Dover on 2 February 1308, Isabella realised that Piers Gaveston, now Earl of Cornwall, would appear the greater in Edward's affections than she did. At Edward's coronation on 25 February, Gaveston not Isabella was guest of honour. It was a grave insult to France and on that day Edward sowed the seeds of his ultimate fate.

From the first too, Edward was mean to Isabella: she was given no dower lands, patronage nor finances to run her household. As a consequence Isabella's father encouraged England's rebel barons to rise up against Edward. The king now tried to mollify France; Isabella was granted title to the English estates in France, and she was given greater honour at court. Nevertheless, her hatred of Gaveston, now exiled with honour as Regent in Ireland, simmered intensely.

Slowly Isabella's influence and wealth increased as Edward loosened the purse strings. All the while Edward was threatened by his barons, and on the borders with Scotland, King Robert I, The Bruce, loomed hostile with guerrilla raids. On 19 May 1312 the barons caught up with the hated Gaveston, long returned from Ireland, and he was executed as a traitor. Edward was devastated. More seriously the country teetered on civil war.

The birth of Isabella's first child in 1312 proved to be another friction with France; Edward had to concede to the barons that the child should not be called Louis (after Isabella's great-grandfather),

and thus was born the future Edward III. Crises continued in
Scotland. By 1313 the English overlordship hammered home by
Edward I was reduced to one castle, Stirling, now under siege by
King Robert's brother. Edward was forced to send troops to support
Stirling's governor Sir Philip de Mowbray. Outnumbered two to one
the Scots still trounced the English at the Battle of Bannockburn on
24 June 1314 and Edward's reputation was at its nadir.

For the next ten years Edward struggled with opposing factions
in his realm which descended into anarchy. He listened only to
his court favourites (the Despencers), an attachment that caused
Isabella's ultimate alienation from Edward. A truce was finally agreed
with Scotland in 1323, but in Wales the most powerful marcher, Lord
Roger Mortimer, saw the Despencers as meddlers in his domain.
Urged on by the Despencers, Edward rode against Mortimer who was
captured and imprisoned in the Tower. Although she bore Edward
four children, Edward, John of Eltham, Eleanor and Joan, Isabella
became more and more distant from Edward. In fact, Geoffrey le
Baker (fl. 1350) in his *Chronicle* (*c.*1341) noted that Isabella worked
out 'the perfect murder' in collusion with Mortimer and the Bishop
of Hereford. Isabella had now formed a close acquaintanceship with
Mortimer which led to her falling in love with him. As the Tower
was also a palace as well as a prison Isabella had early contact with
Mortimer. Again relations with France deteriorated and Isabella
suggested that she try to negotiate with her brother Charles IV.
She went to France and there she was joined by Mortimer whose
escape from the Tower she had engineered. They now dwelt openly
in France as lovers. Thus wrote Elizabeth Longford, 'she was the only
medieval queen known to have been an adulteress'.

Isabella and Mortimer raised an army to depose Edward and replace
him with her son; she now led the revolution that sealed her husband's
fate. Her army landed at Harwich in September 1326 and eventually
Edward was captured in Wales and taken to Kenilworth Castle.

On 25 January 1327 Edward II abdicated in favour of his son and
was taken to Berkley Castle, Gloucestershire. An attempt to rescue
him failed. He must not be allowed to escape and make a resurgence,
said his enemies, so Roger Mortimer made arrangements for his death.
It is too incredible to believe that Isabella did not know the murder
plans. Historians believe that both Isabella and Edward expected the
other to seek their murder. Edward cannot be said to have been a

loving husband. In the Chartulary of Winchester Cathedral is this comment (1334) by the then Bishop of Winchester: 'the king carried a knife in his hose to kill queen Isabella, and [Edward] said that if he had no other weapon he would crush her with his teeth.'

The death of Edward would have to appear natural. Starvation did not work, neither did exposing him to the rotting carcasses of his dead subjects, so said Augustinian friar John Capgrave (1393–1464) in his *Chronicle*:

> Edward [was] slain with a hot spit put into his body [i.e. his anus] which could not be spied when he was dead for they put a horn into his tewhel [rectum] and the spit through the horn that there should be no burning appear outside. This was by the ordinance as was said of Sir John Maltravers [Edward's jailer] and Thomas Gournay, which laid a great door upon him while they did their work.

Edward II was buried at Gloucester cathedral. Edward's death was not avenged until 1330. Roger Mortimer was tried and executed at Tyburn; Isabella was confined under house arrest at Castle Rising, Norfolk. Some chroniclers say that she became unhinged at Mortimer's execution. She died on 22 August 1358 and was buried at Greyfriar's Church, Newgate, London. Hypocritically, historians note she was buried with Edward's heart on her chest.

♦ Could Richard III be innocent of the death of the 'Princes in the Tower'?

> … But after Easter [1484] much whispering was among the people that the king [Richard III] had put the children of King Edward to death.
>
> The Great Chronicle of London, *(1504)*.

In 1951 the Scottish novelist and playwright Josephine Tey (Elizabeth Mackintosh, 1897–1955) produced her book *The Daughter of Time* in which she explored the historical murder story of the 'Princes in the Tower'. She opens the story by having her lead character Inspector Grant stuck in hospital and bored. He is brought a selection of photographs to entertain him, one of which is of King Richard

III taken from his portrait in the National Gallery. At first Grant assumes that the portrait is of a judge, or at least someone in great authority. He is staggered to learn that it is of the 'hunchback who murdered his nephews' as depicted by William Shakespeare. Spurred on he re-examines the evidence and decides Richard was vilified in a Tudor plot. Josephine Tey brought the puzzle once more into the public domain; but was her conclusion of Richard III's innocence of murder plausible?

On May Day 1464 at Grafton Regis, Northampton, Edward IV of the House of York, then 22, married in secret the widow of Sir John Gray called Elizabeth Woodville, daughter of the 1st Lord Rivers; she already had two children. Once the marriage was announced there was consternation. It was rumoured that Edward was already married to Lady Eleanor Butler, daughter of the Earl of Shrewsbury.

By Elizabeth, Edward had ten children, of whom many considered all to be illegitimate. Edward IV died at the Palace of Westminster, 9 April 1483, to be succeeded by his son and fourth child as Edward V, aged 13. He and his brother Richard, Duke of York, became the famous 'Princes in the Tower'. Young Edward grew up in a court circle riven with hostility between Edward IV and his brothers, George, Duke of Clarence (executed in 1478, traditionally drowned in a butt of malmsey wine) and Richard, Duke of Gloucester. On Edward IV's death Gloucester engineered events to become Lord High Protector, a step in his plan to take the throne. He managed to install the youngsters Edward and Richard in the Tower, at that time still a royal residence. Gloucester then took steps to have his nephews accepted as illegitimate, and Edward was deposed as king on 25 June 1483. Gloucester assumed the throne the next day as Richard III. After 31 June 1483 the young boys seem to have vanished from public sight. Down the centuries what happened to them is a matter of conjecture.

A study of contemporary 'evidence', like that found in the *Croyland Chronicle* supplies only gossip, hearsay and rumour. An Italian clerk called Dominic Mancini wrote in 1483 an account of his stay in England. He left one of the few contemporary comments about what people were saying about the princes' fate:

> He [Edward V] . . . and his brother were withdrawn into the inner apartments of the Tower proper, and day by day began to be seen

more rarely behind the bars and windows, till at length they ceased to appear altogether. A Strasbourg doctor, the last of his attendants whose services the King enjoyed, reported that the young King, like a victim prepared for sacrifice, sought remission of his sins by daily confession and penance, because he believed that death was facing him.

Mancini also repeated the rumour:

... that the sons of King Edward had died a violent death, but it was uncertain how.

Documentation only shows one 'outright accusation of murder'. It records a speech made before the Estates General by the French Chancellor de Rochford, dated January 1484. The Chancellor asks delegates to remember and pray for the two children of Edward IV 'whose massacre went unpunished, while the assassin was crowned by popular assent'.

Had the two boys died of natural causes? If so, why did Richard not make this known? Others believe that the boys lived on to be murdered on the orders of Richard III's successor, Henry VII, after the Battle of Bosworth Field. The whole fate of the boys remained so secret that the pretenders Lambert Simnel and Perkin Warbeck were able to achieve some credibility as the lost boys (see chapter 2).

In 1647 the remains of two young children were found buried in an elm chest on a staircase in the Tower. From the location of the box in the White Tower and the approximate ages of the skeletons they were treated as the bones of the two princes and re-buried in Westminster Abbey. The burial urn's Latin epitaph boldly states that Richard III had them 'smothered . . . with pillows'. In 1933 the bones were subjected to forensic examination by anatomist Professor William Wright and Lawrence Tanner. From their study of the bone formation and the development of the teeth it was suggested that the skeletons were of boys aged about 12 and 10. Such ages would tally with the ages of the two princes at the time of their disappearance in 1483. Further research on the skeletons in the early 1960s seemed to confirm the original assessment. The identity of the bones remains inconclusive. Thus the supposed murder of the princes has long been laid at the door of Richard III, but all the evidence is circumstantial, the historical waters muddied by Tudor propagandists Polydore Vergil in *Anglicae Historiae* and Sir Thomas More's *History of Richard III*. Although written in 1513, some thirty years after the events, More's account of the supposed murders by Richard III had a great influence on what people thought about the princes' deaths, and more boldly, declared Richard as ordering their murder:

> And forasmuch as [Richard's] mind gave him that, his nephews living, men would not reckon that he could have right to the realm, he thought therefore without delay to rid them, as though the killing of his kinsmen could amend his cause and make him kindly King. Whereupon he sent one John Green, whom he specially trusted, unto Sir Robert Brackenbury, constable of the Tower, with a letter and credence also that the same Sir Robert should in any wise put the two children to death.

Brackenbury refused to carry out the killing, but Richard, said More, selected Sir James Tyrell, Master of the Horse, to carry out his orders. Tyrell recruited a known murderer Miles Forest and stableman John Dighton to murder the boys. More averred that Sir James had confessed his complicity in the murder; he was executed for treason in 1502. The supposed confession of Tyrell lacks credibility. Every so often a book appears in an endeavour to exonerate Richard III, and his innocence is regularly attested by such as the Richard III Society. Nevertheless, taken even at its lowest value, the circumstantial evidence does show that Richard III committed regicide of one boy and murder of the other.

♦ What made Queen Mary I 'Bloody'?

> Popular opinion inclines to the view that [Queen Mary's subtitle of Bloody] is attributable to her partiality for the executions of persons she disliked, and particularly to her passionate desire to exterminate the leaders of the Protestant Church . . .
>
> *Lord Chief Justice Patrick Hastings (1880–1952),* Famous and Infamous Cases *(1950).*

Born at Greenwich Palace, London, on 18 February 1516, Mary Tudor was the only surviving daughter of Henry VIII by his wife

Catherine of Aragon. She was crowned at Westminster Abbey by Stephen Gardiner, Bishop of Winchester, on 1 October 1553, three months after her accession.

Mary had a troubled childhood. At first she was adored and cherished by her parents, then, as a consequence of her father's divorce from Catherine of Aragon, her loving father turned into a distant, frightening tyrant, intolerant of her defence of her mother. Mary pursued a rumbustious and violent relationship with her new step-mother Anne Boleyn. In 1533 Mary was declared a bastard, unfit to inherit her father's throne, and was made to wait on her baby half-sister Elizabeth, whom Anne Boleyn had given birth to at Greenwich on 7 September. Mary was treated with humiliating cruelty, with Anne Boleyn often urging King Henry to have Mary put to death. Mary never acknowledged Anne Boleyn as queen.

In 1536 Catherine of Aragon died of cancer and Anne Boleyn was executed for adultery and plotting regicide, but Henry's new wife Jane Seymour begged that Mary be allowed to return to court. Henry would only agree if Mary attested to a document that declared that her mother's marriage was incestuous and unlawful. Mary baulked, but pressured by her father and her cousin Charles V, the Holy Roman Emperor, she signed the document. She never forgave herself for betraying her mother which was another poisonous stress in her mind. Mary remained in court circles through her father and brother's reigns, to become, as the Imperial ambassador Eustache Chapuys said, 'universally adored' by the king's subjects.

Mary was well-educated, a keen musician and was deemed a possessor of courage, steadfastness and compassion. Yet she was rigid in her devotion to her Roman Catholic faith which would, in the end, warp her underlying natural kind and affectionate nature. Her declared illegitimacy made it difficult to marry her off to various European princes; she entered spinsterhood, she said, as 'the most unhappy lady in Christendom'. She retreated more into her faith. She despised the Reformed faith gaining strength in England and considered the Protestant faith a threat to 'the traditional concept of an ordered world'. Such a threat she believed must be countered in every possible way; she believed that God wanted all of the 'true faith' to ruthlessly stamp out Protestant 'heresies'.

Mary had red hair, a pale complexion and was of small stature, but her thin lips and piercing stare (caused by poor eyesight) often gave her a sinister expression. As she grew into adulthood she was beset by illness and a longing for marriage and children led her to bouts of frustration. At length she did marry, but her union in July 1554 to the widowed Roman Catholic Philip of Spain, was extremely unpopular in England. Politico-religious opposition to her grew manifest in the insurrection of Sir Thomas Wyatt and Sir James Crofts; the intended coup was badly planned and many of the ringleaders were executed. The failure of the insurrection was a turning point in Mary's reign and marked the beginning of Mary's 'reign of terror' for Protestants and religious dissenters that would earn her the reputation of 'bloody'.

In 1554 the papal legate Cardinal Reginald Pole (whose attainder under Henry VIII was reversed by Mary), announced England's reconciliation with Rome. Protestantism would be crushed and a papal requirement stated that all heretics be burned at the stake. The re-enactment of the *Statute De Heretico Comburendo* led to the burning of bishops like Hugh Latimer of Worcester and Nicholas Ridley of London. The series of pitiful recantations and the courageous death in March 1556 of the aged, frail Thomas Cranmer, Archbishop of Canterbury was a step too far. It is said: 'Cranmer's martyrdom was the death-blow of Catholicism in England'. The dioceses of Canterbury and London saw the most victims of Mary's fanaticism wherein about 300 suffered horrific martyrdom. Generations thereafter learned of Mary's bloody deeds and the sombre tales of Protestant martyrdom from John Foxe's (d.1587) *The Book of Martyrs*. For centuries its volume of gruesome illustrations of hangings, burnings and garottings took its place alongside the Bible as the two books even the uneducated knew. The book has been decried as 'that huge dunghill of your stinking martyrs, full of a thousand lies'. Nevertheless, it is the only record of the horrors of Marian fanaticism and an important volume in the history of perverted religious dogma.

Ultimately the Marian persecutions failed, and Mary's last years were miserable. Although in love with her husband, he found her repellent, largely because of her syphilitic rhinitis. He went back to Spain in 1557 never to return. A phantom pregnancy led Mary to depression and her belief that her reign was a total failure was underlined in 1558 when the Duke of Guise captured Calais, England's last possession in France. Mary's dream of a Roman Catholic Europe with England as a jewel alongside the Catholic Empire of the Habsburgs came to nothing. Mary died at St James's Palace, 17 November 1558 as a consequence of influenza, to be buried in a tomb in the north aisle of Henry VII's Chapel, Westminster Abbey.

Revisionist historians have endeavoured to show that Mary was 'not by nature a cruel or vindictive woman'. The fires of Smithfield, however, were a consequence of her religious bigotry and have assured that the name 'Bloody Mary' has stuck down the centuries.

♦ Which Scottish monarchs were complicit in murder?

Beneath the holy cross a knight he slew.

Old Scots Ballad, Anon.

From the ninth century four monarchs of Scotland were chronicled as being murdered: Donald I, Kenneth II, James I and James III. Others, like James V, caused murder to be committed. This under-educated, sensual, avaricious despot held a vendetta against the Douglas family and caused 'without any substanciall ground', reported Henry VIII's ambassador, the murder of Janet Douglas, Lady Glamis in 1537; she was burned at the stake in Edinburgh on a false charge of conspiring to kill the king.

On another occasion James V, as did so many other brother monarchs, caused the 'judicial murder' of Sir James Hamilton of Finnart, in 1540, once more for an alleged plot to murder him. Ironically some would say, his daughter Mary, Queen of Scots, was murdered 'judicially' in 1587. Two Scots kings, however, stand out as reputed murderers; one did commit murder by his own hand, the other became perhaps Scotland's greatest regicide myth.

Macbeth, son of Findlaech, Mormaer of Moray and Donada, daughter of Malcolm II, ruled Scotland during 1040–57. He was a power politician of his day who ruled with ability. Macbeth's father was murdered when Macbeth was 15, and Macbeth sided with Thorfinn Sigurdsson, Earl of Caithness against Duncan I MacCrinan, High King of Scotland. Together they slaughtered Duncan's army near Pitgaveny, Elgin, on 15 August 1040. Macbeth appears to have fought his way through the mêlée to where Duncan stood and felled him. Duncan, still alive when the battle ceased, was taken to Bothygobharn where he died of his wounds. Shakespeare, quoting Raphael Holinshed (d. *c.* 1580) in his Jacobean play *Macbeth* cemented the myth into history that Macbeth was a murderer.

One Scottish monarch did commit murder with his own hand. Some six weeks before he was crowned at Scone Abbey, 27 March 1306, Robert I, The Bruce, called to a meeting at Greyfriars Church, Dumfries, his co-rival to the Scottish throne, John Comyn, Lord of Badenoch. They were to discuss their rival claims and what to do about Scotland's hated overlord Edward I of England. The two Scots leaders stood before the altar at Greyfriars and began to talk. Their words turned to anger and their old antagonisms and jealousies burst forth. Bruce withdrew his dagger and deliberately stabbed Comyn. From the shadows Bruce's companions emerged to strike at Comyn's prostrate body. In the resultant foray John Comyn's uncle Sir Robert Comyn was killed by Bruce's brother-in-law Christopher Seton. According to the *Chronicle* of Canon Walter of Guisborough, Yorkshire, the Franciscans of Greyfriars Church took the still alive Comyn into the vestry to tend to his wounds and give the last rites. Bruce burst in and dragged Comyn back before the altar where he bloodily dispatched him.

Realising that his act of murder could cause him to be excommunicated and thus lose his claim to the throne, Bruce secured Scotland and precipitated his coronation.

On 29 July 1565, 22-year-old widow Mary Stuart, Queen of Scotland and France married, by Roman Catholic rites at the Palace of Holyrood, Edinburgh, her second cousin Henry Stewart, Lord Darnley (b.1545). Although considered a natural love match, it was unpopular among Mary's aristocracy and its papist ceremonial ruffled the feathers of the Protestant reformers. The birth of their son James on 19 June 1566, and his baptism by Roman Catholic rites, further alienated the Protestants. By this time too, the marriage had turned rocky and although a certain reconciliation occurred after the birth of James, Mary began a liaison with James Hepburn, Earl of Bothwell. Nineteen months after he married Mary, Darnley was murdered at the then lonely house of Kirk o'Field, Edinburgh. On the night of 9/10 February 1567 a vast explosion blew the house to rubble. The body of Darnley was found lying strangled in the garden of the ancient dwelling. Three months later Mary married Bothwell, who was popularly supposed to be Darnley's chief murderer. Whispers of Mary's complicity in the murder were rife. Darnley's mother, Margaret, Countess of Lennox, remained adamant of Mary's complicity in her son's murder. But was Mary guilty of the assertion?

The sequence of events following Mary's third marriage to Bothwell can be simply summarised. On 15 June 1567 Mary's army surrendered to the Confederate Lords at the Battle of Carbery (Bothwell escaped); this was followed by Mary's imprisonment in Loch Leven Castle. On 24 June Mary was forced to abdicate in favour of her son James. By 2 May 1568 Mary had escaped from Loch Leven and her army's further defeat at Langside on 13 May caused Mary to flee her realm to England and captivity.

What could the motives have been for Mary to have Darnley murdered, remembering that there were more than she in Scotland who would have been glad to see the back of him. Did Mary have complicity in the murder? Mary had a number of reasons why she might plot to have her husband murdered. Darnley was a treacherous, debauched and morally worthless being, and she had fallen out of love with him. Had not he been one of the number who entered her chamber at Holyrood the night of 9 March 1566 and murdered her faithful Italian secretary David Rizzio in her presence? With pistols and knives the pregnant Mary had been threatened and forced to watch the butchery. Darnley was jealous of Rizzio's supposed influence over the queen as were the Scots nobles who took part in the murder. Furthermore, Mary strongly suspected that Darnley was conspiring against her life and that of her child in his keenness to rule alone.

Through the good offices of Elizabeth I's intelligence services, Mary's supposed motives were known to those who assembled at York on 8 October 1568 to look into the matter. Elizabeth had decided that her councillors would examine two charges: 1. Why the Scots had made an 'unconstitutional rejection' of their monarch – this would be answered by Scotland's Regent, James Stewart, Earl of Moray, Mary's half-brother; 2. The counter-charges against Mary and the supposed murder complicity.

Moray believed that he could produce evidence of Mary's guilt. The only piece of 'evidence' against Mary was to be found in the famous 'Casket Letters'. A silver casket, embossed with the monogram of Francis II of France, containing eight letters and twelve sonnets allegedly in Mary's own hand and meant for Bothwell, was conveniently found and came into the possession of the Earl of Morton, a confederate of Moray's. The documents were 'astonishingly torrid with sexual feeling and suggestively conspiratorial in the murder of Darnley'. If genuine the letters were damning against Mary, yet the originals have now vanished; it is thought they were destroyed by her son after he became King of England to protect his mother's reputation. However, there were influential voices like scholar George Buchanan who had been Mary's trusted tutor, but was now a hostile witness, who had known Mary's writing and declared them genuine.

The enquiry moved from York to Westminster on 25 November. Elizabeth wanted to give Moray time to gather more details on why she should not help Mary regain her throne. Meanwhile, Mary insisted that the letters were forgeries. She insisted too on facing Elizabeth with her innocence but was denied an audience from captivity. Time passed, the judgement of the assembled councillors was deferred and the enquiry dispersed. No further action was taken. Today the case against Mary as a plotter of her husband's murder is open. It is hard to believe that in her small, gossiping court Mary did not know of any plot to kill Darnley. Already Charles de Guise, Cardinal of Lorraine, had written to her from France warning her 'to take heed whom she trusted with her secrets,' for 'her husband would shortly be slain'. Additionally, her ambassador in Paris, Archbishop David Beaton, had given her similar warning.

♦ How many plots were there to kill Elizabeth I?

> There are more than two hundred men of all ages who, at the instigation of the Jesuits, conspire to kill me.
> *Queen Elizabeth I to the French ambassador, December 1583.*

During her reign of forty-five years Queen Elizabeth I had a number of personal 'alarums'. In October 1583 the clearly insane Roman Catholic John Somerville from Warwickshire, stirred up by anti-Elizabeth Jesuit propaganda, set out with a pistol to assassinate the queen; he hoped, he said, 'to see her head on a pole, for she was a serpent and a viper'. Somerville was arrested, found guilty and condemned to death. Before the hangman could carry out the sentence, Somerville hanged himself in his cell at the Tower of London.

In 1584 a Welsh MP, Dr William Parry, secreted himself in the queen's garden at Richmond Palace, intent on murdering her. On her arrival with her ladies, Parry was 'so daunted with the majesty of her presence in which he saw the image of her father, King Henry VIII' he could not carry out the deed. The reason for Parry's assassination attempt is obscure. He was known to be a spy for William Cecil, Lord Burley, and purported to act as a regicide 'in order to infiltrate papist circles'. This was enough to win him a pension from the queen. Yet there were others who believed he acted with papal blessing on behalf of Mary, Queen of Scots and Parry did boast that he would assassinate the queen if the occasion arose. Whatever the truth was, Parry paid the price for his activities and loose tongue on the gallows.

Again, one day when Queen Elizabeth's barge was plying the Thames, a shot was fired from the shore. One of her bargemen was wounded and the queen handed him her handkerchief to staunch the blood. 'Be of good cheer', she told him, 'for you will never want. For the bullet was meant for me.'

Plots and intrigues against Elizabeth were everyday fodder for the Elizabethan secret service in London, headed by Sir Francis Walsingham (*c.*1530–90) who rose to be Secretary of State. Three plots stand out as the most dangerous to Elizabeth. All were Roman Catholic inspired, for in 1570 Pope Pius V issued the *Bull Regnans in Excelsis of Excommunication and Deposition* against Elizabeth, thus giving Catholics a free hand to oppose her. In 1571 strong penal statutes were passed against Roman Catholics.

1571: The Ridolfi Plot
Intention: To assassinate Elizabeth. To marry Mary, Queen of Scots to Thomas Howard, 4th Duke of Norfolk (1536–72) and thereafter Catholic soldiers would invade England and put Mary, Queen of Scots on the English throne with Norfolk. Philip of Spain and the Pope backed the move in principle.

The plot was named after a Florentine banker and papal agent called Roberto Ridolfi who acted as go-between for Norfolk and the Spanish. Ridolfi had funded the proposed rebellion of the Roman Catholic northern magnates, headed by the earls of Northumberland

and Westmoreland. Ridolfi naively believed that a vast number of Roman Catholics would support the venture. William Cecil, Lord Burleigh's agent, got wind of the plot which collapsed while Ridolfi was abroad. Norfolk was executed in 1572 and Mary, Queen of Scots was greatly discredited.

1583: The Throgmorton Plot

Intention: To assassinate Elizabeth. Supplant her with Mary, Queen of Scots with the help of Spain.

Francis Throgmorton (1554–84), a zealous Roman Catholic, was the player in numerous plots abroad against Elizabeth's government. While organising communications between Mary, Queen of Scots, her agent Thomas Morgan and Spanish ambassador Don Bernardino de Mendoza, Throgmorton was arrested and under torture revealed plans for an invasion from the Spanish Netherlands under the Duke of Guise. The plans were thus thwarted; Mendoza was sent back to Spain and Throgmorton was executed at Tyburn.

1586: The Babington Plot

Intention: To assassinate Elizabeth. The stimulation of a Roman Catholic rising in England in favour of Mary, Queen of Scots, who would be placed on the English throne.

The conspiracy was headed by Anthony Babington (1561–86), one time page to Mary, Queen of Scots. He formed a secret society to aid and protect Jesuit infiltrators to England and linked up with the Scots queen's emissaries on the Continent. The plot was instigated by the Jesuit priest John Ballard, with Babington as leader and the Pope's blessing. The plot was discovered by Walsingham; Ballard was arrested, racked and executed. Babington tried to save his skin by offering information and fled in disguise; he was captured, held in the Tower of London, indicted and executed in September 1586. A special court found Mary, Queen of Scots, then in English captivity, guilty of treason and she was beheaded at Fotheringay Castle, 8 February 1587.

♦ Did James VI plot genocide?

> Gowrie's forfeiture is passed without appropriation to the Crown, the
> dead bodies escartelet with cruelty, all woman and man of the surname
> Ruthven charged to change their surname before Whitsunday next
> under pain of treason …
> *The Master of Gray to Sir Robert Cecil, 15 November 1600, 'Salisbury', MSS III.*

On 5 August 1600 John Ruthven, 3rd Earl of Gowrie (b. *c.* 1578),
supporter of the extreme Protestant party in Scotland, and his
brother Alexander, Master of Ruthven (b. *c.* 1580), Gentleman of
the Bedchamber to King James VI, were murdered at the Ruthven
mansion of Gowrie House, St Johnstone, Perth.

The Ruthvens were notably unfriendly to the House of Stuart.
Had not Patrick, Lord Ruthven, on the occasion of the murder of
the queen's Italian secretary David Rizzio, manhandled Mary, Queen
of Scots? And, had not William Ruthven kidnapped her son James in
the Ruthven Raid? James had managed to escape and William was
executed in 1584. Consequently, the Ruthvens considered James VI
a murderer. For all these reasons James VI loathed and was scared of
the Ruthvens; furthermore, by 1600 he was in debt to them to the
sum of £80,000 and in various state matters they opposed him.

All papers regarding the Ruthven murders have been destroyed in
antiquity, yet, the only contemporary account of the circumstances
of the deaths is that of James himself. This was sent to Elizabeth I's
principal secretary Sir Robert Cecil and is considered dubious in its
content.

It is unclear today why Alexander Ruthven left Perth on 5 August
1600 at an ungodly hour to ride to see James VI at Falkland Palace.
According to James, Ruthven had arrived at Falkland with the story
that 'a stranger, with a great wide pot all full of coined gold in great
pieces' had been arrested near Perth and imprisoned in 'a secret
room' at Gowrie House. James was told that he was the first to hear
of the gold and should accompany Ruthven to Perth to see it.

James VI noted that the gold was not the business of the Crown.
But, said Ruthven, it was in foreign coin; was the stranger a Jesuit
priest who carried the money for seditious purposes? At first James
favoured sending a warrant to detain the stranger but, after a day's
hunting, he agreed to return with Ruthven.

The whole story was a weak fabrication and a crude device for James to give himself an excuse to go to Perth. He told his retainers that he suspected the Ruthvens of a 'treasonable device', but was James now manufacturing a murder plan to rid himself of the Ruthvens? With him James took twenty-five retainers, including the earls of Lennox, Mar and Erskine, and his supposed catamite page John Ramsay. If James suspected treachery his entourage seemed small. Did he know that at Perth there were 300 loyal soldiers under the command of Lord Tullibardine as back up?

A mile from Gowrie House, Ruthven rode ahead to prepare to receive the king. According to James, John Ruthven had no knowledge of the 'pot of gold' and as host, dined with the king, uneasy as to why the monarch should pay a visit. At the end of the meal, the king and William Ruthven retired to view the 'pot of gold'.

After the passage of some time, the rest of the party, who were taking their ease in the garden, were attracted to a turret window where they saw the king 'wanting his hat, his face turned red, and a hand gripping his cheek and mouth', shouting 'Help, my Lord Mar. Treason! Treason! I am betrayed! They are murdering me!' Rushing into the house the party found the turret room door locked; it took half an hour to break it down. Inside a fight was taking place. James was wrestling with Ruthven. Seeing the situation as he entered the room Ramsay withdrew his sword; fumbling the strike on Ruthven in the neck he propelled him down the turret stair, where Ruthven was dispatched by Lord Erskine who was on his way up. John Ruthven had followed the group up the stairs, sword in hand, but on seeing the king lowered his guard to be easily killed by one of the king's party.

Despite an angry mob from Perth crying vengeance for the deaths of the Ruthvens, James was protected by Tullibardine's soldiers and eventually left Gowrie House for the safety of Falkland. James now set about closing in on the remaining Ruthvens. The two younger brothers and their mother escaped to England; one died in exile, the other was captured in 1603 and imprisoned for twenty years without trial. The Gowrie estates were confiscated to the Crown and the Ruthven name made anathema.

The rotting corpses of the Ruthven brothers were given a farcical state trial, with 'testimony' offered from the confessions under torture of Ruthven's friends, employees and close servants to 'establish the

king's innocence'. Bribes of honour and land were distributed to
those who had aided James, or had kept quiet concerning what really
happened. John Ramsay was knighted and eventually became Earl of
Holderness, and Erskine was given Gowrie estates at Dirleton, with
later additional titles of Viscount Fenton and Earl of Kellie.

The Gowrie Conspiracy remains one of the unsolved mysteries of
Scottish history. Some historians have argued that James eliminated
the Ruthvens before they eliminated him. Be that as it may, James
had succeeded in solving all his problems concerning the Ruthvens.
He also re-wrote history to vilify the Ruthvens as perpetrators of a
foul plot of regicide and underlining his 'miraculous delivery of the
affair'. Few believed James's version of the events, the most prominent
doubter being his queen, Anne of Denmark. The murdered men's
sister Beatrice was her favourite lady-in-waiting, and at the queen's
insistence she was granted a pension of £200.

◆ Why was Charles I executed?

> There was such a groan by the thousands then present, as I never
> heard before and desire I may never hear again.
> *Contemporary diarist Philip Henry commenting on the crowd's reaction on
> being shown the severed head of Charles I.*

Charles Stuart was crowned King of England at Westminster Abbey
on 2 February 1626 and King of Scotland at Holyrood Abbey on
8 June 1633. Like his grandmother, Mary, Queen of Scots, he met his
end on the block, being executed at Whitehall Palace, London, on
30 January 1649.

From the first parliament of Charles I's reign in 1625, there began
a slow and steady opposition to royal power, both religious and
constitutional. It is said Charles 'hated the very name of Parliament'
and he ruled without one for eleven years, 1629–40. Among other
things to thwart parliament, Charles raised money without their
leave and ruled with an absolute authority in all matters which he
believed was his divine right. When the Civil War of 1642–6 broke
out between Charles and parliament, the death of the monarch was
not an original aim. Yet, there was an inevitability about Charles's
dire fate as he clashed with MPs over financial, religious and political

issues. Relations irretrievably soured when on 4 January 1642 Charles entered the House of Commons with an armed guard to arrest five members. The members had already fled, and civil war became inevitable. The war advances swayed between Royalists and Parliamentarians, until disaster for Charles at the battle of Naseby, 1645. By 1646 Charles surrendered to the Scots army who handed him over to the English and Charles was imprisoned.

At length Charles was brought to trial in Westminster Hall, before a tribunal of 135 judges. By the laws of the land the tribunal was illegal and unrepresentative. Charles refused to acknowledge the jurisdiction of the court and refused to enter a plea. Charles was accused of treason by levying war against Parliament. In reality Parliament was as responsible for the Civil War as Charles. Only 53 out of the 135 members of the tribunal attended the court. Charles was found guilty and only 59 of the tribunal members signed the sentence of death. Charles's execution was greeted with a general feeling of public horror. Charles met his end with dignity and courage. Contrary to the stated aims of the Parliamentarians they made Charles into a martyr. Charles's comment that he was going 'from a corruptible to an incorruptible crown' assured his saintly status.

Lucy Hutchinson, wife of the Parliamentarian Governor of Nottingham, Col John Hutchinson, wrote, 'Men wondered that so good a man [as Charles I] should be so bad a king'. She brought into focus for many Puritans the marked differences between Charles's undoubted virtues and his failure in politics. Something of the mindset of Charles I can be seen in *Eikon Basilike: The Pourtraicture of His Sacred Majestie in His Solitudes and Sufferings* compiled, it is thought, by John Gauden (d.1662), Bishop of Worcester. It purported to be the meditations of Charles I based on his own papers. Published in the year of his execution it showed how Charles wanted the world to see him. What Charles emphasised was that, although a sinner who made mistakes, he was answerable only to God and not his subjects. He further emphasised that it was his duty to preserve 'the true doctrine of the Christian faith' as set out by the Church of England. Consequently he was against the denominations of Roman Catholicism and Presbyterianism. For these two tenets Charles was prepared to die. The book became a bestseller with thirty reprints in one year.

Charles had a great love for his family, particularly his wife Henrietta Maria, and possessed great charm, modesty and politeness.

He insisted on proper ceremonial and court etiquette, not for his own vanity but for the dignity of his position. Devoutly religious, but not bookish, Charles was described as intellectually weak and lacking in intelligence; certainly the latter was shown in his decisions on political matters. Charles lacked tact and imagination, he was prone to vacillate – promising one thing to one and another to another but never following through – and he was out of touch with public opinion. He also pursued secret plots and intrigues, and tried to be all things to all men. In the end he could have saved his throne and his head if he had agreed to be a 'limited monarch' (as his successor Charles II), with his powers restricted to the will of parliament.

Still today, the anniversary of the execution of Charles I is kept alive by those who believe that Parliament had no right to chop off his head. One, the Royal Martyr Church Union, made up of distant descendants of the Cavaliers, hold a service at St Mary's Episcopal Cathedral, Edinburgh, to mourn his violent death. The liturgy is taken from the King Charles prayer book. Several of their members hope for the return of his bloodline and for the subjugation of Parliament to the Crown. In London the king's execution is remembered by the Society of King Charles the Martyr.

♦ How many attempts were there on Queen Victoria's life?

If Englishmen may beat their wives,
It plainly may be seen,
They must not take the liberty
To strike the British Queen.

Pearson Collection of Nineteenth-Century Ballads.

Despite the regular huffing and puffing by republican groups, Irish agitators, anti-monarchists sheltering within the Liberal Party and the Cromwellian legatees of radical politics, there were eight main attacks and assassination attempts on Queen Victoria during her long reign of sixty-four years.

When Queen Victoria came to the throne in 1837 royal security was at a minimum. Even sixty years later only one policeman was provided for her safety, for instance, when she visited Balmoral. The first attempt on her life occurred at 6 o'clock on the evening of 10 June 1840. Prince Albert and a pregnant Queen Victoria were driving in a low carriage up London's Constitution Hill, after visiting the queen's mother the Duchess of Kent, when the attack occurred. Prince Albert sent this account of the incident to his brother Prince Ernest of Saxe-Coburg:

> 12 June 1840: I saw a small disagreeable looking man leaning against the rail of Green Park only six paces from us, holding something towards us. Before I could see what it was, a shot cracked out. It was so dreadfully loud that we were both quite stunned. Victoria, who had been looking to the left, towards a rider, did not know the cause of the noise. My first thought was that, in her present state, the fright might harm her. I put both arms around her and asked her how she felt, but she only laughed. Then I turned round to look at the man (the horses were frightened and the carriage stopped). The man stood there in a theatrical position, a pistol in each hand. It seemed ridiculous. Suddenly he stooped, put a pistol on his arm, aimed at us and fired, the bullet must have gone over our heads judging by the hole made where it hit the garden wall.

The attacker was a feeble-minded youngster called Edward Oxford. He was grabbed and held until the police arrested him. A crowd gathered around the royal couple cheering enthusiastically at their escape; it was a miracle that Oxford had missed at such close range. A group of gentlemen on horseback escorted the royal couple back to Buckingham Palace. Oxford was imprisoned at Newgate and tried on a charge of high treason at the Central Criminal Court before Lord Chief Justice Thomas Denman. Defended by Sidney Taylor, Oxford was found 'Guilty but Insane'; he was removed to Bethlehem Hospital for the insane at Moorfields. After thirty-five years he was released and went, under surveillance, to Australia.

In spite of this attack no extra precautions were instituted for Queen Victoria's public or private safety. On Sunday 30 May 1842 a second attack occurred. This time Queen Victoria and Prince Albert were driving along the Mall from the Chapel Royal towards Buckingham Palace. Albert, writing to his father later, said: '[I] saw a man step out from the crowd and present a pistol fully at me. He was some two paces from us …' Queen Victoria, looking the other way, saw nothing, but Albert heard the trigger click; the shot misfired and the perpetrator disappeared into the crowd.

Behind closed palace doors it was decided to try to identify the culprit by giving him a second chance. It was a curiously foolhardy scheme sanctioned by Prime Minister Robert Peel. The royal couple set off on that Sunday afternoon with Col Charles Arbuthnot and Lt Col William Wylde as outrider equerries. On the return drive from Hampstead, the assassin struck again. As the carriage sped past him the assassin's shot missed and the man was arrested. He was identified as John Francis, a 20-year-old cabinetmaker. Committed to Newgate, he was tried for high treason and found guilty; he was sentenced to be hanged, drawn and quartered. On Queen Victoria's authority the sentence was commuted to Transportation for Life to Norfolk Island. Francis was ultimately released on 'ticket-of-leave' in 1867.

Although she was anxious to have her security increased, on Sunday 3 July 1842, while driving down the Mall from the Chapel Royal with King Leopold I of the Belgians, the 16-year-old John William Bean made to fire a pistol at the carriage. The weapon was knocked from the boy's hand, but he too disappeared into the crowd. The pistol was found to contain a curious mixture of paper, tobacco and gunpowder. The police gathered a description of the boy who had a noticeable spinal deformity. All males of similar age, who were described as 'hunchbacked', were arrested until Bean was found. Bean was sentenced to eighteen months in prison.

This third attempt on Victoria's life caused the law to be changed. Oxford, Francis and Bean had not been political assassins, but deranged publicity seekers. So the new law backed by Robert Peel provided for 'the further protection and security of her Majesty's person'. It was not now high treason to attack the monarch but a 'high misdemeanour' punishable by up to seven years' transportation or imprisonment, with the options of hard labour and a birching.

On 19 May 1849 Queen Victoria's life was threatened again by an insane Irishman called William Hamilton. His deranged intention was to 'frighten the English Queen with a home-made pistol'. Changing his mind he borrowed a functioning pistol from his landlady and fired a charge at Queen Victoria as she drove down Constitution Hill. The pistol was found to have no bullet in it. Hamilton was transported for seven years.

Robert Pate was bent not on assassination but punishment. On 27 July 1850 the retired lieutenant of the 10th Hussars struck Queen Victoria over the head with a cane as she drove home after visiting her dying uncle Prince Adolphus of Cambridge. As the carriage carrying the queen, the Prince of Wales, Prince Alfred and Princess Alice and lady-in-waiting Fanny Jocelyn, slowed to enter a gate, the escorting equerry was pushed aside by the crowd who had gathered to see the royal party. Pate took his chance. He struck, but was seized by the crowd. Queen Victoria was knocked unconscious, but soon revived to suffer shock, bruising and a headache. Pate too was sentenced to seven years' transportation.

Queen Victoria was informed of a curious threat to her life. On 26 May 1872 a young telegraph clerk called Albert Young appeared before High Court Judge Henry Charles Lopes. Young had sent a letter threatening the life of the queen unless she sent £40 each to some fifty Irish folk who had been dispossessed by their landlords. Young was tried on a charge of intimidation and the bench took a serious view of Young's intent; his sentence after the guilty verdict was ten years' penal servitude.

A weak-minded youth called Arthur O'Connor, nephew of the Chartist leader, the late Fergus O'Connor, took it into his addled head to frighten the queen into authorising the release of Irish Fenian men, then in custody. Towards this end, on 28 February 1872, O'Connor pointed a pistol at her while her carriage paused at the Garden Gate of Buckingham Palace. Prince Arthur jumped out of the carriage to grab the man but was beaten to it by her Highland servant John Brown. Brown was rewarded with a gold medal and a £25 annuity. Prince Arthur received a gold pin in thanks (much to the Prince of Wales's disgust at so paltry a reward when Brown was better favoured). O'Connor was sentenced to a year in prison. Afraid that O'Connor would try to assassinate her on his release Queen Victoria pressed Prime Minister Gladstone to have him deported. In the event O'Connor agreed to a voluntary exile.

As Queen Victoria's carriage stood outside Windsor railway station on 2 March 1882, an imbecile called Roderick McLean fired a pistol at Queen Victoria. Not quite sure what had happened, Queen Victoria was informed by John Brown, who had been riding as postilion, that 'that man fired at Your Majesty's carriage'. Two Eton boys in the crowd ran forward and repeatedly struck McLean with their umbrellas until he was seized by Superintendent George Hayes of the Windsor Police. The Eton boys became the heroes of the hour, and a few days later Queen Victoria 'received 900 Eton boys in the Quadrangle' of their school to thank the two boys personally.

This last attempt on Queen Victoria's life was undoubtedly the most dangerous of all, as McLean's pistol was loaded with six bullets; another firing and McLean might not have missed. McLean was tried at Reading Assizes where he stated that his intent to kill the monarch was to draw public attention to his poverty. He had been awarded the official 6*d* [3p] a week poor relief but demanded that he should get 10*s* [50p]; it was all the Queen's fault that he had not been paid, he said. McLean was declared by the court not fit to be responsible for his actions and he was sent for treatment at asylums in Weston-Super-Mare and Wells. He was released 'cured' in 1884.

With one exception, none of Queen Victoria's assailants was of mature years, and all showed signs of mental derangement. Roderick McLean was clearly insane as well as Robert Pate and Edward Oxford; the others were more of the 'half-baked loner' variety than raving lunatics. Had one of them succeeded, the accelerated reign of Edward VII might have completely altered the structure of British monarchy and perhaps the descent into the First World War.

ATTACKS ON QUEEN VICTORIA'S GRANDFATHER AND SON

On 2 August 1786, just as George III was descending from his coach at St James's Palace for a levee, a domestic servant called Margaret Nicholson stepped forward and offered the king a sheet of paper. He presumed it was a petition. As he took the sheet she quickly drew a knife from her pocket and made a lunge at his torso. The blow was inept and the knife bent, so the king was unscathed and his linen waistcoat was hardly marked. The woman was seized by guards and roughly pummelled. The novelist Fanny Burney recorded what the king said: 'The poor creature is mad! Do not hurt her! She has not hurt me!' The king went on with his engagements in good humour, although when informed of what had happened his daughters and Queen Charlotte were greatly distressed.

During 29 October 1795 George was driving to open parliament when his carriage was attacked by a mob screaming 'Peace and Bread! No War! No War! Down with George!' This was the year of high prices, increasing poverty and in France, Napoleon Bonaparte had dispersed the Paris mob. George Onslow, Lord of the Bedchamber, remarked that

> when we got down to the narrowest part of the street called St Margaret's a small ball, either of lead or marble, passed through the window glass on the King's right hand and, perforating it, passed through the coach out of the other door, the glass of which was down. We all instantly exclaimed, 'This is a shot'.

George III seemed unperturbed, but on his return journey to St James's his coach was pelted with stones; the glass windows were shattered and the king was hit by several missiles.

Again, on 15 May 1800, while reviewing the 1st Foot Guards in Hyde Park, a bullet was fired at the king but struck a navy office clerk who was standing near the king. The monarch refused to move from his position and continued with the review. That evening, while at the Theatre Royal, Drury Lane, John Hadfield fired a pistol at the king and the bullet penetrated the pillar of the king's box. The king insisted that he and his family sit out the performance. At the close of the play the Royal Family were enthusiastically cheered and applauded. The theatre manager Richard Brinsley Sheridan composed an improvised new verse to *God Save the King*:

From every latent foe,
From the assassin's blow,
God save the King!
O'er him thine arm extend,
For Britain's sake defend
Our father, Prince, and friend ...

In Edward VII's time there was no royal protection squad of armed police to protect his every public movement. When the king ventured out incognito to have one of his favourite strolls, he invariably had only one equerry and a detective with him. Often in Paris (under his travelling name of Baron Renfrew), he was accompanied by a solitary aide. On 4 April 1900 as the Prince of Wales, Edward and his wife Alexandra were en route for Copenhagen they made the first stage of their journey to Brussels. Edward's diary entry for the day read: 'Walk about the [Gare du Nord] station. Just as the train was leaving, 5.30, a man fires a pistol at [me] through open window of carriage (no harm done)'. The would-be assassin was a 15-year-old Belgian youth, Jean Baptiste Sipido. He had jumped onto the footboard of the carriage and fired wildly four times; two shots misfired, one went wide but the fourth hit the carriage partition wall between Edward and Alexandra's heads. Sipido had fired maintaining that the prince deserved to die because of the thousands of Boers who had died during the South African War. Edward remained unperturbed, saying only, 'Poor fool'. Commenting to the British Ambassador in Berlin Sir Frank Lascelles, Edward noted: 'Fortunately Anarchists are bad shots. The dagger is far more to be feared than the pistol ...' The bullet is still preserved in the collections at Windsor Castle.

◆ Which monarchs were deemed 'bumped off' by
royal doctors?

The King's life is moving peacefully towards its close.
Bulletin drafted by royal doctor Lord Dawson at Sandringham, 1936.

'My dearest husband . . . passed away on Jan 20th at 5 minutes before
midnight'. So wrote Queen Mary as a final postscript to George V's
holograph diary which he had kept since 3 May 1880. The nation
entered a period of mourning unaware that a royal secret had formed
at Sandringham which would have horrified the thirties generation.

This secret was revealed to the public in 1986 when biographer
Francis Watson disclosed that physician-in-ordinary Bernard Edward
Dawson, Viscount Dawson of Penn (1864–1945), administered a
lethal dose of morphine and cocaine into George V's jugular vein at
11.55 p.m. on Monday 20 January 1936. The surrounding publicity
of Watson's biography of Dawson caused some controversy: 'Was
George V's death treason?' asked the *Independent*. Dawson's reasons
for acting the way he did, according to an incredible statement,
were so that news of the king's death and his obituaries would be
first carried by 'quality' newspapers like *The Times* rather than in
the evening or by more downmarket papers. Some historians have
averred that Dawson's actions were murder.

Just like her husband, the death of Queen Mary, at 10.35 p.m.
on Tuesday 24 March 1953, has been described as a 'mercy killing'.
The reason? So that her approaching death would not disrupt the
coronation on 2 June of her granddaughter Queen Elizabeth II.
Queen Mary's death ten weeks before the coronation assured that
the coronation was outside the official mourning period, and so had
no need to be postponed. Uncorroborated comment suggests that
royal doctors Dawson of Penn and Sir John Weir had discussed the
matter with Queen Mary who agreed that her death should not
interfere with the coronation plans.

The idea that monarchs were 'bumped off' by royal doctors is
not new. Some such instances were moved by politico-religious
reasons. On Saturday 7 June 1594, Dr Roderigo Lopez was hanged,
drawn and quartered at Tyburn Fields after he had been convicted at
London's Guildhall of plotting to poison Queen Elizabeth I. While
Lopez was a player in the Roman Catholic plots to murder Queen

Elizabeth, other doctors were more subtle or cack-handed in ending their monarch's lives.

Charles II died of uraemia, chronic nephritis and syphilis. That's how his death certificate might have read, but in medical history Charles is said to have been murdered by 'iatrogenic regicide'. On Sunday 1 February 1685, the king retired to his chambers with a sore foot to be attended by his physician Sir Edmund King; shortly afterwards the king was struck with an apoplexy. Sir Edmund drew off 'sixteen ounces of blood', risking his own death for treason by not first obtaining the permission of the Privy Council for the bloodletting. Thereafter, as Charles was laid on what would be his deathbed, historian Thomas Babington Macaulay noted that the king was 'tortured like an Indian at the stake'. A total of a dozen doctors now circled Charles's bed. They drew off 'toxic humours' from the king, bled and purged him, shaved his head, applied cantharides plasters and red-hot irons to the skin. For five days, in full view of family, government ministers and hangers-on, Charles was dosed with enemas of rock salt and syrup of buckthorn and an 'orange infusion of metals in white wine'. The king was treated with a horrific cocktail of lethal potions: white hellebore root, Peruvian bark, white vitriol in paeony water, distillation of cowslip flowers, sal ammoniac, julep of black cherry water, oriental bezoar stone from the stomach of a goat and boiled spirits from a human skull. Despite all this the king retained a sense of humour and said to his physicians: 'I am sorry, gentlemen, for being such an unconscionable time a-dying'. Charles's treatment was topped off with 'heart tonics', but to no avail; exhausted, his body raw and aching with the burns and inflammation caused by his doctors, the king lapsed into a coma and died at noon on 7 February 1685.

Queen Anne was a woman of many ills. After her death at Kensington Palace on 1 August 1714, her physician Sir David Hamilton was accused at the autopsy of her body of hastening her death by not spotting, or ignoring, the queen's supposed condition of dropsy. He was not accused of murdering the monarch, but a later sovereign's death was considered to have been 'manipulated'.

Queen Victoria's uncle William IV had a full death certificate of suffering from bronchopneumonia, aortic and mitral valvular disease, myocarditis and syphilis. The king knew he was dying and as Benjamin Disreali reported, 'The King dies like an old Lion'. Following the king's death on Tuesday 20 June 1837, a controversy raged in the medical profession concerning the royal doctors' handling of the king's last days. Each day as the king moved slowly to death medical bulletins were issued. Contemporary doctors considered that royal physicians like Dr William Chambers and Drs James Johnson and William Macmichael had issued bulletins that were mendacious. In them the king was declared not to be terminally ill, and they gave them an optimistic spin. There were those who believed that political pressure had been put on the doctors to play down imminent death. An accusing finger was pointed at William Lamb, Lord Melbourne, the Liberal Prime Minister. Melbourne's cabinet was divided; a general election was due and Melbourne wanted no popular sympathy for the king to be reflected in an increased Tory vote. In the event Melbourne won with a reduced majority. Could future medical bulletins on royal health be trusted again?

◆ Was Amy Robsart, Lady Dudley, murdered by a queen's command?

The Queen of England is going to marry the Master of her Horses, who has killed his wife to make room for her.
Mary, Queen of Scots on Queen Elizabeth I and Robert Dudley.

The Benedictine monks of Abingdon Abbey once used Cumnor Hall, Oxfordshire, as their sanatorium. When the fourteenth-century abbey was suppressed by Henry VIII in 1539, the last abbot Thomas Rowland was allowed to use it as a private residence. It passed into the hands of royal physician Dr George Owen, from whose family Anthony Forster, the Treasurer of the Household of Lord Robert Dudley, rented it for his family and relatives. At Cumnor Hall on the evening of 8 September 1560, Lord Robert's wife Amy Robsart was discovered by servants dead at the foot of a staircase.

Amy's death was extremely convenient for Dudley. The 22-year-old Queen Elizabeth was greatly infatuated with him and it is possible that he was in love with her. Gossip spread in the courts of Europe. Would the widower now marry his sovereign to become King Consort? Was this what Elizabeth wanted too? Did they engineer Amy's death to make the marriage possible?

Pamphleteers had a field day concerning Amy's death. One said this:

> When [Robert Dudley] was in full hope to marry the Queen, he did but send his wife aside to the house of his servant, Forster of Cumnor, where shortly after she had the chance to fall from a pair of stairs [a staircase with a landing in the middle] and break her neck, but yet without hurting of the hood that stood upon her head.

This pamphlet brought into focus what gossips were saying about the mysterious death of Amy Robsart. In 1560 Cumnor Hall had only one storey; if Amy Robsart had so fallen she would have been unlikely to have killed herself. An inquest was held into the death, but the coroner's verdict of mischance and accidental death has vanished. Dudley did not attend the inquest or his wife's funeral. Amy was buried at the Church of St Mary the Virgin, High St, Oxford. Curiously when her coffin was opened in the early 1950s it was found to be empty. Mystery throughout history has attached itself to the name of Amy Robsart.

Robert Dudley and Princess Elizabeth Tudor had known each other from childhood. Dudley met Amy around 1549 when they were both 17. Amy was the daughter and wealthy heiress of Sir John Robsart, Lord of the Manor of Syderstone, Norfolk. Robert was the fifth son of John Dudley, Earl of Warwick and Duke of Northumberland, a great power in the land as Protector during the reign of the boy king Edward VI. Dudley's brother Lord Guildford Dudley, his father and sister-in-law, Lady Jane Grey, were all executed in the intrigue to subvert the succession of Mary Tudor as Queen of England. Dudley escaped the ultimate punishment partly through the intervention of King Philip of Spain.

By this time Robert Dudley had married Amy Robsart on 4 June 1550 at the Royal Palace of Sheen, Richmond, Surrey, and Amy administered his estates while he was in prison over the Lady Jane Grey conspiracy. It is thought that at first their marriage was a love match, but as the pair began to drift apart, William Cecil said the union was 'a carnal marriage, begun for pleasure and ended in lamentation'.

In the Tower at the same time as Dudley was the Princess Elizabeth, for her supposed machinations against her sister Mary, and it is there that romantic history supposes they fell in love. After Elizabeth's succession she openly showed her feelings for Dudley making him Master of Her Horse – she had some 250 horses – and this important court position led to more honours like the Privy Council, the Garter and in 1564 he was created Earl of Leicester. Consequently Dudley's dalliance at court meant that Amy was neglected and she ultimately, after shunting from friend to relative and back again, went to live at Cumnor Hall.

There were many rumours in the courts of Europe that Elizabeth and Dudley would marry, but the presence of Amy Robsart was an obvious obstacle. During April 1559 the Spanish ambassador De Feria sent this report to Madrid:

> Lord Robert [Dudley] had come so much into favour that he does whatever he likes with affairs, and it is even said that Her Majesty visits him in his chamber night and day. People talk of this so freely that they go so far as to say that his wife has a malady in one of her breasts and the Queen is only waiting for her to die to marry Lord Robert.

King Philip of Spain sent Alvaro de Quatro, Bishop of Aquila to London to monitor the situation. He reported thus to his master:

> I have heard from a certain person who is accustomed to give veracious news that Lord Robert has sent to poison his wife. Certainly all the Queen has done in the matter of her marriage is only keeping Lord Robert's enemies and the country engaged with words until this wicked deed is consummated.

Rumour grew on rumour that Dudley would soon divorce his wife or poison her. The libellous document written up by the Roman Catholic enemies of Elizabeth and Dudley called *Leicester's Commonwealth* (1584) even suggests that one Dr Bayley, Queen Elizabeth's professor of physics at Oxford, was approached to supply a deadly 'physic' – he refused.

What can we piece together about Amy Robsart's death? On the day she died there were two other people resident at Cumnor Hall. A widowed housekeeper, the sister-in-law of Forster, Mrs Edith Odingsells, aunt of Dudley's page Richard Verney and one Mrs William Owen, a relative of the property's owner Dr Owen. All the house servants had been released by Amy to attend 'Our Lady's Fair' on this the Feast of the Nativity of the Blessed Virgin. On their return they found Amy's dead body at the foot of the staircase. Both murder and suicide were mentioned. Was she murdered elsewhere then her body placed at the foot of the staircase to cover up the foul deed? The cause of death was certainly a broken neck. Circumstantial testimony suggested that a maid had overhead her mistress pray to God for deliverance. Deliverance from what? Her miserable marriage?

Such a mode of death is hardly credible for suicide; the drop was not high enough. The *Leicester's Commonwealth* publication's assertion that she was murdered by Anthony Forster or page Richard Verney hardly holds water either. Although Dudley had a motive for murder, could it have been an accident? Back in 1559 Ambassador De Feria had mentioned a 'malady in one of [Amy's] breasts'; could this have been cancer that ate into her bones that caused her neck to break after a slippage on the stairs?

When the death was announced few believed that Amy Robsart had met her death by accident. We shall never know the truth. The story of Amy Robsart's death has been expanded, polished, embellished and recounted down the centuries, with the enemies of Elizabeth and Dudley's reputations keeping it alive. Centuries after its happening the story appeared in the fanciful novel of Sir Walter Scott called *Kenilworth* (1821) and the whole mystery was given new life. Hereby, the rumours of Elizabeth and Dudley's love leading to murder will never be stilled.

♦ Did intruders breach the walls of Buckingham Palace?

INTRUDER AT THE QUEEN'S BEDSIDE
She kept him talking for 10 minutes … then a footman came to her aid.
                                    Daily Express, *Friday 9 July 1982*.

Since the increased incidence of possible terrorist attacks, new state-of-the-art CCTV cameras and alarms have been installed at Buckingham Palace and the number of armed officers have been increased. A new royal security coordinator post was created for royal palaces when in 2003 comedian Aaron Barschak gatecrashed Prince

William's 21st birthday party at Windsor Castle, and newspaper reporter from the *Daily Mirror* Ryan Parry obtained a job as a footman. A series of notorious incidences of intruders at royal palaces have occurred in modern times. For instance, in July 1982, Michael Fagan obtained access to the queen's bedroom, but probably the most incredible Buckingham Palace intruder was during the early years of Queen Victoria's reign.

Around 5 o'clock on the morning of 14 December 1838, gentleman porter at Buckingham Palace, George Cox, was going about his duties when he came across a begrimed boy wandering the corridors. On being challenged the boy fled, but was soon arrested in the Marble Hall. He appeared before Magistrate White. Although he gave his name as Edward Cotton, the 15-year-old was really one Edward Jones, whose father Henry Jones was a tailor in Bell Yard, York Street, Westminster, who had thrown him out for bad behaviour. Jones had worked for a time as a builder's apprentice. His intention in breaching the wall of Buckingham Palace, wherein he had successfully avoided the numerous gentlemen porters, duty constables of the A Division and foot guards, was to see Queen Victoria at close quarters, sketch the palace's grand staircase, and attend a Privy Council meeting. All this he had done over a period of eleven months, successfully secreting himself in cupboards and empty rooms. He told the magistrate: 'I was obliged to wash my shirt, now and again', and he lived off 'victuals in the kitchen'. Jones appeared before the magistrate twice on remand for further investigations and was finally to appear at Westminster Sessions on 28 December 1838. His defence lawyer, Mr Prendergast, convinced the jury that Jones's actions were no more than a 'boyish prank' and he was found Not Guilty of a malicious intent to harm the queen.

Edward Jones became something of a celebrity; he was dubbed 'In-I-Go' Jones by the poet Samuel Rogers and was offered a job as a 'turn' on the theatrical stage. Jones turned down the offer.

His thirst for exploring the mysteries of the royal household brought him once more into the public eye. Just after midnight on Thursday 3 December 1840, Queen Victoria's nurse Mrs Lilly was awoken by a noise in the queen's dressing-room. She summoned the page Mr Kinnaird and with Queen Victoria's old governess Baroness Lehzen, they discovered Edward Jones under a sofa. This time proceedings against Jones were conducted in private by the Privy

Council, who discovered that he had scaled the walls of Buckingham Palace somewhere up Constitution Hill and had entered by a window. He said he had enjoyed sitting in Queen Victoria's throne. Jones was committed to the House of Correction for three months as 'a rogue and a vagabond'. Jones's new case was made much of in the comic papers *The Age*, *The Satirist* and *Punch*. Edward Jones, however, was not finished with his palace escapades.

Jones was given a further three months detention in March 1841 for planning a new entry to Buckingham Palace. On his release Jones was again arrested; this time he was found in the royal apartments 'enjoying a hearty meal of cold meat and potatoes'.

The newspaper-reading public were amused at Jones's battle of wits with the palace authorities, who had increased security. The Privy Council took the view that the ease in which Jones entered the palace might tempt an assassin to emulate the boy. Jones was given a further three months sentence, this time with hard labour.

Jones's escapades became a political football to annoy Prime Minister Lord Melbourne. Something had to be done about Jones once and for all. In the end, after official bungling in order to get him a berth, Edward Jones was 'sent to sea' and nothing more was heard of him.

FARMS AND FADS,
VALUES AND VINEGAR BIBLES

♦ Why was George III called 'Farmer George'?

> The King rode with me for two and a half hours, talking farming and
> reasoning upon points ... His farm is in admirable order, and crops all
> clean and fine ...
>
> *Arthur Young (1741–1820), editor of* Annals of Agriculture *(1748–1809).*

George III's nickname 'Farmer George' is well known. The king's
interest in agriculture is hardly surprising, for the majority of his
subjects were employed in agriculture. From the reign of Henry I
there was hunting parkland around Windsor Castle. By the 1780s
George III brought Windsor Castle back to life after some fifty
years of neglect. As George was, as author Michael De-la-Noy has
pointed out, 'far better fitted for the role of country squire than
that of king', he expressed his interest in agriculture by developing
Windsor Castle's parklands. He had the land at Lower Park (Datchet,
or Mastrick Meadows) and Upper Park (Frogmore side) surveyed
for agricultural possibilities, and particularly at Frogmore farm
he indulged his bent in overseeing the husbandry with the help
of the manager Mr Kent. Here George incorporated the farming
methods pioneered in Holland and Norfolk and developed a dairy.
Even so George took almost daily pleasure in inspecting his three
farms at Windsor which covered in excess of 1,000 acres. He created
them in Windsor Great Park and his enthusiasm for them assured
that they ran at a profit. George's academic knowledge of farming
sheep, botany and agriculture in general was thorough. Acting on
the advice of President of the Royal Society, Sir Joseph Banks, he
imported sheep from Spain. His sheep farming acted out a key role
in the breeding of sheep which laid down the ancestor strains from
Australia and New Zealand's Merino sheep. It may be noted on a

more domestic level that George III and Queen Charlotte were the first to import the (German) Christmas tree to England, but it was Prince Albert who popularised it nationwide.

George III wrote letters to the publication *Annals of Agriculture* on farming practices under the pen-name of Ralph Robinson, the name of one of his shepherds. He kept up-to-date with all the latest developments in agriculture and animal husbandry. When Captain Cook set off in *Endeavour* in 1769, the king asked Cook to take with him a number of his farm animals to stock new herds in Polynesia.

The man in the street looked upon George III's love of farming as comical. His agricultural interests gave great scope to the cartoonists of the day who lampooned him as 'Farmer George'. The popular caricaturist James Gillray set society laughing with such depictions of George as 'alarming a cottager at Windsor by his persistent questioning and close inspection'. Gillray also portrayed George and Queen Charlotte in country farming garb riding home to the castle from a country fair. George was satirised as well in words. John Wolcot (Peter Pindar) offered the public the scenario of George hobnobbing with a farm labourer's wife as to how an apple gets into an apple dumpling. George had the habit of adding 'What! What!' to everything he said so Wolcot used that too in the apple dumpling skit:

> In tempting row the naked dumplings lay,
> When lo! the monarch in his usual way,
> Like lightening spoke, 'What's this? what's this? what? what?'
> 'No!' cried the staring monarch with a grin,
> 'How? how? the devil got the apple in?'

♦ Which king brought fun to royal sailing?

'... the year '60 the Dutch gave His Majesty a yacht called *Mary*, whence came the improvement to our present yachts, for until that time we had not heard such a name in England.

Sir Anthony Deane (c. 1638–1721), shipbuilder to Samuel Pepys.

Monastic chroniclers tell us that the English King Edgar was rowed down the River Dee in his royal barge from Chester to the monastery of St John the Baptist in 973. Thereafter, succeeding kings like Edward III, aboard his *Grace de Dieu* had their own vessels dubbed 'royal'. The seed of an idea that ships could be used for 'fun sailing' was sown in 1604 when shipbuilder Phineas Pett was given the commission by the Lord High Admiral to build a ship for James I/VI's 14-year-old son Prince Henry. Alas Henry never got to sail in her as he died in 1612, but the seed was brought to fruition by Henry's great-nephew Charles II.

While in exile in Holland, Charles II became familiar with the Dutch *jacht* (yacht) and formed an enthusiasm for sailing. After his Restoration to the British throne, Charles II pursued his love of sailing. In 1661 he commissioned for £1,335 the 90-ton royal yacht *Katherine* (named after his future wife Catherine of Braganza, Infanta of Portugal). In all, Charles II was to have twenty-seven royal yachts and thus became the 'father of sailing yachts' and the first king in Europe to own a royal yacht and inject fun into sailing. The apotheosis of 'fun sailing' was probably in the reign of Edward VII; his yacht, £8,000 Clyde-built *Britannia*, designed by G.L. Watson, won 231 firsts in 635 races.

BRITISH ROYAL YACHTS 1660–1997

Charles II

Mary – 1660. Considered the first ever official royal yacht.

Royal Escape – 1660. Formerly *Surprise*. Took the king to exile.

Anne – 1661.

Bezan – 1661. A present from the Dutch. A racing vessel.

Catherine – 1661. Named after Queen Catherine of Braganza.

Minion – 1661.

Greyhound – n.d. Racing vessel.

Royal Charles – 1662. Present at the battle of Lowestoft.

Jemmy – 1662. Named after James, Duke of Monmouth.

Henrietta – 1663.

Merlin – 1666. The king ordered special Holland quilts for his bed on the vessel and fine chamber pots.

Monmouth – 1666.

Navy – 1666.

Saudadoes – 1670.

Cleveland – 1671.

Queensborough – 1671.

Deale – 1673.

Isle of Wight – 1673.

Kitchen – 1674.

Catherine – 1674. Second yacht so named after the queen.

Portsmouth – 1674.

Royal Charles – 1675. Second yacht so named.

Charlot – 1677.

Mary – 1677. Second yacht so named.

Henrietta – 1679. Second yacht so named.

Izabella Bezan – 1680.

Fubbs – 1682. Perhaps the first royal yacht named after a royal mistress. 'Fubbs', from the English word 'chubby' was the king's nickname for his mistress Louise Kéroüalle, Duchess of Portsmouth. Vessel broken up, 1770.

Isabella – 1683.

William III & Mary II

William & Mary – 1694.

Squirrel – 1694.

William III

Scout – 1695.

Queensborough – 1701. The second yacht so named.

Soesdyke – 1702.

Portsmouth – 1702. The second yacht so named.

Queen Anne

Isabella – 1703. The second yacht so named.

Drake – 1705.

Dublin – 1709.

Bolton – 1709.

Charlot – 1710. The second yacht so named.

Carolina – 1710. *Royal Caroline*, 1733. Originally *Peregrine*.

Chatham – 1710.

George II

Chatham – 1741. The second
yacht so named.

Portsmouth – 1742. The third
yacht so named.

Royal Caroline – 1749. Renamed
Royal Charlotte, 1761.

Dorset – 1753.

Plymouth – 1755.

George III

Augusta – 1771. Renamed *Princess
Augusta*, 1773.

Portsmouth – 1796. The fourth
yacht so named.

Plymouth – 1796. The second
yacht so named.

Royal Sovereign – 1804. Became a
depot ship after 1830.

William & Mary – 1807. The
second yacht so named.
Became a depot ship after 1830.

Royal George – 1817. Broken up,
1905. Used by George IV for
his trip to Scotland.

Prince Regent – 1820. Presented to
the Imam of Muscat in 1836.

George IV

Royal Charlotte – 1824. The second
so named. Broken up after 1830.

William IV

Royal Adelaide – 1833. Broken up,
1877.

Queen Victoria

Victoria & Albert – 1842.
Renamed *Osborne*, 1855.

Fairy – 1844. Vessel in which the
queen toured the west coast of
Scotland in 1847. *Victoria &
Albert* in attendance.

Elfin – 1848. Broken up, 1901.

Victoria & Albert – 1854. The
second yacht so named. Broken
up, 1904.

Alberta – 1863. Broken up, 1913.

Osborne – 1870. The second yacht
so named. Sold, 1908.

Victoria & Albert – 1899. The third
so named. Broken up, 1855.

Edward VII

Alexandra – 1908. Sold, 1925 to
Norway as the *Prince Olaf*.
Sunk by German bombs, 1940.

Edward VII (as Prince of Wales)
raced his yachts:
Dagmar, 1866; *Princess*, 1869;
Alexandra, 1871; *Zenobia*, 1872;
Hildegarde, 1876; *Formosa*, 1880;
Aline, 1882, and *Britannia*.

Elizabeth II

Britannia – 1953.

Decommissioned, 1997. Now
permanently moored as a
tourist attraction at Leith.

♦ Who rank as the most superstitious monarchs?

Should any salt be spilled in the royal presence, Queen Elizabeth II is
likely to throw a pinch over her left shoulder to avoid bad luck.

Royal Court Gossip.

The roots of Scottish and English medieval monarchs' superstitions
were largely imbedded in religion, from the worship of holy relics
to the fears that the Devil might take a hand in mortal affairs. James
I/VI was particularly obsessed with the supposed machinations of
the Devil and witches, and wrote an account of his superstitions
concerning them in his book *Daemonologie* (1597). And writing on
James II/VII, John Evelyn said that the king 'spoke of some relics of
our Blessed Saviour's cross, that healed a gentleman's rotting nose by
only touching'. James I/VI also had some strange beliefs concerning
superstitious cures. As a sufferer from arthritis and gout, the king
attempted to cure the conditions 'by standing up in the belly of
bucks and stags slaughtered in the hunting field'.

The diaries and journals of courtiers are awash with comment on
the supposed superstitions of monarchs. Caroline Amelia Elizabeth,
uncrowned queen of George IV is said to have made wax 'devil'
figures of her estranged husband, stuck pins in them and threw them
in the fire, in a superstitious attempt to cause him a quick demise.
She died in 1821, preceding her husband by nine years.

Queen Victoria had a number of superstitious quirks – touching
wood for good luck was one. She followed the old Scots superstition
that it was unlucky to marry in May, forbidding her children to do
so. Detractors had lampooned Mary, Queen of Scots, for marrying
James Hepburn, 4th Earl of Bothwell as her third husband on
15 May 1567, quoting the line by Ovid: 'Wantons marry in the month
of May.' It was also, too, as if Queen Victoria harked back to the
cult of relics. Her desk was strewn with artefacts relating to relatives
dead and alive; visitors found it gruesome to see her tables exhibiting
plaster casts of the hands and feet of her children.

Edward VII was extremely superstitious; he had a dread of crossed
knives on a table as an omen of bad luck; similarly a misplaced medal
on a tunic, he said, was an evil omen. His valets and footmen were
forbidden to turn his mattress on a Friday lest it bring ill-fortune for
the rest of the week. Neither would he sit down at a table if there

was a company of thirteen. On one occasion Lady Londonderry remembered that as they sat down to a party of thirteen the king was nervous, until his mistress Alice Keppel pointed out that one of the ladies present was pregnant. The king's pockets usually contained a mascot or two. When Sir Luke Fildes prepared to draw the scene of Edward VII's deathbed in 1901 he was surprised to see that the bed head was decorated with a number of charms and talismans. The king's daughter, Princess Victoria, enlightened Fildes: 'The old dear used to think they brought him luck.'

◆ Which king would have liked to be a fireman?

> The King has always been a man of many interests, some of them so diverse as to seem to the superficial observer contradictory. He has ... always been keenly concerned in the scientific side of fire extinction.
> *J. Penderel Brodhurst,* King Edward VII *(1911).*

It was a fire in the nursery at Marlborough House in 1864, the home of the Prince and Princess of Wales, that stimulated a new interest for Albert Edward, Prince of Wales. The fire was quickly under control and Edward assisted by chopping at burning floorboards and organising the servants in forming a human chain to carry buckets and jugs of water. The location of the fire meant that Chief of the Metropolitan Fire Brigade Captain (later Sir) Eyre Massey Shaw attended. Stimulated by the event, Edward asked Shaw to let him know of any significant fires in London in which he might assist. Shaw agreed. Not long after this, Edward joined the fire crew at the blaze on 23 February 1865, which destroyed seventeenth-century Saville House, Leicester Square. Once the royal residence of Queen Charlotte, wife of George II, the building had later uses, 'mostly downward' as one commentator remarked. Thirty minutes after the blaze began Edward attended with his friend George Leveson-Gower, 3rd Duke of Sutherland. Biographer J. Penderel Brodhurst recounted:

> The Prince, who was much cheered by the crowd, put on a fireman's helmet and jacket and approached as near to the flames as safety would permit, that he might the better watch the work of extinction.

It was not unusual for Edward to leave the dinner table with friends and equerries to attend a fire. Queen Victoria did not approve of such 'gallivanting', but to no avail.

♦ Why does Queen Elizabeth II have corgis?

> Have a footman enter with a silver tray each afternoon. On it should be: a jug of gravy, a plate of dog biscuits, a bowl of dog food and three spoons.
> *Queen Elizabeth II's advice on the care of corgis, as noted by Craig Brown and Lesley Cunliffe (1982).*

In 1933, when she was 7 years old, her father King George VI (then Duke of York) gave Princess Elizabeth her first corgi. Thereafter the dog, and subsequent additions, became a part of her life. As a general rule visitors and staff are wary of the dogs. The princess's nanny, Marion Crawford, remembered how one corgi, Dookie, 'took a piece out of Lord Lothian's hand'. His lordship dismissed the incident as 'nothing'. 'All the same', said the princess, 'he bled all over the floor'. Wherever she went, even on honeymoon, the princess, and then as queen, took the corgi too, whether by car or aircraft of the Queen's Flight.

In 2006 the queen chartered the vessel *Hebridean Princess* for a tour around the coast of Scotland as part of her 80th birthday celebrations. The company owning the vessel had a strict no dogs policy. As part of the £125,000 charter, the queen insisted that the ban be lifted to accommodate her beloved corgis – it was. Over the years the queen has had in excess of thirty corgis, and in 2007 the tally was five, Emma, Linnet, Monty, Holly and Willow.

More than one courtier has expressed the opinion that to Queen Elizabeth dogs are the 'real love of her life' – along with horses.

The queen is following a long tradition of royal 'pet keeping'. The chronicler Goscelin, writing in the *Life of St Edith* (c.1080) about Princess Edith (d.984), the daughter of Edgar I of the House of Cedric and Denmark, noted that she cared for a personal 'suburb' (i.e. precinct) of native and foreign animals at Wilton Nunnery, which had been founded by Ealhswith (d.902), queen of Alfred the Great. The animals may have been gifts to the princess and her mother Queen Athelfleda, Abbess of Wilton. Perhaps this was the first zoological collection in England. Nevertheless, a collection of wild animals for court pleasure and display began when Henry I maintained his menagerie in his park at Woodstock, near Oxford. His animals included lions, camels and a porcupine, gifted to him by brother monarchs.

Royal pets have been immortalised in paintings and photographs. Van Dyck portrayed the five children of Charles I in 1637, with the Prince of Wales (later Charles II) leaning his arm on the head of a huge dog. Queen Victoria spent regular sums on having her animals photographed. For example, in 1854 photographer William Bambridge took about a month to photograph the royal dogs; his bill for the mounted album was £25.19s (£25.95: about £1,650 today). Queen Victoria also pioneered the royal animal memorial. When her beloved King Charles spaniel Dash died in 1840, the dog, a gift from her mother the Duchess of Kent and which had been painted in oils by Edwin Landseer, was given this epitaph:

> His attachment was without selfishness,
> His playfulness without malice,
> His fidelity without deceit.
> Reader, if you would live beloved and die regretted, profit by the example of Dash.

When Queen Victoria married Prince Albert, his German greyhound Eos went with them on honeymoon. Victoria had Eos painted by Landseer in a portrait she gave Albert as a Christmas present in 1841. Eos died in 1844 and was buried in Windsor Castle Home Park; a statue, based on the Landseer portrait, was erected in memory of the dog. The policies of all Queen Victoria's homes were bespotted with the graves of her pets. As her journals, photographs and portraits show, Queen Victoria favoured dachshunds, pomeranians and collies. When she showed interest in the latter breed the collie became fashionable; so much so that the dog's photographs were sold as cartes-de-visite.

Kennels were built in Windsor Home Park in 1840–1 and at any one time the queen had upwards of 100 dogs. When Edward VII succeeded to the throne in 1903 he had the kennels moved to Sandringham. Perhaps Edward VII's most famous dog was Caesar, a terrier bred by the Duchess of Newcastle. A mischievous dog that had disdain for all but the king; it went with him everywhere from Balmoral to Biarritz. He was even immortalised as a Carl Fabergé jewelled chalcedony figurine; Caesar sported a specially made collar with the inscription: 'I am Caesar. I belong to the king.' In 1910 Caesar won international fame when he walked behind the coffin at the monarch's funeral procession.

Today the queen remains one of the most famous breeders of Pembroke corgis in the world, each dog sharing the bloodline of her first corgi, Susan. Thus corgis and royalty now go together.

◆ Who was Britain's first royal car owner?

[John Montague as driver in] April 1902 is notable as being the first time
a reigning monarch of England [*sic*] had been driven in a motor-car.
Lord Montague, The Motoring Montagues.

The motor car had many detractors as 'dirty' and 'evil' when Albert Edward, Prince of Wales, had his first drive. Called the 'autocar', or 'horseless carriage' in its early form, the machine caught the prince's imagination when at 55 he had his first drive on 14 February 1896 at the Imperial Institute, South Kensington. The vehicle was a Cannstall-Daimler and the driver was The Hon. Evelyn Ellis, cousin of the prince's equerry Gen Sir Arthur Ellis. The car had rubber-tyred carriage wheels, carriage lamps, flat mudguards and a large leather hood. Steering was the 'tiller' type and the engine was mid-mounted. A second demonstration by Daimler took place in the grounds of Buckingham Palace on 27 November 1897. The prince's first drive on public roads was in June 1898 when he visited the Earl of Warwick at Warwick Castle. A fleet of Daimlers took the royal party to Compton Verney, the home of Lord Willoughby de Broke. The prince bought his first Daimler in the early part of 1900; this had the Model A frame with a twin-cylinder 6hp engine with bodywork by Hoopers of London. The prince was taught to drive by Oliver Stanton (who had taught him to cycle). By 1905 the now King Edward had purchased seven Daimlers. In 1904 Queen Alexandra became the first crowned queen of Great Britain to own a car; in this year she took delivery of a 24hp Wolseley landaulette.

◆ Which monarch had the most hobbies?

A vulgar business.
Queen Charlotte when George III expressed interest in horseracing as a pastime.

Writing of her time as private secretary to Edward, Prince of Wales, as the then exiled King Edward VIII, Duke of Windsor, Dina Wells Hood saw at first hand how his devotion to the pastimes of dancing, socialising and particularly golf, came before public duties. Following his abdication in 1936 and his marriage to the former Mrs Ernest Simpson, the activities of the new Duke and Duchess of Windsor was constant fodder for the international press. The duke's hobbies of bagpipe playing, toy animal and shell collecting were all given column inches, and stimulated the lasting thirst for gossip about royal hobbies.

The duke's father, George V, was a stickler for duty and his hobbies were largely threefold: yachting, shooting game and philately. In the former two he followed his father Edward VII, but he did not pursue his father's additional hobbies of gambling and serial adultery. George V's enthusiasm for stamp collecting was aroused by the collection of his uncle Prince Alfred, Duke of Edinburgh, whose albums form the basis of the present Royal Stamp Collection. When he died in 1936 George V's collection of stamps had swelled to 250,000 in 325 large volumes. As for Queen Mary, her interest was in the collection of royal iconography, particularly that of the descendants of George III and Queen Charlotte, as well as for miniature *objets d'art* and doll's house furniture. The famous 'Queen Mary's Doll's House' of 1924 at Windsor Castle was designed for her by Sir Edwin Lutyens. The suggestion for such a house was that of Queen Victoria's granddaughter Princess Marie-Louise (erstwhile Princess Aribert of Anhalt). The interior collection was amassed from many sources and is on permanent public display.

Although he was not a monarch – Queen Victoria made him Prince Consort in 1857 – her husband Prince Albert of Saxe–Coburg made hobbies and pastimes the source of practical inventions and designs. From his childhood, Prince Albert's hobbies had a definite practical purpose. His collection of (sea) shells, for instance, became an addition to the Naturmuseum at Coburg. In adulthood he designed hats, medals, houses, furniture and room decorations and supported the arts and sciences, daily scouring sources for new ideas. In this he was an arch-hobbyist. On several occasions Queen Victoria had toyed with the idea of creating Prince Albert 'King Consort'; Prime Minister Lord Melbourne ruled this out entirely but Albert could be considered 'King of Hobbyists'.

♦ How did James I/VI come to commission a new Bible?

[I] could never yet see a Bible well translated in English.
James I/VI at the Hampton Court Conference, 1604.

James Charles Stuart was born at Edinburgh Castle on 19 June 1566, the only son of Mary, Queen of Scots, and Henry, Lord Darnley. He was crowned King of Scots at Stirling Castle when just 13 months old. He ruled Scotland for thirty-six years before he added the realm of England to his monarchy in 1603 on the death of Elizabeth I. James I/VI was dubbed 'the wisest fool in Christendom' by King Henry IV of France; he was loud, boorish, unwashed and weak of limbs, yet in 1611 he introduced his own Authorised Edition to the Bible, which is known today as the King James Bible, the language of the Anglican church.

In January 1604 James called the Hampton Court Conference with the determination to hear of 'things pretended to be amiss in the church'. Ostensibly to hear complaints levelled by the Puritans. Although the revision of the Bible – a factor which had been discussed for decades – was not on the agenda, the Puritan president of Corpus Christi College, Dr John Reynolds, asked the king that there be a new translation of the Bible as those versions of Henry VIII and Edward VI's reigns were 'corrupt and not answerable to the truth of the Original'. King James was in full accord with this idea. The Geneva Bible was the one in common use and James considered it to be the worst. He had already proposed a new version of the scriptures to the General Assembly of the Kirk of Scotland in 1601 and had made his feelings about the Geneva Bible well known. He thought the marginal notes in the Geneva Bible to be subversive. For instance, he quoted the note on Exodus 1:19, wherein the midwives opposed to Pharaoh were allowed 'disobedience to Kings'. Thoughts of the execution of his mother Mary, Queen of Scots were engendered by the note at 2 Chronicles 15:16 where Asa is criticised for merely deposing his mother Maachah 'and not killing her'. So, a resolution for a new translation was set in motion.

James set about selecting fifty-four 'learned men' to carry out the work; only forty-seven are known to have actually set about the task of translation in six groups, working at Westminster under Lancelot Andrews, then Dean of Westminster; at Cambridge, under Edward Lively, Professor of Hebrew; and at Oxford under John Harding. A final revison of all the work was undertaken by Myles Smith, later Bishop of Gloucester and Thomas Bilson, Bishop of Winchester. The completed work was issued in 1611 with a dedicatory epistle to King James. Thus, the Authorised Version eclipsed all previous versions of the Bible.

Over the years, versions of the Bible have appeared with various typos that have made them rarities. One such was published in 1717 by King's Printer John Bask of Oxford. In Luke 20, the Parable of the Vineyard is rendered Parable of the Vinegar, thus producing the 'Vinegar Bible', copies of which sell at large prices in auction rooms.

◆ What were Victorian values, and did Queen Victoria have them?

Many of the 'Victorian values' which are well remembered and discussed today came to the fore in [the nineteenth century] to form part of a code of behaviour designed to govern every aspect of life.

James Walvin, Victorian Values *(1987).*

Today we do not resemble the Victorians; it is almost as if they lived in a different Britain to us for we have almost nothing in common with them. Victorians were the last generations to know real self-confidence that their world would endure. Victorians enjoyed a strong sense of national security, patriotism and belonging, all based on a rigid code of social behaviour that is in conflict with the twenty-first century concept of personal freedom. The brutal consequences of world war, financial depression and nuclear uncertainty expunged the last vestiges of Victorianism.

Chronologically the Victorian age ran from Queen Victoria's accession to the throne, on the death of her uncle William IV at 2.12 a.m. of 20 June 1837 at Windsor Castle, to her death at 6.30 p.m. on 22 January 1901 at Osborne House.

At the moment of Queen Victoria's death, Britain was undoubtedly one of the world's leading powers; the nation was at the peak of its economic and imperial achievement; the Royal Navy ruled the waves and the country ruled vast tracts of the earth and her industries dominated the markets of the world.

The cement that kept Victorian society together was its supposed 'values'. Many of these 'values' had their roots in past ages, but the Victorians honed their own variations. A selection of these, and there were many more, might be quoted thus: *Chastity* – Victorian society was not sexually repressed, chastity was largely conformed to because of fear of pregnancy, the shame of bastardy, contraction of venereal disease and a strong religious feeling that 'being unchaste' before marriage was improper. *Prudery* – As the age progressed doctors gave more attention to the physiology and psychology of sexuality; bastardy, prostitution, homosexuality and lesbianism (Queen Victoria did not think the latter was possible) became more openly debated. Printed (rather than visual) pornography was circulated among middle- and upper-class males, featuring mostly the sexual adventures of lower-class women. Albert Edward, Prince of Wales, is said to have been supplied with such pornography by the notorious philanderer Sir Frederick Johnstone.

The Victorians also promoted a huge amount of nudity in art, from the nude bather pictures of William Etty and Lawrence Alma Tadema to the wide range of naked statues in museums and gardens. People bathing nude at the seaside was not unusual. One who enjoyed such public nudity was the Revd Frances Kilvert, who in his *Diary* under the date Thursday 5 September 1872, wrote:

> I was out early before breakfast this morning bathing from the sands. There was a delicious feeling of freedom in stripping in the open air and running down naked to the sea, where the waves were curling white with foam and the red morning sunshine glowing upon the naked limbs of bathers.

The Victorians then slipped in and out of prudery and permissiveness with relish. But what of Queen Victoria in these matters? Although a virgin on her wedding night, Queen Victoria and Prince Albert seem to have had a vigorous sex life – 'fun in bed' as the queen described it – producing nine children. Publicly stiff and serious, Queen Victoria was not a prude; in a letter of 1859 to her daughter Victoria, then wife of the Crown Prince of Prussia, she opined that women were 'born for man's pleasure and amusement'. But she considered childbirth *die Schaltenseile* (the shadow-side) of marriage. Her art collection did not exclude the nude pictures of the day, and nude statues were to be seen in her various residences. Overall though, Queen Victoria insisted on the Victorian virtue of *Decorum*, propriety of conduct in all things.

Hard work, *Industry*, *Respect for the Law*, *Thrift*, *Honesty*, *Sense of Duty* and *Patriotism* were all Victorian values. Queen Victoria had a high sense of them all. The poor had to work hard to exist, Queen Victoria did it because she felt it her role and her own sense of duty was exemplary.

'*Cleanliness* is next to godliness', quoted by John Wesley in his *Sermons*, No. xciii 'Dress', is one of the clichés associated with Victorians. Wesley also recited that 'God's in his heaven – All's right with the world', from Robert Browning's *Pippa Passes*. The construction of new sewers was a great Victorian municipal drive, and by the 1860s many of the gentry bathed daily, while the middle-classes bathed weekly. The poor, whose constant struggle against dirt led to defeat, bathed hardly at all, often despite the development of public baths and the passing of the Public Health Act, 1866. The death of the Prince Consort from the consequences of typhoid focused Queen Victoria's attention on cleanliness.

Victorian values continued to be a part of the public consciousness long after Queen Victoria's death. But in many ways their demise began on that fateful day, 28 June 1914, when Archduke Franz Ferdinand was assassinated at Sarajevo, plunging Europe into total war.

COURTIERS, CROWNS
AND CORONATIONS

♦ Did King John lose the Crown Jewels?

> King John lost his Crown in the Wash.
>> *Schoolboy 'laundry joke', nineteenth century.*

John Lackland, King of England from 6 April 1199 to 18 October
1216, the youngest son of Henry II and Eleanor of Aquitaine, is
probably best remembered today for being forced to sign the *Magna
Carta* (Great Charter) by rebel barons at Runnymede on 15 June
1215. Harshly blackened as an 'evil king' in the Robin Hood myths,
John did create a whole raft of enemies and it was during the last
civil war of his reign that he is believed to have lost his treasure and
the Crown Jewels.

King John had a great liking for jewellery and the loss of his
treasure greatly grieved him. Chroniclers note that his treasure chest
included:

> a clasp ornamented with emeralds and rubies, given him by the
> Bishop of Norwich, four rings of emerald, sapphire, garnets and
> topaz, presented to him by Pope Innocent III, 143 cups of white silver,
> a wand of gold with a cross given him by the Knights Hospitaller
> and the regalia which his grandmother Matilda wore when she was
> crowned Empress.

How did John manage to lose his treasure?

During the last civil war, John successfully took Cambridge from
the rebel barons and rode through Huntingdonshire and Lincolnshire
to subdue eastern England. After recovering from dysentery at Kings
Lynn, he led his army south-west to Wisbech on 11 October 1216.
His target was Swineshead Abbey. To achieve his goal he had to

cross the Wellstream (the old River Ouse), which flowed into the
Wash. As his soldiers advanced the baggage train containing supplies,
armaments, the royal treasure and the Crown Jewels lumbered
behind. The intention was to traverse the 4½ mile-wide mouth of
the Wellstream (now much further inland than it is today) at low
tide. In the autumn fenland mist the wagons lost their way, became
entrapped in quicksand and were stuck as the tides rushed in. The
chronicler Roger of Wendover in his *Flores Historiarum* noted, 'the
ground was opened in the midst of the waves, and bottomless
whirlpools engulfed everything, together with men and horses, so
that not a single foot-soldier got away to bear tidings of the disaster
to the king'. Dog-tired and wracked with dysentery, John died two
days later at Newark Castle; he was 48.

Biographer of John, Professor W.L. Warren, has a cautionary
comment for those who would 'treasure hunt' John's possessions.
He quotes the story of how a priest, who went to Newark Castle to
say the requiem mass for John, told Ralph, Abbot of Coggeshall, 'that
he had seen men leaving the city laden with loot'. Whether John
lost his treasures and Crown Jewels in the Wash, or was robbed of
them on his deathbed, remains a mystery. Only one thing is certain:
identifiable artefacts from such an event have never ever turned up.

◆ Which kings pawned their crowns?

> So lavish was his bounty ... that all the property attached to the
> Crown, in common with the revenues belonging to the royal
> exchequer, was virtually dealt out piecemeal to various people who
> presented demands ...
>
> The Westminster Chronicle *on Richard II.*

War and extravagance compelled some monarchs to pawn the
symbols of their sovereignty. England's regalia was first pawned by
Henry III (r.1216–72) to merchants in Paris. The regalia was new
– King John had lost the previous set (see previous entry) – and for
his first coronation at the age of 9, Henry was crowned with his
mother Isabella's torque. Henry was crowned again in 1220 with the
new regalia. The king pawned his crown to fund a crusade to the
Holy Land. The crusade never took place.

Edward III (r. 1327–77) pledged his crown to the merchants of Flanders, while it seems the sum of £20,000 was raised by Henry V (r. 1413–22) in pledging his crown and jewels. Undoubtedly the most profligate of the medieval monarchs was Richard II (r. 1377–99) who in 1386 pledged his crown and regalia to the City of London for £2,000. His receipt of redemption still exists. Richard had a penchant for extravagant habits. According to Holinshed's *Chronicles*, he employed 300 domestics in his kitchens alone and daily fed an entourage of courtiers, hangers-on and visitors of around 6,000. He soon spent the dowry of 200,000 marks brought to him when he married Isabella; the wedding alone cost 300,000 marks. Richard was continually borrowing money from his subjects who, when tipped off that the king was on the cadge, found urgent business elsewhere.

How many crowns are there in the English regalia?
… within the hollow crown
That rounds the mortal temples of a king.
                                   William Shakespeare, Richard III, *3, ii.*

Within the royal regalia of England – for Scotland has its own regalia – are set eight crowns, all to be found in the Royal Jewel House, Tower of London. Most of the Crown Jewels of the time were melted down by Oliver Cromwell after the establishment of the Commonwealth in 1649, with a gem-breaking price of £3,650. On the Restoration of Charles II in 1660 much of the regalia was replaced at a cost of £31,978.

St Edward's Crown: Gold. The Crown of Coronations, made in 1661 for Charles II's coronation, although it has been altered several times since. It includes 444 precious stones. The design consists of four crosses pattée and four fleur-de-lis, with two arches on top surmounted by a jewelled cross. The crown remembers the diadem of Edward the Confessor, King of England, 1042–66; he was crowned with it at Winchester on 3 April 1043 and the Saxon crown was used at coronations for six hundred years. (Queen Elizabeth II for her coronation chose a stylised representation of the 1661 crown in 1953.)
Imperial State Crown: Gold. The monarch's personal crown, made 1937. The design is similar to one made for Queen Victoria's

coronation, 1838. It reflects the design of St Edward's Crown. Over 3,000 precious stones, including the spinel of Edward, Prince of Wales and Aquitaine, known as the Black Prince's Ruby and the Cullinan II diamond.

Imperial Crown of India: Made in 1911 for George V's visit to India as Emperor of India. Containing 6,000 diamonds it cost £70,000. It is not now used since British rule ended in India in 1947; it was made for use at the special coronation Durbar in India as an ancient law stated that the Crown of England should never leave the country.

George IV's State Diadem: Made in 1820 for use at George IV's coronation in 1821. It appeared in the coronation processions of Queen Victoria and Queen Elizabeth II.

The Crown of Mary of Modena: Worn by Mary of Modena, second wife of James II/VII, at his coronation in 1685. The cost of £110,000 caused public criticism. The crown was thereafter used by queen consorts.

Queen Alexandra's Crown: This was an update of the Crown of Mary of Modena and was worn by Queen Alexandra at the (delayed) coronation of Edward VII in 1902.

Queen Mary's Crown: Made in 1911 for the coronation of George V.
Queen Elizabeth (the Queen Mother): Crown made in 1937 for the coronation of George VI. The crown last appeared on her coffin at the funeral of the Queen Mother in 2002.

◆ Does Scotland have its own Crown Jewels?

Uneasy lies the head that wears a crown.
        William Shakespeare, King Henry IV, *Part 2, I, ii.*

With eight of Scotland's monarchs murdered – nine if you include Mary, Queen of Scots – many a Scots monarch's head has lain uneasy. Yet there are no finer symbols of Scotland's monarchy and feelings of independence and nationhood than its crown regalia. The Crown Jewels of Scotland are known as The Honours of Scotland and comprise three main artefacts.

The Crown: The foundation is the circlet of gold which is said to come from the helmet of Robert I, The Bruce, and which he wore at the Battle of Bannockburn, 24 June 1314. Bruce was crowned with the circlet in 1306. Surmounted by four golden arches and topped with a blue enamel celestial globe, the crown was altered for James V in 1540. This is the oldest crown of the British regalia. It is known that King John Baliol had a set of regalia but this was taken away from him by Edward I when he made Baliol his puppet ruler. The extant crown is set with carbuncles, jacinths, rod crystals, topazes, amethysts, diamonds and pearls. All these enclose a crimson bonnet.

The Sceptre: Presented to James IV in 1491 by Pope Alexander VI. It was re-modelled for James V in 1536.

The Sword of State: Of all these elements it is perhaps the Sword of State that has had the most adventurous life. During 2007 a special reception took place at the Palace of Holyrood to mark the 500th anniversary of the coming of the sword to Scotland. It was a gift to James IV from Giuliano della Rovere, known to history as Pope Julius II. During a celebration of solemn High Mass at the Abbey of Holyrood on Easter Sunday 1507 the sword was presented by *cavaliere* Antonio Inviziati, on behalf of the Pope.

The 1.4m steel-bladed sword was crafted by Italian cutler Domenico Da Sutri and came with a wooden scabbard covered with red velvet and a belt of silk and gold. The overall decorative design is based on the heraldic arms of Pope Julius II – oak tree, leaves and acorns, plus dolphins; the former representing the risen Christ and the latter his church. On the blade, which has been broken in two at some time in history, appear the figures of St Peter and St Paul on alternate sides; beneath each are the letters JULIUS II PONT[IFEX] MAX[IMUS] for 'Julius II, Supreme Pontiff'. With the sword came a consecrated hat of dark crimson velvet, lined with ermine. This too had symbolic designs of an embroidered gold dove decorated with pearls to signify the Holy Spirit.

From medieval times the Honours were kept at Edinburgh Castle to be produced for state occasions and for coronations. It seems they were first used together at the coronation of Mary, Queen of Scots at the Chapel Royal, Stirling Castle, 9 September 1543. Cardinal David Beaton, Archbishop of St Andrews placed the Crown symbolically on the head of the weeks old infant and guided her tiny hand around the shaft of the sceptre and wrapped the belt of the Sword of State around her waist. The Honours appeared again at the coronations of James VI at the Holy Rude Church, Stirling, 29 July 1567, Charles I at

Holyrood, 18 June 1633, and the impromptu coronation of Charles II at Scone on 1 January 1651.

For safe keeping, after Charles II's coronation in what was now Cromwell's occupation of Scotland, the regalia was moved to Dunottar Castle, near Stonehaven, the stronghold of the Earl Marischal of Scotland. The castle was besieged by Cromwellian troops for eight months, but before its surrender the regalia was spirited away by two courageous women, Mrs George Ogilvy of Barras, wife of the Governor of Dunottar and Mrs Christian Granger, wife of the Revd James Granger, minister of nearby Kinneff, aided by a servant girl. Until the Restoration in 1660 the regalia lay buried among some pews at Kinneff church. Incandescent that the regalia was missing, the Cromwellian commander ordered the castle governor Sir George Ogilvy and his wife to be vigorously interviewed into revealing where the regalia was. They never disclosed the secret location although Mrs Ogilvy died of her treatment. In Charles II's reign the regalia were back in Edinburgh Castle to be produced for sittings of the Scottish parliament. When this was dissolved on the Act of Union of 1707 a pledge was made that the regalia should never leave Scotland and they were locked away in an oak chest in the castle where they remained 'lost' for a century.

By the 1800s rumours circulated that the regalia had long been sent to England. Sir Walter Scott was one who believed that a search should be made for them. The chest was located, but could only be unlocked by Royal Warrant. Sir Walter persuaded the Prince Regent, later George IV, to grant the warrant and on 4 February 1819 the chest was opened. Sir Walter described the scene:

> The blows of the hammer echoed with a deep hollow sound . . . even those whose expectations had been most sanguine felt at the moment the probability of disappointment. . . . The joy was therefore extreme when the ponderous lid of the chest being forced open, at the expense of some time and labour, the Regalia was discovered lying at the bottom covered with linen cloths, exactly as they had been left in the year 1707. . . . The discovery was instantly announced by running up the Royal Standard above the Castle, to the shouts of the garrison and the multitude assembled on Castle Hill.

The Honours of Scotland are on permanent public display in the Crown Room of Edinburgh Castle, where they have rested since 1617 (apart from during the Cromwellian adventures and when they were hidden in the castle's King David's Tower, 1941–5). They play a pivotal role in Scottish constitutional life. They were formally presented to Elizabeth II (Elizabeth I in Scotland) at St Giles's Kirk, Edinburgh, on 24 June 1953, following the sovereign's London coronation; and they would appear in a similar role for future coronations. The Crown alone has been present at the state openings of the Scottish parliament since the first of 1999. Thereat the crown is carried by the Hereditary Keeper of the Palace of Holyroodhouse, the Duke of Hamilton and Brandon.

♦ Who stole the Crown Jewels?

> Blood that wears treason in his face,
> Villain complete in parson's gown,
> How muche he is at court in grace
> For stealing Ormond and the crown!
> Since loyalty does no man good,
> Let's steal the King, and outdo Blood.
>
> *Satirical verse on Colonel Thomas Blood (c. 1618–80).*

At one time the Crown Jewels were housed in Westminster Abbey, and it was 'one of the biggest burglaries in the history of crime', wrote Lewis Broad, that caused them to be transferred to the Tower of London. It was Edward the Confessor who granted the Abbey of St Peter at Westminster the privilege of housing the national regalia. The Crown Jewels were kept in the crypt of the Chapter House, a place secured by a huge double door locked with seven great keys. Herein too, was the wealth in jewels and coin of the Norman kings, who held the Benedictine monks of Westminster in great favour.

Before setting out for campaigns in the north in 1303, King Edward I accumulated a large sum of money in this strong-room. As he rested at Linlithgow, Scotland, a messenger appeared to tell him that the strong-room had been breached and a large part of the contents removed. On Edward's orders Father Wenlock, Abbot of Westminster was arrested, along with forty-eight monks, and thrown into the Tower. The Lord Mayor of London and the Master of the Wardrobe were put in charge of the investigation. The king was now assured that his diadem was safe, but his wealth had vanished. After some two years' of investigation the Sub-Prior and Sacrist were found guilty of the robbery, along with a merchant called Richard de Podlicote. Their fate is not known, but Edward I ordered that the Crown Jewels should now go to the Tower of London to be housed there in perpetuity. Even so, the Crown Jewels were not entirely safe.

The issue of 8–11 May 1671 of the *London Gazette* gave an account of perhaps the most outrageous robbery of the seventeenth century:

> This morning about seven of the clock, four men coming to Mr. Edwards, Keeper of the Jewel House in the Tower, desired to see the Regal Crown remaining in his custody, he carries them into the room where they were kept, and shows them; but according to the villainous design they it seems came upon, immediately they clap a gag of a strange form into the old man's mouth; who making what noise and resistance he could, they stabbed him a deep wound in the belly with a stilleto [a dagger with a narrow blade], adding several other dangerous wounds on the head with a small beetle [heavy wooden mallet] they had with them, as is believed, to beat together and flatten the Crown, to make it the more easily portable; which having, together with the Ball [i.e. Orb], put into Bags, they had to that purpose brought with them; they fairly walked out, leaving the old man grovelling on the ground, gagged and pinioned . . .

The leader of this gang was one Thomas Blood whom the *London Gazette* dubbed 'that notorious traytor and incendary'.

Thomas Blood was born around 1618 at Sarney, Dunboyne, County Meath, Ireland. From a Protestant landowning family Blood began his military career fighting for the Royalists during the Roman Catholic rebellion in Ireland. In 1646 a peace treaty was agreed between the Roman Catholics under Sir Phelim O'Neill and the Royalist James Butler, 12th Earl of Ormonde, which was unacceptable to many devout Protestants and Thomas Blood switched sides from Royalists to Parliamentarians. Thus he went to England to fight alongside his new comrades. In 1649 he was back in Ireland with Cromwell's troops. When Ireland was subjugated, Thomas Blood was rewarded with confiscated lands and a position as JP. Returning to England

Blood married Maria, daughter of Parliamentarian Col John Holcroft in 1650. Following the Restoration of 1660, Blood was involved in the religious struggles in Ireland for the nonconformist cause. Thus Blood was involved in the 1663 plot to kidnap Charles II's new Lord Lieutenant of Ireland, the Duke of Ormonde, from Dublin Castle. The plot was discovered. Blood fled in disguise to England to be a player in a number of escapades which included an attack on the Tower of London and plots to murder Charles II and his brother, the devoutly Roman Catholic Duke of York. A backer of some of these schemes was George Villiers, 2nd Duke of Buckingham who was violently opposed to any Roman Catholic succession through the Duke of York. Throughout, Thomas Blood, who now called himself Colonel Blood, evaded arrest and punishment and 1671 saw the beginnings of his boldest plot yet; to steal the new Crown Jewels which had replaced those ancient pieces sold off by Oliver Cromwell. These were under the protection of The Keeper of the Jewel House, Sir Gilbert Talbot, at the Martin Tower, Tower of London. As he did not live in the Tower, the day to day responsibility for the jewels fell to a septuagenarian assistant keeper, one Talbot Edwards. Edwards had the perk of charging visitors a fee to view the jewels.

Even though security for the Crown Jewels was a shadow of what it is now the breaching of the Tower of London was no mean feat in the seventeenth century. Huge walls, a deep moat, a battalion of the King's Guards and a squad of the Yeomen of the Guard would all have to be evaded. Carefully Blood noted the comings and goings of the Tower's civilian and military staff, most of the former going about their business unchallenged. The Crown Jewels were not directly guarded. A few weeks before the robbery, Blood surveyed the immediate location of the Jewel House dressed as a clergyman paying his visitor's fee and being accompanied by a young actress called Jenny Blame, who threw a bogus faint to distract the assistant keeper and his wife while Blood made his detailed examination. Over a period of time Blood ingratiated himself with the Edwards's.

Blood set out to act on 9 May 1671 and on that day visited the Tower with his son (alias Tom Hunt) and two known criminals Robert Perrott and Richard Halliwell. Outside was William Smith waiting with horses. Taking the 'visitors' to the Jewel House, Edwards was assaulted and bundled up in a cloak, his struggles causing a severe beating. He was stabbed in an attempt to keep him quiet. Blood selected the pieces he wished to steal and made to leave. Aroused from his state of shock Edwards shouted 'Treason! Murder! The Crown is stolen!' as the robbers fled. Now pursued by Edwards's son and a visitor Captain Martin Beckman, the robbers made to escape in the crowd outside the Tower, but they were caught and arrested.

Over the centuries historians have tried to fathom out Blood's motives in stealing the jewels. Could it be financial gain? This was considered unlikely as Blood's other exploits had never included personal monetary profit. Was the capturing of the crown the opening gambit of a plot to depose Charles II? And was the ambitious Duke of Buckingham behind it all? Buckingham believed that through his Plantagenet ancestors (through his mother's family) he had a right to the throne. All in all the theft was probably a political gesture. Triumphing over the authorities would have been a piece of fine propaganda to draw attention to the cause of the Protestant nonconformists in Ireland. Or, was it a piece of bravado to feed Blood's ego and a 'see what I can do' recklessness?

Whatever the motive, Blood seems to have lived a charmed life. He talked his way out of punishment and remarkably found favour with Charles II at court, being granted a pension of £500 per annum. This caused some suspicion in court circles with the supposition that Charles II used Blood as a spy on the nonconformists. Blood died on the 24 August 1680 to be buried at New Chapel, Tothill Fields, London. Such was his reputation for trickery that many thought he had feigned death as a ruse to vanish; his body was even dug up to make sure he had died. Yet, whatever the truth about the Thomas Blood Crown Jewels incident, thereafter greater precautions were made to secure their safety.

♦ Who had the most controversial coronation?

The Bishop of Durham [Edward Maltby] never could tell me what was to take place. . . . Poor old Lord Rolle, who is 82, and dreadfully infirm, in attempting to ascend the steps fell and rolled quite down . . . The Archbishop [of Canterbury, William Howley] . . . was so confused and puzzled and knew nothing . . . [he] put the ring on the wrong finger . . . I had great difficulty to take it off again . . . great pain.

Queen Victoria's account of her coronation, 28 June 1838.

Down the centuries coronations have thrown up their caprices that have led to feelings of national insecurity or suspicious dread that the monarchy was doomed. When Henry Bolingbroke was crowned as Henry IV (r.1399–1413) at Westminster Abbey in 1399, he lost one of his shoes in the procession and then one of his spurs. At the coronation feast a sudden gust of wind blew his crown off his head. His rumbustious reign was considered a consequence. At his death, as his body was being borne by ship down the Thames to burial at Trinity Chapel, Canterbury, the vessel was lashed by a sudden squall. The story goes that his body was washed overboard. Panic-stricken the mariners substituted another cadaver. This recurrent story led to an investigation of the royal body in 1832. A bearded cadaver was found in the tomb and the simplicity of the burial did not lead to any final conclusion. Had the coronation mishaps led to Henry IV's substitution, the superstitious wondered?

Queen Mary I was extremely picky at her coronation in 1553. She refused to sit in the coronation chair or be anointed with the consecration oil, because both had been used in the coronation of her brother Edward VI, whom she considered a heretic. At Queen Anne's coronation in 1702 she had to be carried in a chair everywhere in the Westminster Abbey ceremony because she was so fat and gouty.

Taking into consideration the riot when the Jews gave presents to King Richard I, Lionheart, at his coronation in 1189, perhaps the coronation that caused the most public controversy was that of George IV at Westminster Abbey on 19 July 1821. At the time he was estranged from his wife and cousin Caroline Amelia Elizabeth, daughter of Charles, Duke of Brunswick-Wolfenbüttel, who he had married in 1795 through financial and dynastic expediency. As Prince of Wales, George had been drunk throughout the marriage ceremony, and after the birth of their daughter Charlotte Augusta, George and Caroline separated and he went back to his mistress Mrs Fitzherbert, whom he had married 'illegally'. On his accession to the throne George IV was determined that his legal wife should never be recognised as queen. He insisted too, that her name be excluded from the liturgy. George was set on a divorce. Caroline, however, who had been cutting an outrageous and adulterous swathe through society on the Continent, was equally determined to return to Britain to claim her 'undoubted legal rights'.

Caroline arrived in Britain on 5 June 1820 to a tumultuous welcome stage-managed by one of the king's political enemies, the radical Alderman Sir Matthew Wood. London was engulfed in 'queen-fever' stirred up by her supporters. The king fumed in exasperation telling all that he would rather abdicate than have a coronation that included Caroline as his crowned queen.

Matters developed so that parliament received a Bill of Pains and Penalties, designed to enquire into Caroline's rumoured adulterous conduct and deprive her of her title. Caroline appeared in the House of Lords for what amounted to, and has been accepted as, her 'trial'. The Bill went to a third reading and was passed only by a majority of nine and the government thought it best to drop it. On hearing this George sulked in Brighton.

It was hoped that matters would cool down and Caroline would drop her campaign; a satirist expressed the public feeling:

> Most gracious Queen, we thee implore
> To go away and sin no more;
> Or if that effort be too great,
> To go away at any rate.

Meanwhile George came out of his sulk and prepared for his coronation. It was to be a sumptuous affair of pomp and circumstance. There had not been a coronation for sixty years since that of George III in 1761 and George studied precedents from the coronation of James II. There were general mutterings as to the proposed cost of the coronation; the coronation robes alone cost £24,000. All the while George was anxious about what Caroline would do to humiliate him on coronation day. Public sympathy had drained from her cause but she still had supporters in the mob. Lady Sarah Lyttleton noted the mood:

> The mob are rather too cross, and too fond of the Queen to [permit] a ceremony in which she is not to take part. They will make some bustle on the occasion. We are all in a fright about it. As it is they make bustle enough; every day there is a gathering of some account or other. And her Gracious Majesty takes care to keep it up, by showing herself all about London in a shabby post-chaise and pair of post-horses and living in the scruffiest house she could think of,

to shew she is kept out of the palace. Lord Temple reported that fears of riots were making it difficult to sell seats in the stands along the processional route.

The day of the coronation dawned. Queen Caroline arrived at Westminster Abbey and approached the west door. The doors were shut in her face. Through the doorway Caroline's Chamberlain Viscount Hood argued with a door-keeper to admit the queen; the official said she could not come in without a ticket. The party moved to the north door to have that slammed shut too. Caroline retreated in despair; once back home she wrote to the king to demand that she be crowned 'next Monday'. George did not reply.

On the night of the coronation Caroline had been at Drury Lane Theatre and had a relapse of her recurrent bowel trouble. She took to her bed and on 7 August 1821 she died. Caroline died around the same time as Napoleon Bonaparte. When news of the exiled emperor's death was told to George IV, who was waiting for news of Caroline's condition, the messenger said: 'Sir, your bitterest enemy is dead.' To which Goerge replied: 'Is she, by God.'

♦ Which monarchs of Scotland and England were the first to have coronations?

Now this Edwin ... aims at bearing the crown from the North to the South.
Thirteenth-century reference to ninth-century Edwin of Northumbria in The Chronicle of Pierre de Lonqtoft.

The concept of placing a diadem on the head of a ruler as a token of sovereignty and the seeking of a Divine Providence upon a reign, is much older than any of the British kingdoms. Six thousand years before even the Pictish kings emerged in the fifth century, the rulers of Ancient Egypt were crowned with white and red crowns of their dynasties. Yet, the first recorded coronation we can be sure of was that of the Saxon King Egfrith of Mercia; he was consecrated monarch in 787 by Hygeberht, Archbishop of Lichfield. Egfrith was the son of Offa (r. 757–96) and his queen Cynethryth, and was thus crowned during his father's rule to secure the succession. Egfrith's rule was

short; he died on 14 December 796 having ruled 141 days. After
the crowning of Athelwolf of Wessex, son of Egbert (r.802–39) and
Redburga, in 839 by Ceolnoth at Kingston, all English coronations
were carried out by the Archbishop of Canterbury.

There were no formal crownings in Scotland until the coronation
at Scone Abbey of Robert I, the Bruce, in 1306. Before that, probably
from the time of St Columba's anointing of Aedan mac Gabhrain,
ruler of the Dal Riata Scots, in 574, rulers of what became Scotland
were only ordained to title.

♦ Who was the first woman to have a coronation?

[It is] contrary to God's prohibition and Christian dignity, and also
against the usage of all pagans.
>   *Asser, Bishop of Sherborne, in his* Life of Alfred.

Athelwolf, of the old English ruling house of the line of Cerdic
of Wessex, who was born around 795 and ruled the Kingdom of
the West Saxons, 839–58, was married twice. On 1 October 856 he
married secondly the 13-year-old Judith, daughter of Charles the
Bold, King of the Franks, at Verberie-sur-Oise. The marriage was of
political importance, and Charles decreed that at a special coronation
Judith be crowned queen of Athelwolf's realm. This queen-crowning
was a common practice among the Frankish rulers, but by this time
had been discontinued by the West Saxons. The ceremony was
carried out by Hincmar, Archbishop of Rheims.

By his first wife, Osburgh, daughter of Oslac of Hampshire,
Athelwolf had five children, including Alfred the Great and Athelbald.
To the consternation and shock of the people, on Athelwolf's death
his successor Athelbald married his step-mother. The scandal was
made a matter of historic record by Alfred's biographer, Bishop Asser.

QUEENS OF ENGLAND AND SCOTLAND KNOWN TO BE CROWNED

Judith, second wife of Athelwolf	1 October 856	by Hincmar at Verberie-sur-Oise.
Elfrida, wife of Edgar	11 May 973	by Dunstan at Bath Abbey.
Edith, wife of Edward	23 January 1045	by Eadsige at Winchester.
Matilda, wife of William I	11 May 1068	by Ealdred of York.
Matilda, first wife of Henry I	11 November 1100	by Anseim at Westminster Abbey.
Adeliza, second wife of Henry I	2 February 1122	by Ralph d'Escures at Westminster Abbey.
Matilda, wife of Stephen	22 March 1136	by William de Corbeil at Westminster Abbey.
Eleanor, wife of Henry II	25 December 1158	by Theobald at Worcester Cathedral.
Margaret, wife of Henry, 'The Young King'	27 August 1172	by Rotrou Archbishop of Rouen at Winchester Cathedral.
Berengaria, wife of Richard I	12 May 1191	by John FitzLuke, Bishop of Evreux, at St George's Chapel, Limasol, Cyprus.
Isabella, second wife of John	8 October 1200	by Hubert Walter at Westminster Abbey.
Eleanor, wife of Henry III	20 January 1236	by Edmund Rich at Westminster Abbey.
Eleanor, wife of Edward I	19 August 1274	by Robert Kilwardby at Westminster Abbey.
Isabella, wife of Edward II	25 February 1308	by Henry Merewell, Bishop of Winchester, at Westminster Abbey.
Philippa, wife of Edward III	20 February 1328	by Simon de Meopham at Westminster Abbey.
Joan, wife of David II, King of Scots	24 November 1331	by James Ben, Bishop of St Andrews, at Scone Abbey.
Euphemia, wife of Robert II, King of Scots	1372	by Alexander de Kyninmund, Bishop of Aberdeen, at Scone Abbey.

Anne, first wife of Richard II	22 January 1382	by William Courtney, at Westminster Abbey.
Annabella, wife of Robert III, King of Scots	14 August 1390	by Walter Trail, Bishop of St Andrews, at Scone Abbey.
Isabella, second wife of Richard II	8 January 1397	by Thomas Arundel at Westminster Abbey.
Joan, second wife of Henry IV	26 February 1403	by Thomas Arundel at Westminster Abbey.
Katherine, wife of Henry V	24 February 1421	by Henry Chichele at Westminster Abbey.
Joan, wife of James I, King of Scots		by Henry Wardlaw, Bishop of St Andrews, at Scone Abbey.
Margaret, wife of Henry VI	30 May 1445	by John Stafford at Westminster Abbey.
Mary, wife of James II, King of Scots	3 July 1449	by James Kennedy, Bishop of Dunkeld, at Holyrood Abbey, Edinburgh.
Elizabeth, wife of Edward IV	26 May 1465	by Thomas Bourchier at Westminster Abbey.
Margaret, wife of James III, King of Scots	13 July 1469	by James Kennedy, Bishop of St Andrews, at Holyrood Abbey, Edinburgh.
Anne, wife of Richard III	6 July 1483	by Thomas Bourchier at Westminster Abbey.
Elizabeth, wife of Henry VII	24 November 1487	by John Morton at Westminster Abbey.
Margaret Tudor, wife of James IV, King of Scots	8 August 1503	(probably) by William Scheves, Archbishop of St Andrews, at Holyrood Abbey, Edinburgh.
Catherine of Aragon, wife of Henry VIII	24 June 1509	by William Warham at Westminster Abbey.
Anne Boleyn, second wife of Henry VIII	1 June 1533	by Thomas Cranmer at Westminster Abbey.
Marie de Guise-Lorraine, second wife of James V, King of Scots	22 February 1540	by David Beaton, Archbishop of St Andrews, at Holyrood Abbey, Edinburgh.

Mary, Queen of Scots	9 September 1543	by David Beaton, Archbishop of St Andrews, at Stirling Castle.
Mary I	1 October 1553	by Stephen Gardiner, Bishop of Winchester, at Westminster Abbey.
Elizabeth I	15 January 1559	by Owen Oglethorpe, Bishop of Carlisle, at Westminster Abbey. (This was the last coronation to be conducted according to the medieval Latin rubric.)
Anne, wife of James VI, King of Scots	17 May 1590	by David Lindsay, Chaplain to James VI, at Holyrood Abbey, Edinburgh.
(Anne was crowned once more on 25 July 1603 by John Whitgift at Westminster Abbey when James VI became James I of England.)		
Mary, wife of James II/VII	22 April 1685	by Roman Catholic rite at Whitehall Palace, London, and again the next day by Anglican rite, by William Sancroft, at Westminster Abbey.
Mary II	11 April 1689	by Henry Compton, Bishop of London, at Westminster Abbey.
Anne	22 April 1702	by Thomas Tenison at Westminster Abbey.
Caroline, wife of George II	11 October 1727	by William Wake at Westminster Abbey.
Charlotte, wife of George III	22 September 1761	by Thomas Secker at Westminster Abbey.
Adelaide, wife of William IV	8 September 1831	by William Howley at Westminster Abbey.
Victoria	28 June 1838	by William Howley at Westminster Abbey.
Alexandra, wife of Edward VIII	9 August 1902	by William Maclagan, Archbishop of York.
Mary, wife of George V	22 June 1911	by Randal Davidson, at Westminster Abbey.
Elizabeth, wife of George VI	12 May 1937	by Cosmo Gordon Lang at Westminster Abbey.
Elizabeth II (and I of Scotland)	2 June 1952	by Geoffrey Fisher at Westminster Abbey.

♦ Which King was the first to have a crown?

> A crown! What is it?
> It is to bear the miseries of a people!
> To hear the murmurs
> Feel their discontents,
> And sink beneath a load of splendid care.
>
> *Hannah More (1745–1833), 'Daniel', Part VI.*

It is a matter of some controversy among historians as to whether or not the early Saxon kings wore a head covering during their coronations. Some say they wore a ceremonial helmet. It is now generally believed that the first king to have a crown at his coronation was Edward the Elder, King of the West Saxons, who ruled 899–924. His coronation took place around 8 June 900 at Kingston-upon-Thames, and was conducted by Plegmund, Archbishop of Canterbury. The second son of Alfred the Great, Edward, probably at his coronation, proclaimed himself as 'by the gift of God's grace, King of the Anglo-Saxons', the first use of the title. At his death at Farndon, in Mercia, on 17 July 924, Edward had fulfilled the new symbolism of his coronation by building on the foundations laid by his father Alfred to create a new Kingdom of England from the English Channel deep into English Northumberland as far as the Firth of Forth.

♦ Who was the first to be crowned at Westminster Abbey?

> Behold, ye builders, demigods who made England's Walhalla …
> *Walter Theodore Watts-Dunton (1832–1914), 'The Silent Voices – No. 4 –*
> *The Minster Spirits'.*

An abbey was built close to his palace on Thorney Island by Edward the Confessor (r. 1042–66), sometimes called 'last of the English kings'. The buildings were completed in 1065 and stood surrounded by the many ancillary buildings needed by the society of Benedictine monks who formed the religious community here. Around the time of the abbey's consecration, Edward died and it was only natural that his burial place should be herein abutting the high altar. By 1269 Henry III had ordered important structural changes to house a new focal point for the abbey: a magnificent shrine to contain Edward's body, befitting his canonisation of 1163. A new nave was begun in 1376, but the abbey was not completed until 150 years later.

Edward the Confessor had died at Westminster on the night of 4/5 January 1066, aged 61. On the day of his funeral plans were set in place for the first coronation in Westminster Abbey. Edward's successor, Harold II of the House of Godwin, was thus crowned on 6 January. The religious ceremony was conducted by Ealdred, Archbishop of York, who adapted continental coronation rites. Ealdred performed the crowning because Stigand (d. 1072), Archbishop of Canterbury, had been excommunicated and his appointment by Pope Benedict X was considered uncanonical. Norman historians were later to twist the truth, saying that Stigand had officiated to undermine Harold's legitimacy as king.

The Normans, too, considered the first king crowned at Westminster Abbey to be William I, The Conqueror, who was crowned by Ealdred on 25 December 1066. Harold II, however, was not to hold his monarchy long as he died on the bloody field of Hastings on 14 October 1066.

◆ Who was the first noblewoman to crown a king?

> The countess ... by command of King Edward of England, was placed in a little house of timber in a tower in the castle of Berwick, the sides latticed so that all there could gaze on her as a spectacle.
>
> Scalacronica, *130.*

For Scottish coronations, the officiate was the contemporary Bishop of St Andrews. However, there were five exceptions: On 25 March 1437, Michael Ochiltree, Bishop of Dunblane, crowned the 6-year-old James II at Holyrood Abbey church. On 29 July 1567, Adam Bothwell, Bishop of Orkney, crowned the 1-year-old James VI at the parish church of Stirling, and on 17 May 1590, the eminent Edinburgh divine, the Revd Robert Bruce, assisted by David Lindsay, royal chaplain, crowned James VI's wife Anne of Denmark at Holyrood Abbey in a 7-hour ceremony. On 1 January 1651, Archibald

Campbell, Marquess of Argyll, crowned Charles II at Scone Abbey; and in 1306 a Scottish king was crowned by a noblewoman.

Robert I, The Bruce (r. 1306–29) was inaugurated on 27 March 1306 at the Augustinian Abbey of Scone; the first recorded crowning of a Scottish monarch. His coronation was controversial mainly because of the woman who crowned him and who she was, remembering, of course, that six weeks previously, Bruce had murdered John Comyn, Lord of Badenoch and Guardian of Scotland, at Greyfriars Church to facilitate his path to the throne.

The Chronicle of Walter of Guisborough tells us that Bruce's coronation was 'attended and consented to by four bishops, five earls and the people of the land'; a hostile land, for by 1305 Edward I of England had completed his conquest of Scotland. No detailed account of the ceremony remains. We know that robes for the occasion were made in the sacristy of Glasgow Cathedral and Robert Wischard, Bishop of Glasgow brought to Scone 'The Banner of Scotland' which he had hidden from the English. By this time Edward had removed the famous Stone of Scone upon which Scots monarchs had been traditionally inaugurated. The only recorded rite was the placing on his head of a coronella or coronetta of gold by 20-year-old Isabel of Fife, Countess of Buchan, representing her husband, then at his Leicestershire manor of Whitwick. Curiously she was the cousin-in-law of the murdered John Comyn. William de Lamberton, Bishop of St Andrews, performed a pontifical high mass. For her pains Isabel was later arrested by Edward I and was lodged in cages of timber and iron within towers at Roxburgh and Berwick castles consecutively. She was so incarcerated until 1310 when she was released into house arrest at the Carmelite convent at Berwick. Thereafter, she was in the custody of Sir Henry de Beaumont, nephew of Edward I. Although she then disappears from history, she is secure in the history of Scottish coronations as the only woman to crown a king.

♦ Who had the most sumptuous coronation?

The river was crowded with boats – the banks and the ships in the Pool swarmed with people; and fifty of the great barges formed the procession all blazing with gold and banners.

James Anthony Froude (1818–94) on the 1533 coronation of Anne Boleyn.

Coronations in the Middle Ages tended to be spectacular occasions. When Richard I, Coeur-de-Lion (r. 1189–99) was crowned at Westminster Abbey on 3 September 1189 by Archbishop Baldwin, it was a ceremony 'befitting so great a knight of chivalry'. So magnificent was its panoply that Jean de Wavrin of Bruges depicted it specially for Edward IV in his *Chronique d'Angleterre*. Richard's was the first detailed account of a coronation in English history. A huge body of clergy attended, including four archbishops – of Canterbury, Rouen, Trier and Dublin – to form a magnificent procession. While Richard walked under a splendid canopy, supported by four lances carried by four nobles, from the Palace of Westminster to the Abbey church, his feet never touched common soil as he walked on a cloth of the Tyrian dye. Four more barons bore the golden candlesticks and tapers; Godfrey de Lucy carried the Royal Cap, John Marshall bore the Royal Spurs of gold, while William Marshall, Earl of Pembroke carried the golden Rod and Dove. Six barons carried the Regalia and Robe table, while the great golden crown was carried by William de Mandeville, Earl of Essex. Controversially Richard picked up his crown from the altar and handed it to the archbishop, who put it on the king's head; thus Richard showed to all present that he held his crown directly from God.

Richard III's coronation, along with that of his wife Anne Neville, on 6 July 1483 by Cardinal Thomas Bourchier, was perhaps the most magnificent of the Middle Ages. Edward, Prince of Wales, the deposed Edward V – one of the 'murdered Princes in the Tower' – had had rich ermines, velvets and cloth of gold made for his coronation; these were now appropriated by Richard. Richard and Anne walked barefoot in procession to the Abbey. Behind them came the senior clergy, the Earl of Northumberland with the Sword of Mercy, Lord Stanley with the Constable's Mace, John de la Pole, Duke of Suffolk with the sceptre and John, Earl of Lincoln with the orb; John Howard, Duke of Norfolk followed with the crown and Thomas Howard, Earl of Surrey with the Sword of State. The huge congregation watched as Richard and Anne stripped to the waist to be anointed with the chrism, to change into cloth of gold to be crowned. Contemporaries claimed it was the most magnificent coronation ever seen. More than anything it was a political statement of Richard's position and power; propaganda of the boar badge of his heraldry was everywhere – 13,000 white-boar on fustian hangings

alone decorated Westminster. The magnificence of the coronation
was soon to be soiled with blood and disaster. In April 1484 Richard
received news that his son Edward, Prince of Wales, was dead and in
March 1485 Queen Anne was dead too. Richard's short reign came
to an end when he died in battle at Bosworth Field, Leicestershire,
on 22 August 1485, aged 33.

Throughout his reign Henry VIII was a devotee and promoter of
courtly magnificence, or maiestas. Henry spent lavishly on his court
with the intention of attracting men of consequence and talent
to his service. Henry came to the throne on 22 April 1509 at the
age of almost 18. Six weeks after the death of his father Henry VII,
Henry married Catherine of Aragon (his brother Arthur's widow)
on 11 June 1509 in the oratory of the friary church outside the walls
of Greenwich Palace. Thereafter on 24 June they shared a joint
coronation. Historian Edward Hall (d.1547) described the scene:

> . . . the noble prince with his queen left the Palace of Westminster
> at the appointed time. The barons of the Cinq Ports held canopies
> over the royal couple who trod on striped cloth of ray, which was
> immediately cut up by the crowd when they had entered the Abbey.
> Inside, according to sacred tradition and ancient custom, his grace
> and the queen were anointed and crowned by the Archbishop of
> Canterbury [William Warham] in the presence of other prelates of
> the realm and the nobility and a large number of civic dignitaries. The
> people were asked if they would take this most noble prince as their
> king and obey him. With great reverence, love and willingness they
> responded with the cry 'Yea.Yea'.

All who observed were overwhelmed by the great amounts of
glittering gold. Over £1,500 was spent on Queen Catherine's
coronation alone, with £1,700 on Henry's; from the court accounts
it can be seen that 2,000 yards of expensive red cloth were needed
and 1,500 yards of 'superior scarlet cloth' for clothes, thrones and
decorations. The streets were all lined with tapestries, and pageants
were performed all along the route to the Abbey; the livery
companies lavished decorations on their halls and after the ceremony
a sumptuous banquet was held followed by weeks of feasting, royal
tournaments and civic celebrations. The coronation splendour was
not to be rivalled for another 300 years.

Prince George Augustus Frederick, the eldest son of George III, had ruled (with limitations) as Prince Regent since 1811 and on his father's death at Windsor Castle, on 29 January 1820, became King George IV. Known to all, with varying degrees of affection and loathing as 'The Prince of Pleasure', George had cut a dash through society for sixty years before he became king and was determined that his coronation would be no dull, grey affair. The total cost would rise to the phenomenal sum for the age of £243,000.

George's coronation took place on 19 July 1820. The focal points for the splendour were Westminster Abbey and Westminster Hall where the coronation banquet would be held after the ceremony. Both places had been transformed with lavish decoration, but nowhere outdid the king himself. He made a stunning entrance to his coronation, sporting a 27ft train of crimson velvet and gold stars, topped off with a black Spanish hat with great plumes of white ostrich feathers. The painter Benjamin Robert Haydon said: 'The way in which the King bowed, was really royal. As he looked towards the peeresses and foreign ambassadors, he showed like some gorgeous bird of the East'. For the last time in coronation history the king's procession was preceded by the king's herb woman and six maids strewing herbs along the monarch's blue-carpeted path. Overall the procession and ceremony took 6 hours to complete and thereafter 312 people sat down to a feast of medieval proportions. Curiously, after the company had finished their first course of soup, the Lord High Constable (Duke of Wellington), the Lord High Steward (The Marquis of Angelsey) and the Deputy Earl Marshal (Lord Howard of Effingham) entered on horseback. There followed the Ceremony of the Challenge in which the king's champion (young Sir Henry Dymoke), on white charger, challenged all who might deny the king his sovereignty. Unsurprisingly no one picked up the champion's gauntlet and the king drank to his champion from a gold cup. The company proceeded to attack their full repast:

160 tureens of soup
160 dishes of fish
160 hot joints
160 dishes of vegetables
480 sauce boats of lobster, butter and mint sauces
80 dishes of braised ham
80 plates of savoury pies

80 dishes of goose
80 plates of savoury cakes
80 dishes of braised beef
80 dishes of braised capons
320 dishes of mounted pastry
320 plates of small pastries
400 dishes of jellies and creams
160 dishes of shellfish (lobster and crayfish)
160 dishes of cold roast fowl
80 dishes of cold lamb

The feast was an all-male affair, so the hungry peeresses in the galleries erected above could only watch the gourmandising. The great day of splendour ended with fireworks and coloured balloons in Hyde Park. Overall, as Sir Walter Scott remarked, 'Never monarch received a more general welcome from his subjects ...'

♦ Which king first adopted the title 'King of England'?

There was not English armour left,
Nor any English thing,
When Alfred came to Athelney
To be an English king.
        'Ballad of the White Horse', Gilbert Keith Chesterton (1874–1936).

Over the years historians have argued which king qualified as the first to be dubbed 'King of All England'. Three kings have been so identified:
1. Egbert of Wessex (r. 802–39); one charter is known to exist which gives him the title *Rex Anglorum* (King of the English), although his rule of Northumbria and East Anglia was tenuous.
2. Alfred the Great (r. 871–99); he accepted sovereignty of the entire kingdom, so he was King of England, but was never crowned as such.
3. Edward the Elder (r. 899–924); Alfred's eldest surviving son was crowned King of England in 901.

Athelstan (r. 924–27), of course, called himself King of the English. However, it may be remembered that at his coronation on 25 January 1603, James I/VI was proclaimed as 'King of England, Scotland, France and Ireland, Defender of the Faith'.

CORONATION TRADITIONS, LORE AND GOSSIP

A trawl through the diaries, journals and reports of those performing crowning rituals for English and Scottish monarchs throws up a range of unusual facts. An early example refers to Edgar the Peaceable, King of the English (he was also King of Mercia and Northumbria). Dunstan, Archbishop of Canterbury, at first refused to crown Edgar because he considered him immoral. Edgar had many amorous adventures with talk of illegitimate children, and there were those who said he had fornicated with and led into adultery one Elfrida, who became his second wife. The gossips added that with Elfrida, Edgar had conspired to murder her husband to make her free to marry him. Thus Edgar was not crowned and anointed until 11 May 973 at Bath Abbey by Dunstan, some fourteen years after he succeeded as king and just two years before he died in 975.

At the coronation of Adeleza, second wife of Henry I, in 1122, the senile and confused Archbishop Ralph d'Escures lost his temper. He believed that he was crowning the king instead of Adeleza, and realising his mistake knocked Henry's crown off in exasperation. By this time, crowning diadems were being passed from monarch to monarch; before the coronation of Edward the Confessor in 1043 monarchs were buried with their crowns at death.

For reasons of political speed, restoration and re-establishment of fealty, King Stephen had three coronations at Westminster Abbey, Canterbury and Lincoln in 1135, 1141 and 1146. Richard I had two coronations in 1189 and 1194, the latter following his release from captivity in Emperor Heinrich VI's castle of Durrenstein. Richard I was considered doomed by the superstitious as a bat flew round his head at his first coronation. His brother John had no time for pomp and ceremonial and, to the consternation of the clergy and nobility at his coronation in 1199, succumbed to fits of the giggles. Edward I and his wife Eleanor had the first double coronation in 1274 for over 100 years and for the first time the street conduits ran with wine in celebration.

David II, King of Scots, was one of the 'junior kings' to be crowned aged 7 in 1331. A miniature set of regalia was made for him. The youngest monarch to be crowned was Mary, Queen of Scots in 1543 at the age of 9 months and 2 days; she had succeeded to her father James V's throne at the age of 7 days. Richard II was only 10 when he was crowned in 1377, and the omen mongers were aghast when he lost a shoe, a spur and when his crown fell off at the time of his coronation. His reign was thus perceived as doomed. Richard abdicated in 1399 and was probably murdered in 1400. For a monarch to stumble or lose a part of the regalia during a coronation was considered bad news. Charles I, who had both English and Scottish coronations in 1626 and 1633, stumbled at his, and a jewel fell from George III's crown at his coronation in 1761 – Charles lost his head and George his mind.

♦ What was the 'Star Chamber'?

> From an early period subjects' petitions were heard by the king and
> his council. The council in its judicial aspect over criminal matters
> thus became the Court of the Star Chamber.
>
> Munn's Legal Notes & Queries *(1887)*.

When Henry Tudor became King of England as Henry VII, after his
triumph over Richard III's army at the battle of Bosworth Field in
1485, he came to kingship untutored. After all, he had spent his adult
life in exile in Brittany and as a youth probably never journeyed
out of Wales after his birth in Pembroke in 1453. It was important
therefore that he surrounded himself with able advisors. One such
was Cardinal John Morton (*c.*1420–1500), who was made Archbishop
of Canterbury in 1486 and Lord Chancellor the following year.
A talented ecclesiast and politician, Morton was the most learned
and devoted of Henry VII's courtiers. Henry wisely chose his
advisers from both the Lancastrian and Yorkist camps and during his
reign he was served by some 200 'royal councillors'. They were a mix
of noblemen, lawyers, clerics and assorted gentry. The councillors
gathered in the presence of the king from 1487 in the Court of the
Star Chamber, Westminster Palace, so named because there were
stars on the ceiling of the meeting place. From the first the Star
Chamber had three main functions: To dispatch legal cases brought
by aggrieved individuals; attend to poor men's legal suits at sessions
known as Requests; to take care of general business. At first, Star
Chamber rendered great service as it weakened baronial power, a
facet later built upon by Cardinal Thomas Wolsey.

The Star Chamber, too, was a rich source of revenue; for instance,
the Earl of Oxford, though a faithful servant to the Crown, was
fined £15,000 for keeping retainers. In the seventeenth century this
facet was greatly abused by cash-strapped monarchs. Later, owing
to the absence of a jury and to the right of arrest enjoyed by every
member, the Star Chamber came to gravely limit the freedom of
the subject. It was employed extensively by Henry VIII because it
was able to enforce the law when other courts were unable to do so.
Consequently, in the opposition to Charles I, the Star Chamber was
considered a symbol of oppression. It was abolished in 1641 under the
Redress of Grievances of the first session of the Long Parliament.

♦ When were jesters and dwarves made courtiers?

The skipping king, he ambled up and down
With shallow jesters and rash bavin wits.

William Shakespeare, King Henry IV, *Part I.*

The earliest societies recognised the importance of clowns and jesters. The Ancient Egyptians imported pygmies from Central Africa to be acrobats and comedians. The great Aztec ruler Montezuma hired clowns to amuse his court. Slowly such entertainers evolved in Europe as permanent court performers. There were jesters at the Saxon courts some 900 years ago, and the heyday of the jesters was in the days after the Crusades when the kings of Europe would employ a superior jester to be an almost constant attender at court. They were given a license to say the unsayable and to burst the balloon of pomposity. Jesters in English courts were more than just stand-up comics, or tellers of witty jokes. In the Middle Ages the jester was expected to dance, turn cartwheels, juggle, sing, and compose satirical verses. Sometimes a jester would set up a company to enact burlesques. By the sixteenth century they were real professionals, enacting elaborate spectaculars. The job was, therefore, a very demanding one and long hours were worked.

Eventually jesters developed a distinctive costume. The hood, asses' ears, or cockscomb, or black and white chequered coat, all developed from primitive allusion to the basic elements of natural life. In time the trappings, which at one time had represented the colourings of animals, the gestures and dancing also mimicking the movements of animals, all became the stock in trade of the jester. So the greens, whites, blacks and yellows of the jester's clothes once represented the elements of Earth, Fire, Water and Air, and man's fear of death and so on.

Slowly the importance of jesters began to be reflected in court records, with some jesters playing significant parts in social history. One such was Rahere, jester in the court of Henry I. Rahere, who died in 1144, had come to court as a minstrel, mime and jester. Some time after Henry succeeded to the throne in 1100, Rahere entered the church. During a pilgrimage to Rome he fell ill with malaria and on his recovery vowed to build a hospital for the poor. The site of the hospital at London's Smithfield was said to have come about in a vision of St Bartholomew, who also urged that a priory be built on site. Rahere had amassed funds as a court jester and commenced the building of the hospital in 1123; it received a royal charter in 1133 and Rahere became its first master. The hospital developed into the famous St Bartholomew's Hospital.

By the reign of Edward I, the Master of the Wardrobe was responsible for the payment of jesters' fees. The Prioress of Wilberforce pressed the Master for compensation when the king's retinue visited and the same account showed payment to 'Martinot of Gascoigne, a fool'.

Another jester to appear in court records was one Scoggins at the court of Edward IV. It is recorded that Scoggins had been a student at Oxford, introduced to court by Sir William Nevill. 'A Master of Arts is not worth a fart', Scoggins is reputed to have declared. Instead he set about making money out of the court. Scoggins, who received a house in Cheapside and a mansion in Bury, specialised in what records call 'base humour', exhibiting his bare backside when the king said he did not wish to see his face again. Once, when in the queen's chamber entertaining her women, he was so outrageous in unbuttoning his trousers that they threatened to beat him with stones enclosed in napkins. He escaped a beating by inviting the greatest whore among them to hit him first.

Some jesters earned a great deal of unpopularity. Will Sommers (d. 1560) was one. The jester of Henry VIII was greatly disliked by Cardinal Thomas Wolsey, on whom Sommers played regular practical jokes. Sommers specialised in riddles, one of which was said to have made King Henry 'exceeding merry'. 'What is it', asked Sommers, 'that, being born without life, head, lip, or eye, yet doth run roaring through the world till it die?' The answer was: 'A fart'. Henry collapsed in a giggling heap.

Jesters also appeared in the Scottish court. James Geddes was jester to Mary, Queen of Scots; he had taken over from one of the very few women jesters Jenny Colquhoun. But head and shoulders above all others in Scotland was Archie Armstrong. He is believed to have been one of the family of the laird of Subholm, near Langholm. His date of birth is unknown, but it must have been in the late 1500s. As an Armstrong his early career was one of sheep and cattle stealing, for which he was condemned to death. On receiving a last request from King James VI, Armstrong said that he would like to read the

Bible through with his eyes shut. James considered this to be funny and appointed him court comedian. In the documents of the day Armstrong was referred to as *joculator domini regis* and received official regalia of his office: pointed cap, silver bells and quartered jacket. When James VI became James I of England in 1603 Armstrong went with the court to Greenwich. He was so popular at court that those who wished to find favour with the king paid tribute to the jester. Cities like Coventry and Nottingham gave him suits of clothes and he even received the Freedom of Aberdeen in 1617. Some of his pranks did get him into trouble. On one occasion he jested with the king while at Newmarket races, that the crowd favoured Prince Henry over the king. James rose to the bait and quarrelled with Prince Henry. Prince Henry's retainers, every time they could catch Armstrong, threw him up in a blanket. When King James died in 1625, his son Charles I kept Armstrong on and gave him a grant of 1,000 acres in Ireland. Armstrong's downfall came through his antagonism towards William Laud, Archbishop of Canterbury. He overstepped the mark with his comments on episcopacy in Scotland and he was banished from court in 1637. Nevertheless, Armstrong had done well for himself. He acquired pensions from the government, his book *A Banquet of Jests* (1630) sold widely, he was granted a patent to make tobacco pipes and in time he bought himself an estate near Arthuret, Cumberland and there he died in 1672.

Thomas Killigrew, jester to Charles II seems to have been the last one of note; he built the Theatre Royal, Drury Lane in 1663 and rose to be Gentleman of the Bedchamber, with his wife Keeper of the Sweet Coffer of the queen's court. Killigrew had great influence over the king. As E.S. Turner wrote, 'It was within Killigrew's power to persuade the King to attend to business, even though others failed'. But Killigrew made enemies. Henry Wilmot, 1st Earl of Rochester, sick of Killigrew's personal barbs, boxed his ears at a banquet given by the Dutch ambassador. Sir Henry Coventry, Master of the Revels, was another who clashed with Killigrew, who succeeded him as Master in 1673. Killigrew remains known in English literature for his plays.

Charles I's wife, Henrietta Maria of France, who he married in 1625, had a fancy for dwarves in her retinue. At a banquet given by the Duke of Buckingham, the 18in high Jeffrey Hudson stepped out of a pie to bow elegantly to the queen. Eventually Hudson achieved the height of 3ft and the queen kept him on at court employing him from time to time as a messenger. When the queen went into exile in 1644 Hudson went with her. In France Hudson had a verbal spat with one Will Croft, who mocked him for holding a commission in King Charles I's cavalry. Hudson challenged him to a duel. Played out on horseback, Croft did not take it seriously and armed himself only with a water squirter; Hudson did take it seriously and killed Croft with a single pistol shot. The queen dismissed him. There were more dwarves at the Stuart court besides Hudson; Richard Gibson and his equally diminutive wife served both king and queen, while Gibson won fame as a gifted painter.

◆ When did ladies-in-waiting first come to court, and what influence did they have?

For a king with any pretensions to majesty … chief courtiers were essential. … If he married, his queen would demand her own establishment, consisting in the main of various idle women to keep her amused.

E. S. Turner, The Court of St James's, *(1959).*

Until the twentieth century the Royal Court was one of only a few British institutions in which women of quality had an influential role to play. Undoubtedly the consorts of early English monarchs had women around them. But the earliest record of a queen's official entourage of ladies-in-waiting dates from the eleventh century. In 1068 Matilda, wife of William I, The Conqueror, arrived in England from Normandy, with a 'stately cortege of . . . ladies'. Again, Matilda (formerly Edith), daughter of Malcolm III, King of Scots, wife of Henry I of England, who he married as his first wife in 1100, had three ladies-in-waiting, in particular recorded as Emma, Gunilda and Christian, said to be 'three virgins of God, sacred damsels who belonged to the chamber of Matilda …' On her death in 1118 they entered a convent. By the reign of Edward III, 1327–77, ladies-in-waiting had become an integral part of the court. His wife Philippa of Hainault, had some thirty such women, including lesser gentry such as Elizabeth Chaundros and Philippa de Lisle, entitled simply as *demoiselles*. Edward IV's queen, Elizabeth Woodville, who he married in 1464, had a female court which would be reflected in structure in future years. By Tudor times the ladies, now salaried, were grouped as Great Ladies, Ladies of the Privy Chamber, Maids of Honour and Chamberers. Elizabeth I called her 'Great Ladies', Ladies of the Bedchamber, a title which was retained down the succeeding centuries.

The duties of ladies-in-waiting varied down the centuries, from serving the queen's meals in her privy chambers to reading, singing to her, writing letters and gossiping. The influence of such women could be great, especially in obtaining royal favours for family and friends. Others could scale great heights. One such was Jane Seymour. She had originally been a maid of honour to Queen Catherine of Aragon, and transferred her service smoothly to Anne Boleyn, Henry VIII's second wife. She proved to be Anne's nemesis, coached by the queen's enemies to infiltrate gossip into the king's ear; Jane became Henry's third wife.

Some ladies-in-waiting entered royal folklore, for example, the 'Four Maries' of the court of Mary, Queen of Scots. We first hear of them in detail when Mary sailed from France to her kingdom of Scotland in August 1561. Thus Mary Seton, Mary Beaton, Mary Livingston and Mary Fleming entered history. All were of noble birth, were well-educated for the time and are woven into the romance of Mary Stuart's life. Mary Seton was the only one to remain unmarried and passed into English captivity with her mistress in 1568, there she served for another fifteen years until ill-health forced her to retire to the Convent of St Pierre des Dames at Rheims. The 'Queen's Maries' are remembered in the haunting ballad with this refrain:

Last night the Queen had four Maries
Tonight there'll be but three
There's Mary Seton and Mary Beaton
And Mary Carmichael and me.

The ballad is eighteenth century in origin and the 'me' is one Mary Hamilton; the ballad refers to Mary, Queen of Scots's court but was mixed up with other circumstances later on of Mary Hamilton's affair with Tsar Peter the Great. (There was no Mary Carmichael at Mary's court.) Nevertheless, the verses touched the heart of Sir Walter Scott who gave it on-going life within the 'romance of Mary, Queen of Scots', for Scott's romanticism often overrode historical fact.

Other balladeers were not as polite when it came to 'immoralising' ladies-in-waiting. One was Arthur Maynwaring who commented on a lady-in-waiting 'scandal' at the court of Queen Anne:

> When as Queen Anne of great Renown
> Great Britain's Sceptre sway'd
> Besides the Church, she dearly lov'd
> A Dirty Chamber-Maid.
>
> O! Abigail that was her Name
> She stich'd and starch'd full well
> But how she pierc'd this Royal Heart
> No Mortal Man can tell.
>
> However, for sweet Service done
> And Causes of great Weight
> Her Royal Highness made her, Oh!
> A Minister of State.
>
> Her Secretary she was not
> Because she could not write,
> But had the Conduct and the Care
> Of some dark Deeds at Night.

Abigail Hill, later Lady Masham (d.1734), the 'Dirty Chamber Maid' alluded to by Maynwaring, was the first cousin of Sarah, Duchess of Marlborough, who was made Bedchamber Woman to Queen Anne through Sarah's influence. Abigail is a fine example of how by the eighteenth century, lesser women could achieve great favour at court. More than that, Abigail was able to influence Anne on court matters. She acted as go-between for Robert Harley, 1st Earl of Oxford, the Tory statesman, and is said to have played a role in the fall of Sidney Godolphin, 1st Earl of Godolphin and also her cousin Sarah at court. Abigail was able to influence Queen Anne by amusing and 'soothing' her through her daily duties known as 'royal body service'. Queen Anne's passionate relationships with women have been an on-going matter of historical conjecture with suggestions of lesbianism. Emptying the royal slops and chamber pots could lead to great things.

Ladies-in-waiting enter modern history with Queen Victoria. After her own widowhood in 1861, Queen Victoria built up a group of court ladies which Elizabeth Longford described as 'a Sacred College of Vestal Widows'. Aristocratic widows were a good source of ladies-in-waiting as 'they were free and glad of an occupation'. One such devoted lady was Jane, Marchioness of Ely who became one of the queen's closest confidantes, and a 'go between' for the queen on 'delicate matters'. She also acted as a conduit for politicians and for 'unfortunate news' if members of the Royal Family could not pluck up courage to approach the queen themselves. As Jane Hope-Vere she had married John Henry Loftus, 3rd Marquis of Ely in 1844 but was widowed in 1857 and soon after became 'Lady of the Bedchamber' to Queen Victoria.

Queen Victoria's selfish and demanding nature placed a restrictive hand on her ladies-in-waiting (and gentlemen). They were not allowed to take a walk at Osborne or Balmoral until the queen had had her walk or drive; those on duty had to be summonable at all times, and the queen became tetchy if their family matters interfered with her own comfort. All this had a great strain on Lady Ely, who once had to ask the queen to restrict her stint on the rota to 'six weeks at a time'. During the summer of 1890 Queen Victoria realised that Lady Ely was dying, 'Yet the final telegram was a shock and she cried bitterly', said Maid of Honour Marie Mallet. Jane died on 11 June and had she been at Windsor the queen would have gone to her funeral, an unheard-of gesture, for Queen Victoria did not even 'attend ... family funerals'. Lady Ely was buried at Kensal Green Cemetery and the queen visited her tomb on 27 June; of this she wrote in her journal:

> There were crowds out, we could not understand why, and thought something must be going [on] but it turned out, it was only to see me. Got out and walked a short way along a path, where the vault is in which dear Janie Ely rests. Placed our wreaths there. Unfortunately, there were such crowds that the privacy of my visit was quite spoilt; still, I felt glad so many bore witness to this act of regard and love paid to my beloved friend.

In 1900 Victoria's 'ladies' were grouped under the Department of the Mistress of the Robes, Louisa Jane Hamilton, wife of William Montague Douglas Scott, 6th Duke of Buccleuch, into three categories: Ladies of the Bedchamber (8 + 1 'Extra'); Bedchamber Women (8 + 9 'Extras') and Maid of Honour (8 + 1 'Extra'). Still some forty years after Prince Albert's death, the queen and her ladies-in-waiting dressed in black. The Maids of Honour were allowed to wear white, grey, mauve or purple, unless mourning.

Down the centuries queens have been harsh when their 'ladies' have stepped out of line; Queen Elizabeth I, for instance, became hysterical and vindictive when a lady married without her permission. Queen Victoria, despite being demanding all her life, learned a salutary lesson when dealing with the more personal aspects of the lives of her ladies-in-waiting.

Lady Flora Hastings entered royal service as Lady of the Bedchamber to Queen Victoria's mother, the Duchess of Kent. Lady Florence Elizabeth Hastings, known to all as Flora, was born in 1806, the eldest daughter of the soldier and statesman Frances Rawdon Hastings, Viscount Loudoun and Earl Rawdon, 1st Marquess of Hastings. Queen Victoria was prejudiced against Lady Flora believing that she schemed against her in her mother's court. In 1839 Lady Flora's state of health was seen to deteriorate and she complained of stomach pains. Her 'protuberance of the stomach' became noticeable. Queen Victoria developed the idea that the unmarried Lady Flora was pregnant. The court ladies were in uproar and Queen Victoria was aghast, and was party to scurrilous gossip about Lady Flora's morals. A reluctant Lady Flora was medically examined, found to be a virgin and in July 1839 died of a tumour of the liver. Her family were angry about the way Queen Victoria and the court ladies had gossiped against their relative and threatened legal action. The queen eventually gave the family a (half-hearted) apology for her part in the calumny and the whole thing was 'hushed up'. Nevertheless, the anti-royal pamphleteers had a field day concerning the 'Lady Flora Case' and at Royal Ascot Queen Victoria was booed, and from the grandstand balcony was 'hissed' by the Duchess of Montrose and Lady Sarah Ingrestre.

From Queen Victoria's time the households of senior royal ladies like Alexandra, Princess of Wales, were fully developed. The princess, for instance, had eight ladies-in-waiting led by the Dowager Countess of Morton, chief Lady of the Bedchamber. Today Queen Elizabeth II has some fifteen ladies-in-waiting, who serve part-time on a rota basis still within the categorisation of Queen Victoria. They assist as companions of the queen publicly and privately, and help with such tasks as correspondence.

QUAINT AND QUIRKY

♦ Who was the last British king to lead his troops into battle?

His Majesty was all the Time in the Heat of the Fire; but is in perfect Health.
John Carteret, Earl Granville (1690–1763) to Thomas Pelham-Holles, 1st Duke of Newcastle (1693–1768), The Gentleman's Magazine.

Elector George Augustus of Hanover ruled Great Britain as George II on the death of his father George I on 11 June 1727 until his own death at Kensington Palace, 25 October 1760. On 27 June 1743 he commanded and led his troops onto the battlefield at Dettingen, Bavaria; the site being the north bank of the River Main some 70 miles east of Frankfurt and 3 miles west of Aschaffenburg. This was during the Austrian Succession War 1740–8, caused by Prussia's rejection of the Pragmatic Sanction wherein the rights of Maria Theresa to succeed to the Habsburg throne of her father Emperor Charles VI were enshrined. France also repudiated the sanction.

George II gathered a 52,000-strong national army of British, Dutch and Hanoverian troops, with pro-Austrian German allies, and mustered on the lower Rhine; support was given by the infantry led by John Dalrymple, 2nd Earl of Stair. George advanced slowly into the Main and Necker valleys; meanwhile a 60,000-strong French force under Adrien Maurice, 3rd Duke of Noailles (d.1766) moved into position to block the advance. With tactical skill Noailles virtually blockaded George's force in the Main defiles. His Hanoverian stubbornness to the fore, George extricated his army from the situation, but the initial French cavalry charge of Comte de Grammont almost overwhelmed the allies. 'Now boys,' shouted George, 'now for the honour of England; fire and behave bravely and the French will soon run.' George's horse bolted, however, and threw him; he walked back to the front saying: 'I can be sure of my own legs. They will not run away with me.'

As the day closed George's force held the field, and Noailles retreated after the French Black Musketeers were decimated by the Royal Dragoons, and the French Household Cavalry were routed by the Scots Greys. Some 5,000 French were killed, wounded or taken prisoner, with British losses at around 265 dead and 560 wounded. This was the last occasion on which a British sovereign commanded an army on the battlefield. To commemorate the victory Georg Friedrich Handel composed his *Dettingen Te Deum*.

(Richard III was the last English king to die in battle at Bosworth Field in 1485. Edward, Prince of Wales (later Edward VIII) served as a staff officer in the First World War but was not allowed to fight on the front line. In 1916 he was visited in France at the HQ of His Majesty's Brigade of Guards by his brother Prince Albert (later George VI). On 31 May 1916 Prince Albert was present on board HMS *Collingwood* at the Naval Battle of Jutland when his vessel came under fire; *Collingwood* suffered no casualties.)

◆ Which king invented the handkerchief?

A dress of white satin embroidered with leeches, water and rocks, hung with fifteen silver-gilt mussels and fifteen cockles of white silver, doublet embroidered with gold orange trees on which were set a hundred silver-gilt oranges.

Sacherville Sitwell (1897–1988) commenting on Richard II's quirky sense of dress (1969).

King Richard II was 10 when he ascended the throne of England in 1377 and ruled for twenty-two years. Before he came to a sticky end at Pontefract castle, Yorkshire, his court was deemed effete. Historians have claimed that he was homosexual citing his over-affectionate behaviour towards certain male favourites like Robert de Vere and Michael de la Pole and his foppish dress. Richard's interest in what to wear and choice of cloth is supposed to have led to him inventing the handkerchief. The Household Rolls note 'little pieces [of cloth] for the lord King to wipe and clean his nose.'

Other monarchical inventions include the George Cross, based on a design by George VI, the John Brown Memorial Brooch designed by Queen Victoria, and the Windsor Uniform of dark blue tail-coat with red collar and cuffs designed by George III.

Perhaps the most quirky invention was the title 'Sirloin of Beef'; this appellation was invented by James I/VI – who certainly had need of a handkerchief to mop up his disgusting personal habits – when he knighted a loin of beef at Hoghton Tower, near Preston, Lancashire. The Revd E. Cobham Brewer, however, in his *Dictionary of Phrase and Fable* showed that James was being neither witty nor original in this act, given prominence by writer Jonathan Swift in his *Polite and Ingenious Conversation II* (1738). Brewer quotes *Church History of Britain* (1655), by Canon Thomas Fuller, chaplain-in-ordinary to Charles II, who noted this of Henry VIII:

> Dining with the Abbot of Reading, [Henry VIII] ate so heartily of a loin of beef that the abbot said he would give 1,000 marks for such a stomach. 'Done!' said the king and kept the abbot a prisoner in the Tower, won his 1,000 marks, and knighted the beef.

♦ Which monarch was the greatest gambler?

The whore and gambler, by the state
Licensed, build that nation's fate.
                    William Blake (1757–1827), 'Auguries of Innocence'.

Henry VIII spent a little time each evening gambling at cards or dice with his intimates. This kept Sir Anthony Denny, Chief Gentleman of the Privy Chamber and Keeper of the Privy Purse, busy as he had to pay out substantial sums in gambling debts.

In the court of James I/VI, gambling was not the major vice, except perhaps on Twelfth Night. On such a night in 1607 no one was allowed to sit at the king's table who could not produce a purse of £300. Curiously, others gambled on behalf of the Royal Family: Philip Herbert, the Earl of Montgomery, played for the king and won £150 (he was allowed to keep the winnings); William Parker, Baron Monteagle, played for Queen Anne and lost £400, while Sir Robert Carey lost £300 for Prince Charles. Charles II endeavoured, with little success, to discourage ladies-in-waiting from gambling on Twelfth Night, but John Evelyn noted that Charles did not discourage his 'great courtiers' from playing for stakes as high as £2,000 in gold at court.

George II was an enthusiastic gambling monarch though he tended to use his winnings on good causes, including bailing-out indigent servants. On one occasion he put his £1,000 winnings into the funds of the Foundling Hospital founded by Captain Thomas Coram in London in 1742. During one of his periods of illness he was discomfited to learn that his subjects were wagering 'ten Guineas [£10.50] to a hundred' that he would live no longer than twelve months. He bet fifty guineas [£52.50] on himself and after a year drew 500 guineas [£525]. On learning that the king was to lead his troops into battle on the Continent in 1743, underwriters offered bets on his demise on the battlefield at 4:1. The king lived.

George IV, as Prince of Wales, was a frequenter of the fashionable houses where private gambling games of Faro took place; often they were run by aristocratic ladies like Lady Archer, 'a woman steeped to the crown of her head in infamy and vice'. George's mistress Maria Fitzherbert was also a keen gambler, and the Prince of Wales took a perverse pleasure in seeing others 'broken' at the gambling tables. Once in 1814 the Prussian General Gebbard Blücher was the prince's guest at his home at Carlton House. Gleefully George encouraged the fleecing of him of around £25,000, which led him to leave London almost destitute. (Blücher came to the rescue of the Duke of Wellington the next year at the Battle of Waterloo.)

During the early years of marriage, Queen Victoria and Prince Albert were fond of playing card games like *vingt-et-un* usually with courtiers. Should they lose to the sovereign they were required to pay up in newly minted coins, 'a stock of which the ladies and gentlemen-in-waiting always kept in readiness'.

Perhaps the best-known royal gambler, both as Prince of Wales and king, was Edward VII. As Prince of Wales he ran up so much debt from card playing that Lord Palmerston became alarmed, writing to Queen Victoria to warn her. She delegated the prince's secretary Sir Francis Knollys to issue a reprimand; this had little or no effect, for over two nights Edward lost £700 at the tables at White's Club. Edward's favourite game was baccarat, a French card game that was illegal in Britain; for this he had his own ivory chips made with the Prince of Wales feathers as an emblem. The game was to win him serious public opprobrium. In September 1890, during the St Leger Week at Doncaster races, the prince and his cronies attended a house party gathered at Tranby Croft, near Hull, the home of Arthur Wilson. After a game of baccarat one of the players, Lt Col Sir William Gordon-Cumming, was accused of cheating. Gordon-Cumming was a distinguished soldier and a personal friend of the prince, and he was now accused of a criminal offence. He was given an ultimatum that in exchange for the silence of the parties in the know he must sign a written testimony that he would never play cards again. Unable to force his fellow players to withdraw their accusation he brought a civil action for slander against his accusers.

The case was the sensation of the decade; crowds of fashionable folk flocked to the law courts to hear the case presided over by the Lord Chief Justice, Lord John Coleridge, and to see the Prince of Wales as a witness. For the first time in 300 years, an heir apparent to the throne took the oath and gave evidence. The jury found against Gordon-Cumming who was now a broken man. He was cashiered from the army and lost his place in society; yet, to his death in 1930, Gordon-Cumming insisted on his innocence.

The case brought Edward's gambling lifestyle into the public eye once more and he was censured by church and nation. Queen Victoria was appalled that her son had appeared in court and made a terse suggestion that he give up gambling. Edward refused and said that if she ever suggested such a thing again, he would cease to visit her at Windsor. The queen was silent on the matter thereafter.

In his latter years Edward was a keen owner of race horses and between 1886 and 1910 he received some £400,000 in stake money and stud fees. Records show that his largest bet was £600 on Baron Maurice von Hirsch auf Gereult's horse Matchbox in the 1894 Paris Grand Prix. Edward lost. After retiring from the dining table most evenings when he got old, Edward usually played a few rubbers of bridge, but at this time in his life the stakes were not as high as back in the day when he was perhaps Britain's most enthusiastic royal gambler.

♦ Which queen pretended to be invisible?

> It was so clear and solitary, it did one good as one gazed around; and the pure mountain air was most refreshing. All seemed to breathe freedom and peace, and to make one forget the world and its sad turmoils.
>
> *Queen Victoria, journal entry, September 1848.*

Queen Victoria first took up residence at Balmoral castle in 1848; in 1852 the queen and Prince Albert bought the castle with ambitious plans to rebuild. Although she always held the castle dear as another tribute to Prince Albert's design skills, it was the Scottish countryside she loved best. In particular she had a passion for the shiels and bothies. The former are huts or cottages – originally shepherd's summer shelters – the latter the name of a cottage used in common by farm labourers. Over the years she refurbished, rebuilt, or built several such dwellings on her estate and often went to them to enjoy the 'wilderness around [them] that beckoned her'. From their windows she could see the tracks that wound away into the distant heather hills and the forests that reminded Prince Albert of the Thuringian Forest of his native Coburg. The shiels and bothies were the gateways to the privacy that the queen longed for and needed. Courtiers noted that when she went out walking on her estate the protocol was that folk 'had to pretend not to see her'. In her illusion of privacy – her attendants were never far away – she pretended to be invisible. When abroad she tried to be incognito, travelling under a pseudonym like the 'Countess of Balmoral'; no one was fooled hailing her with 'Vive la Reine d'Angleterre' or 'Viva la Reina d'Inghilterra'.

♦ Which queen is buried under a railway platform?

> Goaded by much mutual encouragements, the whole island rose under the leadership of Boudicca, a lady of royal descent . . .
>
> *Roman orator Publius Cornelius Tacitus (c. 55–120),* Annals.

Boudicca, or Boadicea, Queen of the Iron Age tribe the Iceni, led a famous revolt against Roman rule in Britain in 60 AD, sacking Londinium (London), Verulamium (St Albans) and Camulodunum (Colchester), throwing the Roman province into chaos. She was finally defeated by Provincial Governor Suetonius Paulinus at a place, the location of which historians still cannot agree, ranging from Mancetter in Warwickshire to Gop Hill, Flintshire.

Historian Dio Cassius tells us that she 'fell sick and died', while Tacitus says she took poison after her defeat. However she died, Dio says that she was given a costly funeral by her people; but where is she buried? Again this is in dispute, but curiously it has long been suggested that she was buried in a grave where Kings Cross Station, London, now stands, while some even narrow down the site to Platform 8.

♦ Was King Richard III really a hunchbacked monster?

> He left such a reputation behind him that even his birth was said to have proclaimed him a monster.
> *James Gairdner (1828–1912),* History of the Life and Reign of Richard III.

John Rous (d.1491), the Warwickshire cleric and antiquary was not the first to curry royal favour with his writings. Yet his *Historia Regum Angliae* is said to bear much of the blame for promoting the Tudor myth that Richard III was a 'crook back'. Rous wrote:

> Richard was born [2 October 1452] at Fotheringhay in Northampton-shire, retained within his mother's womb for two years and emerging with teeth and hair on his shoulders.

This was clearly nonsense but historians have been thwarted concerning Richard's appearance for there is no contemporary description of him. Yet, look at the portrait of Richard (artist unknown) in the National Portrait Gallery; apart from a rather absent-minded expression, there is no sign of deformity, nor is there in the *c.*1520 copy of the portrait of Richard (possibly when he was the Duke of Gloucester) in the collection of the Society of Antiquaries of London. Both must have appeared in Tudor times but neither show the anti-Richard propaganda of the Tudor court.

The sixth and youngest son of Edmund of Langley, Duke of York and his wife Cecily Neville, it is likely that the 37-year-old duchess had a difficult birth with Richard. As Shakespeare wrote in King Henry VI, Part III: 'For I have often heard my mother say I came into the world with my legs forward.'

Following the description of Richard's birth by Sir Thomas More in his *The History of King Richard the Third* – remembering that More was one of Richard's foremost character assassins – Shakespeare is probably describing a breech birth. Perhaps, too, Richard was hauled out in the days before forceps and suffered a slightly raised right shoulder. More also describes a 'withered arm', but there is no conclusive evidence that Richard had any of these deformities. To the medieval mind, deformity was a mark of being born, if not evil, at the very least of dubious character only a step away from being a creature of witchcraft. It was easy therefore for Tudor detractors like Rous, More and Polydore Vergil to use the superstition of the day concerning deformity to blacken Richard's character, especially when linking him to the murder of his nephews, 'The Princes in the Tower'.

◆ Which king was afraid of witches?

About this time [c.1590] many witches were taken in Lothian, who deposed concerning some designs of [Francis] the Earl of Bothwell's against his Majesty's person …

Sir James Melville (1535–1617), Memoirs *(1827 edition).*

It was while James VI still only ruled Scotland that he developed his physical fear of witchcraft. A thorn in the side of James was his cousin, the Catholic Lord Francis Stewart Hepburn, 5th Earl of Bothwell, who had been one of a group conspiring against him. Bothwell had got off lightly, but soon James's displeasure with him turned to an undying hatred, and through him James became personally involved in one of the most famous cases of witchcraft in Scotland, which was to become the inspiration for an internationally famous drama.

During the winter of 1590/1 there took place, in the Lothians, a series of witch trials. Because of his taste for the creepy and abnormal King James had taken a great deal of interest in them. One such prosecution, known as the Trial of the North Berwick witches, particularly fascinated him. So much so that James had a few of the supposed witches appear before him, to tell of their caperings and antics in attempting to call up the Devil. James considered witchcraft to be a branch of theology, and believed witches to be the mortal creations of Satan lured to thwart God's purpose on earth. James set down all his beliefs in his book *Daemonologie* (1597).

James was horrified to discover, from where it is not clear, that the witches he had spoken to at court were employing their devilish arts to cause his murder on land or sea at the instigation of the Earl of Bothwell. Under torture the witches confessed to poisons being concocted to kill James, of waxen images of him being thrown into the fire to cause his death, and special spells to cause sea tempests to drown him. Far more terrifying for James was the confession which implied that Bothwell was the witch leader and his ultimate aim was to have James murdered by witchcraft and replace him on the throne.

Bothwell was imprisoned in Edinburgh Castle on 16 April 1591, but escaped three months later before he could be arraigned for treason. He fled to his castle in the Scottish Borders, lived as an outlaw, and mounted a daring raid on Holyrood Palace. He fled, unable to kidnap James as had been his intention. Captured once more Bothwell was tried at the Tolbooth, Edinburgh, on 10 August 1593 on a charge of inciting witchcraft. The king's advocate placed before the court the depositions of the Lothian witches extracted by torture; the testimony reflected all the superstition of the day including witches flying through the air, having cats as confidants and so on; this was offered as evidence that Bothwell was to use witchcraft to kill the king. The 'evidence' was laughable, said the defence lawyers who pointed out that 'no reasonable' person could believe such nonsense. Bothwell spoke in his own defence saying that the charge was purely political in intent to get rid of him. The jury returned a verdict of not guilty. After various lunatic escapades against James, Bothwell fled to the Continent and died in poverty in Naples in 1624.

James retained his fear of witchcraft until his death in 1625. Many believe that it is more than likely that when Shakespeare was composing his *Macbeth* (1606), he had the North Berwick witch trial in mind, and those ludicrous attempts to kill James by magic.

♦ Which British reigning monarch was the first to wear a kilt?

Aloud strike the harp, for my bosom is cold,
And the sound has a charm on my fears.
A City new-clothed as a Bride I behold,
And her King as her Bridegroom appears.

'Tis he whom they love, and who loves them again,
Who partakes of the joy he imparts,
Who over three nations shall happily reign,
And establish his throne in their hearts.

George Crabbe (1754–1852) on George IV's arrival in Scotland.

When painting his official portrait of King George IV in Highland dress in 1829, Sir David Wilkie (1785–1841) said that it took 3 hours to dress the monarch in his Highland outfit and 'to lace up all the leggings and excrescencies'. The effect, Wilkie further remarked, was like 'a great sausage stuffed into the covering'. Why was this Hanoverian sovereign dressed in a kilt in the first place?

In 1822 Scotland was thrown into a panic when it was announced that George IV had decided to pay an official visit to his northern realm. George had just been to Ireland and wanted to see the land of his Stuart forbears. The last of the Jacobite pretenders to his throne (Henry Stuart, Cardinal of York) had died in 1806 and danger from that quarter had gone, with the Jacobites now put firmly into Scottish romanticism and myth. No ruling monarch had visited the country since Charles II's coronation in 1651 and consequently there was no one who knew anything about arranging such an event. However, the whole pageant would be stage-managed by Sir Walter Scott at the invitation of the Lord Provost of Edinburgh (soon to be Sir) William Arbuthnot. With his romanticism blowing at full blast, Scott filled Edinburgh with invented tartan nonsense which would stereotype Scottish culture for generations.

George arrived at the Port of Leith on 15 August 1822 aboard the *Royal George.* Dressed as a full admiral George was processed along Leith Walk to Holyrood Palace. (George did not stay there; he preferred the Duke of Buccleuch's residence of Dalkeith House outside the city). George was lauded wherever he went with triumphal arches and banner mottoes. One such took the first line of Robert Burns's *Address to the Haggis* as a compliment: 'Fair fa' your honest, sonsie [cheerful] face.' Thankfully the next line was omitted: 'Great chieftain o' the puddin'-race.'

At the royal levée at Holyrood on Saturday 17 August, George appeared for the first time in his kilt of Royal Stuart tartan devised for him by Col David Stuart of Garth. The sight of rotund George in a kilt caused an intake of breath among the 2,000 'gentlemen of Scotland' present. George's corpulence did not suit the kilt, which when on was too short. George ensured that the effect was more ludicrous by wearing flesh-coloured leggings to hide his unflattering Hanoverian knees. Delighted by his appearance, George was unaware of his comical persona. Luckily his buffoon-like figure did not dampen the enthusiasm for all things Scottish which would be given a further boost by his niece Queen Victoria decades later, when she added 'tartanitis' to Scotland's themed designs.

♦ Who was the first monarch to install a flushing lavatory?

> Even in the goodliest and stateliest palaces of our realm, notwithstanding all our provisions of vaults, or sluices, or gates, or pains of poor folks in sweeping and scouring, yet still the same whoreson saucy stink!
> *Sir John Harrington (1561–1612) author of* Metamorphosis of Ajax *(1596).*

Sir John Harrington was a Cambridge-educated noted wit and author who took his place in royal circles as a godson of Elizabeth I. He was exiled from court for the composition of ribald satires. Yet, when his rehabilitation had taken place he won an important place in the history of British sanitation through a more useful invention.

For centuries the disposal of human waste posed a problem. Great abbeys like the Benedictine foundation of Fountains, Yorkshire, had extensive latrine blocks (reredorters) above quick-flowing streams, and in castles lavatories were built out over walls with drops into moats. The common man defecated where he could and physician Andrew Boorde in his *Brevyary of Health* (1547) noted that there was much 'pissing in chimneys'. By the reign of Elizabeth I middle-class and aristocratic houses had cupboards containing chamber pots, often of pewter, known as 'jordans'. While the queen had more elaborate lidded pots in her chambers, concealed in close-stools, and emptied by ladies-in-waiting. Other courtiers, say, at Hampton Court, used 'the great house of easement' or relieved themselves in the palace courtyard. Then along came Sir John Harrington with his new idea.

During 1584–91 Sir John built a house for himself at Kelston, Bath, and in it he constructed a flushing lavatory which he called an Ajax. His water closet had a pan with an opening at the bottom, sealed with a leather-faced valve. There was a system of handles, levers and weights to flush the pan from a cistern. When Elizabeth I used the facility during her visit she was much taken with it and in 1597 had one installed at Richmond Palace. Thus Elizabeth was the first monarch to have a flushing lavatory installed, the first in any royal palace.

The device did not catch on with her subjects who preferred to carry on as they had before, many emptying their potties directly into the street. In Scotland outriders preceded any royal procession from Edinburgh Castle to Holyrood Palace down the Canongate in case anyone made a direct hit of excrement on the person of the monarch; usually the householder would shout *gardez l'eau* before emptying their container to warn those below. In time this cry was reduced to *gardy loo* from which the modern word for lavatory, 'loo', is taken. A flushing lavatory was not patented until 1775 by Alexander Cumming of London.

♦ Who was the 'Carpet Queen'?

> Ye curious carpet knights, that spend your time in sport and play,
> Abroad, and see new sights, your country's cause calls you away.
>   *Humphrey Gifford (1550–1600), 'For Soldiers: Posie of Gilloflowers'.*

Tapisary history identifies Eleanor of Castile (1241–90), first wife of Edward I, 'Longshanks', as the first to introduce carpets into England in 1255, dubbing her the 'Carpet Queen'. For a long time their use did not spread, although by the reign of Edward III (r. 1327–77), his palace was carpeted. Most folk sneered at carpets as effeminate and chose to perpetuate the use of rushes as a floor covering. Not until

1301 is there a mention of carpets for sleeping chambers. Rushes were used in Queen Mary I's presence chamber from 1553–8, but her sister Elizabeth I had a Turkish carpet. Their brother Edward VI introduced carpets for setting before the altar of his chapel as one courtier noted:

> Carpets full gay
> That wrought were in the Orient.

By the reign of James I/VI carpets were commonplace at court, particularly those woven in the works of Sir Francis Crane (d. 1636) at Mortlake, Surrey.

♦ Which monarchs had nicknames or were immortalised in nursery rhymes?

> I was first of all the kings who drew
> The knighthood-errant of this realm and all
> The realms together under one, their Head,
> In that fair order of my Table Round,
> A glorious company, the flower of men,
> To serve as model for the mighty world,
> And be the fair beginning of a time.
>   *Alfred, Lord Tennyson (1809–92), 'Idylls of the King'.*

The Royal Family calling Queen Elizabeth II 'Miss Piggy', when she gives them her famous 'Hanoverian frown', is one in a long history of nicknames for royal personages. Long before the Benedictine monks of Glastonbury Abbey found a grave in 1191, which they believed to be the last resting place of King Arthur and advanced his presence in British myth, his name was already legendary. In the sixth century the Celtic monk John of Exeter described Arthur as *Flos Regulorum* (The Flower of Kings), adding one more listing to the king's nomenclature. While the cleric was using the sobriquet to be flattering, most royal nicknames are double-edged.

Queen Isabella, the adulterous wife of Edward II, who he married when she was 12 at Boulogne Cathedral in 1308, was known as 'The She-Wolf of France', largely because of her ruthless pursuit and total destruction of her husband and his favourite, Hugh de Spencer. Popular history has long stated that Edward II was murdered at the order of his wife. Others, like Charles II, had more jokey nicknames. He was known as 'Old Rowley' for his sexual nature and carnal exploits. The nickname came from the name of a horse in the royal stables known for its procreative potency. Charles's mistress Nell Gwynn called him 'Charles III', for she had already bedded Charles Sackville Buckland, (later) Earl of Dorset and Shakespeare's grand-nephew, actor Charles Hart.

George III is well known as 'Farmer George' (see chapter 5), while George IV was called 'Fun the Fourth' in Lord Byron's *Don Juan*. Queen Victoria was given a set of nicknames by the anti-monarchy radical press. The best known were 'Empress Brown', or just 'Mrs Brown'. These derived from her devotion to her Highland servant, John Brown, the stable-boy who rose to be her royal confidant (see chapter 1). Her son Edward, Prince of Wales, had no sense of humour for nicknames about himself. One late night in the billiard room at Sandringham with pals, his friend the philanderer Sir Frederick Johnstone was behaving boisterously. The Prince of Wales reprimanded him with 'Freddy! Freddy! You're very drunk'. Johnstone pointed to the prince's ample stomach, and rolling his r's in imitation of Edward's Germanic accent, replied: 'Tum-Tum, you're verrrry fat!' Furious, the prince turned on his heel and instructed an equerry to have Sir Frederick's bags packed. 'Tum-Tum' became the prince's nickname in society, but not again to his face. In time Sir Frederick was forgiven.

While serving on the vessel *Britannia* in 1877, Prince George of Wales (later George V) and his brother Albert Victor, Duke of Clarence were nicknamed 'Sprat and Herring' by their fellow midshipmen. George V's son, Edward VIII (Duke of Windsor), had most nicknames arising from his association with Mrs Wallis Simpson. 'Peter Pan' is what Ernest Simpson called him, while the Court referred to the couple as 'King Edward the Eighth and Mrs Simpson the Seven-Eighths'. He had already received a different nickname from the staff for a previous mistress Mrs Dudley Ward. Every morning the king called, 'just like the baker's van', so they called him 'The Baker'.

Within the Royal Family nicknames abound. Henry VIII called his fourth wife Anne of Cleves, 'The Dutch Cow' and 'The Flanders

Mare'. George IV called Queen Caroline, 'That She-Devil', while his niece Victoria called him 'Uncle King', and she called William IV 'Uncle Pineapple'. In turn her grandson Kaiser Wilhelm II called her 'Duck'. Edward VII called his daughters princesses Louise, Victoria and Maud, 'Toots, Gawks and Snipey' after their names for themselves. His son, the Duke of Clarence, he called 'Collar and Cuffs' after the prince's mode of dress of high starched collar and length cuffs. Queen Elizabeth II called her grandfather George V, 'Grandpa England' and George VI referred to his family as 'The Firm'. For his wife, her in-laws the Duke and Duchess of Windsor reserved the more scathing titles of 'The Monster of Glamis', 'The Fat Scotch Cook' and 'The Dowdy Duchess'.

The nursery rhyme which begins 'There was an old woman who lived in a shoe' was adapted by such papers as *Punch* to describe Queen Victoria's family of (eventually) nine children. The point was a political one, suggesting that the royal nursery was a drain on the public purse. The nursery rhyme, with its second line, 'She had so many children she didn't know what to do', had originally referred to Queen Caroline, wife of George II, who had nine children (one stillborn).

Henry VIII probably had the most nursery rhymes attributed to his activities. Here's one:

Little Jack Horner, sat in corner
Eating a Christmas pie.
He put in his thumb, and pulled out a plum
And said, 'What a good boy am I'.

Tradition has it that Jack Horner was the steward of Richard Whiting, the doomed last Abbot of Glastonbury Abbey, Somerset. At the Dissolution of the Monasteries, Whiting was pressed to give up his title to monastic properties. In an attempt to persuade Henry not to dissolve the abbey, Whiting had the deeds of the Manor of Mells baked in a pie for Henry to find. One source noted that instead of travelling to London to deliver the pie, Horner opened it and misappropriated the Mells deeds for himself. Henry had the abbot executed. Again the rhyme 'Sing a song of sixpence' is thought to relate to more Henrician property confiscations as attested in the line, 'Four and twenty blackbirds baked in a pie'. The 'blackbirds' being property deeds. Then there's the rhyming game:

Oranges and lemons said the bells of St Clements ...
Here comes a candle to light you to bed, Here comes a chopper to
chop off your head.

The verse is said to refer to the marriages of Henry VIII which led to
the executions of Anne Boleyn and Catherine Howard.

The popular rhyme 'Ride a cock horse to Banbury Cross' (in
Oxfordshire) traditionally identifies the 'fine lady upon a white horse'
as Queen Elizabeth I. While the thorn in her side, Mary, Queen of
Scots is remembered in:

Mary, Mary, quite contrary, how does your garden grow?
With silver bells and cockle shells, and pretty maids all in a row.

The 'pretty maids' being the queen's 'Maries'.

'Rock-a-bye-baby' with the wind blowing a cradle doomed to
fall, is said to refer to the birth of Prince James Francis Edward
Stuart, the son of James II/VII. Roman Catholic Prince James never
succeeded to the throne of his father as 'the wind' came putting
Protestant Prince William of Orange on the throne. Prince James's
son Prince Charles Edward Stuart would also be the source of
rhymes and songs in the verse 'Charlie over the water' and 'The Skye
Boat Song'. Again two monarchs – Charles II and George I – are
linked in one rhyme, the first as 'Rowley Powley' and the latter as
'Georgie Porgie':

Rowley Powley (or Georgie Porgie), pudding and pie,
Kissed the girls and made them cry.
When the boys came out to play,
Rowley Powley (or was it Georgie Porgie?) ran away.

♦ Which monarchs used pseudonyms?

Your high self you have obscur'd
With a swain's wearing, and me poor lowly maid,
Most goddess-like prank'd up.

William Shakespeare, The Winter's Tale.

When Queen Anne (as princess) and her favourite, Sarah, Duchess of Marlborough, sent each other *billets doux* they used pseudonyms. In her *Conduct* (1742), Sarah explained why:

> [Queen Anne] grew uneasy to be treated by me with the ceremony due to her rank and with the sound of words that implied superiority. It was this turn of mind which made her one day propose to me that whenever I should happen to be absent from her we might in all our letters write ourselves by feigning names such as would import nothing of distinction of rank between us. Morley and Freeman were the names her fancy hit upon & she left me to choose by which of them I would be called. My frank open temper naturally led me to pitch upon Freeman, and so the Princess took the other; and from this time Mrs Morley and Mrs Freeman began to converse as equals, made so by affection & friendship.

George III appeared under the pseudonym of Ralph Robinson when he wrote an article for *Annals of Agriculture* in 1787. But his son George IV used the more whimsical name of 'Florizel' when sending letters to his first mistress the actress Mary Robinson. The name was taken from David Garrick's 1756 version, *Florizel and Perdita*, of the first two acts of Shakespeare's *The Winter's Tale*. George imagined himself in love with Mary who appeared as Perdita; 'she is I believe almost the greatest and most perfect beauty of her sex,' he said. She died in 1786 aged 28.

As a midshipman William IV was known as 'William Guelph'. This was the name of one of the major ruling families of Germany from early medieval times, from which the House of Hanover was a descendant branch. Also as a midshipman, aboard the battleship HMS *Collingwood* George VI was referred to as 'Mr Johnson' for security reasons.

Both Queen Victoria (Countess of Balmoral and Countess of Lancaster) and Edward VII (Earl of Renfrew) used pseudonyms when travelling unofficially, as did Queen Mary (Lady Killarney). In her journal describing her 'First Great Expedition' to Glen Fishie and Grantown in the Scottish Highlands in 1860, Queen Victoria described how she and Prince Albert used pseudonyms:

> We decided to call ourselves Lord and Lady Churchill and party, [Jane] Lady Churchill [Lady of the Bedchamber] passing as Miss Spencer,

and General [The Hon. Charles] Grey as Dr Grey! [John] Brown [Queen Victoria's Highland servant] forgot this, and called me 'Your Majesty' as I was getting into the carriage; and [John] Grant [Head Keeper] on the box called Albert 'Your Royal Highness'; which set us off laughing, but no one observed it.

When Queen Victoria's grandson Prince Albert Victor, Duke of Clarence visited the notorious Hundred Guineas Club – which had a rule that all members be given a female Christian name – he chose 'Victoria'.

When King Edward VIII and his mistress Mrs Ernest Simpson spoke to each other on public telephones they used the pseudonyms 'Mr James' and 'Janet'. Edward also travelled as the 'Duke of Lancaster' – like Edward VII using one of his titles – when on a private trip to the Mediterranean with Mrs Simpson in the summer of 1936 aboard Lady Yule's yacht *Nahlin*.

◆ Why can't Queen Elizabeth II eat 'Granny's Chips'?

Queen Mary glittered with five diamond necklesses about her neck. She was in blue with literally mountains of jewels, [Lady] Pamela Berry whispered to me – 'She has bagged all the best.' She has.

Sir Henry Chips Channon (1897–1958), Diaries, 16 November 1938.

Those who have studied the history of jewels in the royal collection agree with one-time fashion editor of *The Times* Suzy Menkes, that Queen Mary, wife of George V, had an 'avaricious acquisition of jewels'. One official photograph portrait of her depicts her in regal pose bedecked with coronet and myriad jewels. On her garter ribbon is pinned one of 'Granny's Chips'.

The Cullinan Diamond was the largest gem diamond ever found. Weighing around 3,106 carats in its rough form it was discovered on 26 January 1905 at the Premier Mine, Transvaal, South Africa, and named after the discoverer of the mine Sir Thomas Cullinan. It was presented to Edward VII as a token of the loyalty of the people of the Transvaal (annexed to the British Crown in 1900), following the end of the South African (Boer) War. As a safety precaution, to deter criminals, the diamond was sent to London by parcel post, while a dummy stone was sent by sea. Chief of the General Staff, Viscount Esher, advised the king not to accept the diamond, but King Edward demurred and said the 'great and unique' diamond would be preserved 'among the historic jewels which form the heirlooms of the Crown'.

The great Cullinan Diamond was 'cleaved' by Asscher's of Amsterdam into three masses. The smallest of the three – the marquise – King Edward gave to his wife Queen Alexandra. The rest of the Cullinan stones – six large brilliants and ninety-six smaller diamonds – were ultimately presented to Queen Mary. Thereafter the Cullinan cleavings were referred to by the Royal Family as 'Granny's Chips'. They are a part of the personal jewels worn by Elizabeth II on state and semi-state occasions.

♦ Which king joined a sex club?

> It is with these lusty monks of Pittenweem, and their guardian Knights Templar of the Dreel, that the Society or Brotherhood of the Beggar's Benison undoubtedly had its origin. Its motto is the monkish blessing 'Be fruitful and multiply'.
>
> *Col M.R. Canch Kavanagh*, Résumé of the History of the Order.

Present-day Anstruther, on the south coast of Fife overlooking the Firth of Forth, is made up of two historic settlements: Anstruther Easter and Anstruther Wester divided by a burn known as The Dreel. Long famous for its prosperous maritime traditions, the Burgh of Anstruther west of The Dreel was granted a Royal Charter by James VI on 21 October 1587. By The Dreel's mouth there stood a now vanished castle known as the Castle of Dreel, once the home of the influential Anstruther family.

In a room of the castle met the gentleman's club of The Most Ancient and Puissant Order of the Beggar's Benison and Merryland. Primarily it was a dining club but its fundamental interests were erotic in nature with phallicism of great interest. Records show that it was founded in 1732, while some suggest an earlier medieval provenance. Two main stories persist. Out in the Firth of Forth is the Isle of May and on it, in his monastery, St Adrian was slain by marauding Vikings around 870 AD. Adrian's tomb was soon considered to have miraculous powers wherein pagan fertility rites became attached to his Christian shrine and barren women flocked here to be made fertile. James IV of Scots and his Queen Margaret came here to receive the blessing of the Augustinian Prior, 'Be fruitful and multiply'. Thus the Club had its roots.

The Club, too, was long associated with the (apocryphal) tale of how James V of Scots, nicknamed 'the Gudeman of Ballangeich', a pseudonym he used when travelling, came to Anstruther and was unable to cross The Dreel. A local 'buxom gaberlunzie [i.e. beggar] lass' hitched up her skirts and carried the monarch piggy-back over the burn so he could continue his journey to the Castle of Dreel. In recompense James V gave the woman a gold sovereign. She curtseyed to him and gave him her benison:

> May your purse ne'er be toom [empty]
> And you horn aye in bloom.

That night James V dined at the Castle of Dreel and supposedly initiated the Club. Be all that as it may, the Club (which referred to itself as the Order and their members as Knights), met twice a year at Candlemas (February) and St Andrews's Day (30 November), in a room of the Castle of Dreel which they called The Temple. (When the castle was no longer habitable they met at a nearby inn.) In 1738 the members devised a seal with its device a purse of money hanging from a phallus with the anchor of Anstruther's arms in the background. At this time membership cost ten guineas (£10.50), a diploma of membership three guineas (£3.15) and a gold medal to wear five guineas (£5.25). The membership was headed by a 'Sovereign', and several local notables held the office from 'Sir' John McNaughton, Collector of Customs at Anstruther to 'Sir' John Lumisdaine, a local estate owner. The 'Sovereign's' deputy was the 'Remembrancer', with a 'Chaplain' added in 1767. The membership was composed of thirty-two 'Knights' and the founder members were all from this part of the country known as the East Neuk of Fife; its membership included landowners and merchants, smugglers and peers as well as Jacobites, Whigs, Presbyterians and Episcopalians.

The main meeting was held on 30 November with a dinner, with an initiation for new members to follow; the whole ethos of the meeting has been described as 'the pagan glorification of the phallus and the puerile initiation ceremony concerning its display and measuring'. Thereafter a new member was toasted in wine from glasses engraved with the Club Seal of the Order. The toast was 'To the beggar maid and joy'. During the evening of lasciviousness naked local girls danced around to arouse sexual desire. The dissolution of the Order occurred on 30 November 1836.

A Chapter of the Order, known as the Wig Club, was founded in the 1760s at Edinburgh. The Chapter took its name from a Benison Club relic of a wig made from the pubic hair of the mistresses of Charles II, which had been originally given by Charles to the Earl of Moray. It was into this Club that George IV (then Prince of Wales) was given honorary membership at the suggestion of Sir Walter Scott. As the late Alan Bold points out in his introduction to the reprint of the 1892 edition of the Records of the Club: 'Apparently George IV suggested that the knights fashion a new wig and, as a right royal gesture, presented them with a silver snuffbox containing the pubic hair of his mistress.'

PALACES, CASTLES
AND LOVE NESTS

♦ Which monarch built a love nest for his mistress?

> They say – What say they?
> Let them say.
> *Sentiment inscribed in the plasterwork of 'The Red House', Bournemouth,*
> *by Lillie Langtry.*

One day in April 1877 the young painter Walford Graham Robertson was making his way across the road at Hyde Park Corner, London, when he noticed a young woman approaching. He glanced at her garb of black bonnet and dress and thought she might be 'a miliner's assistant', or a 'poorly paid governess'. As he passed 'the girl looked up and I all but sat flat down in the road', he later recounted. Stunned, he observed: 'For the first and only time in my life I beheld perfect beauty!' The beauty who captured his attention was Mrs Lillie Langtry.

Born on 13 October 1853 at the Old Rectory, St Saviour, Jersey, Lillie was christened Emilie Charlotte Le Breton, the only daughter of The Very Revd William Corbet Le Breton, Dean of Jersey and his wife Emilie Martin. On 9 March 1874 she married an Irish widower called Edward Langtry and eventually moved to London. Lillie entered London society with a will and her beauty won her many compliments. Daisy, Countess of Warwick left this description of her:

> She had dewy violet eyes, a complexion like a peach. How can words convey the vitality, the glow, the amazing charm that made this fascinating woman the centre of any group she entered?

At a reception at the opulent home in Lowndes Square of Sir John and Lady Sebright, Lillie made a profound impression on the distinguished company which comprised several of the outstanding artists of the day. Albert Edward, Prince of Wales (later King Edward VII) heard of the beautiful Mrs Langtry, now called the 'Jersey Lillie' following the public display of her portrait by Sir John Millais. At a discreet dinner party at Stratford Place, engineered by his equerries Sir Allan Young and Lord Suffield, the Prince of Wales met Lillie. Soon after she was to be seen riding with the prince in Hyde Park and it was inevitable that she became his mistress. By the end of 1877 he would not go out socially without being accompanied by Lillie.

Edward Langtry and Lillie's house in Eaton Place was not very suitable for royal seduction; after all, Lillie's husband could be a constant interruption. The building of love nests by royals for mistresses was nothing new, but it was for the Prince of Wales. He chose the rising seaside resort of Bournemouth as the location for the love nest, on the cliffs overlooking the sea. The foundation stone was laid in 1877 with Lillie's initials carved in its surface. She called the building 'The Red House' and on the south wall was inscribed the Latin tag *Dulce Domum* (a sweet house). The mock-Tudor house had a huge drawing room and dining room with a minstrels' gallery. The decoration included lovers' symbols and a number of mottoes; on the outside wall of the suite of rooms occupied by the Prince of Wales were the words *Stet Fortuna Demesis* (May fortune attend those who dwell here). Off the prince's rooms were hidden passages and stairways which led to Lillie's bedroom, but the prince's Jacobean bed was huge for night-time gymnastics. A tiny hatch was built into the wall of the dining room so that the Prince of Wales could inspect the company unseen before going in to dine. The Red House became a refuge for the prince from the pomposity of the court and with both in trying marriages they could enjoy 'playing house'. Lillie and the Prince of Wales's love nest, in what became Derby Road, later developed as a hotel (The Langtry Manor), and although Edward as Prince of Wales and king became distracted by other beauties, his friendship with Lillie continued until his death in 1910. Lillie, who divorced Edward Langtry in 1887, enjoyed a career as an actress, and remarried in 1899 to become Lady de Bathe. Lillie died at Monaco on 12 February 1929 aged 75, to be buried at St Saviours Church, Jersey.

Lillie and the Prince of Wales had another love nest with its private beach. This was at the eighteenth-century stone-built home of the Malcolm family, called Portalloch House, on the Isle of Taynish, Argyll, on the west side of the Mull of Kintyre, Scotland. The Prince of Wales and Lillie would travel to Scotland separately on the night train to what the prince described as 'this Enchanted Isle'. He enjoyed the days out stalking and locals spoke of his skinny dipping with Lillie from the secret bathhouse by the shore.

The Prince of Wales in his long career of serial adultery had a variety of love nests. St Hubert's, near Gerard's Cross, Buckinghamshire, was another house where royal seductive history was made. Strangely, during the ownership of Col The Hon. William de Poel Trench (Commander-in-Chief of the Ordnance Survey), the house disappeared from maps. Also, a road that ran close to the front of the house was diverted by a private Act of Parliament, all to preserve the privacy of the Prince of Wales for his seductive pleasures. When the Prince of Wales was present the many household staff were banished from the main house to cottages on the 50-acre estate. Here the Prince of Wales entertained various mistresses from Lillie Langtry to Daisy, Lady Brooke and Alice, The Hon. Mrs George Keppel, his last great love.

♦ How did Buckingham Palace become the prime royal residence?

'Everything is so straggly, such distances and so fatiguing.' – *Queen Victoria*.
'A sepulchre.' – *King Edward VII*.
'It has a dank and musty smell.' – *King Edward VIII*.
'An icebox.' – *King George VI*.

Monarchs' opinions of Buckingham Palace.

Buckingham Palace, with its address of Pimlico, London SW1, was originally the town house of the dukes of Buckingham. The palace was constructed during 1702–5 by William Winde for John Sheffield, 1st Duke of Buckingham and Normanby (1648–1721), who was given a parcel of land at the western end of St James's Park to add to his Buckingham House estate. It was rumoured that Queen Anne admired him as he had made advances towards her in 1682 when she was Princess Anne and was banished from court for his pains. The gift of land was a token of her remembrance.

In earlier days James I/VI had used the land for the cultivation of black mulberry trees. At the time the English aristocracy were much taken with the idea of making vast fortunes out of silk making; it was noted that the prime step towards such a fortune was to plant groves of mulberry trees in which the silk worms could breed. Alas for King James, it was *white* mulberry trees that nurtured silk worms. Thus the royal experiment failed. But the plot he set out became known as the Mulberry Garden and was a popular rendezvous for young lovers. Today a mulberry tree is still extant in the gardens of Buckingham Palace.

By 1633 George Goring, Earl of Norwich paid Charles I £400 for the rights to the Mulberry Garden and built himself a mansion known as Goring House. Alas in 1674 it was gutted by fire destroying the new owner, Henry Bennet, Earl of Arlington's fabulous antiques collection. Arlington, who is remembered in history as a procurer of pretty girls for Charles II, rebuilt Goring House as Arlington House and by purchase of land from Sir Thomas Grosvenor, expanded the estate. Thus the house and estate was sold by Arlington's daughter, the Duchess of Grafton, to John Sheffield.

Sheffield developed Buckingham House out of the property he had bought and it remained within the same family until it was bought for £21,000 in 1762 by George III. For a time it was known as Queen's House, the residence of George III's wife Queen Charlotte. The king spent £47,506 on alterations to the house which now resembled a country gentleman's property. The house became a focal point for Londoners to promenade and gossip outside its railings in the hope of catching a glimpse of the Royal Family. Here, too, in the Royal Mews was housed the State Coach purchased by George III in 1762 for £7,567 19s 9½d (£7,587.95); the coach is still in use today for state occasions. George III collected a fine library of books at Queen's House, which was to form the nucleus of the British Library. The first marriage to be conducted at the house was that of Frederick, Duke of York, George and Charlotte's second child, who married in 1791 Princess Frederica, eldest daughter of Frederick William II of Prussia.

When George IV succeeded to the throne in 1820 he decided to make the Queen's House his principle London residence and persuaded parliament to vote £252,690 for its repair. In the event George spent three times as much on its reconstruction and died before the palace was completed to the design of John Nash. George's successor and brother, Prince William, Duke of Clarence (later King William IV) was born at Buckingham Palace in 1765; the first royal to be born here. He hated the place, but finished off the work his brother had started to include gas lighting. Proving to be an open drain for cash Buckingham Palace was ready for occupation in May 1837. William IV died the following month. Queen Victoria inherited the palace and all but one of her children were born there, including Edward VII who was the only monarch to die at the palace. Final alterations to the palace were made in 1913 by the addition of the west front of Portland Stone to the design of Sir Aston Webb.

There are some 600 rooms in the palace including those used by the staff as offices and domestic quarters. The rooms privately occupied by the Royal Family are few in number. The queen and the Duke of Edinburgh have a suite of about a dozen rooms on the first floor of the north wing overlooking Green Park. The gardens of the palace, landscaped by W. T. Aiton, run to some 45 acres and extend to Hyde Park Corner.

♦ Which railway station can be dubbed 'the most royal'?

Guests usually arrived at Sandringham House by train at the small station of Wolferton, some two miles away, to be met by smartly turned-out carriages with coachmen in the Prince of Wales's livery; luggage and servants arrived separately in less ostentatious vehicles.
Raymond Lamont-Brown, Edward VII's Last Loves: Alice Keppel & Agnes Keyser *(1998).*

Several railway stations have entered history as being associated with royalty. When Queen Victoria made her 'Scottish home' at Balmoral the Ballater railway station – the terminus for the line from Aberdeen – became a focal point for the public to gather to see the comings and goings of the Royal Family and their celebrated guests. The line to Ballater station was completed in 1867 which helped to make the village a popular spa resort. The station lies 8 miles west of Balmoral Castle and was rebuilt in 1886 to incorporate a royal waiting room. Proposals were put forward to extend the line to Braemar, but tradition has it that Queen Victoria strongly objected to a railway line passing through her estate so the extension line was never built.

The arrival of the royal train at Ballater was a great event and The Great North of Scotland Railway published special timetables which became collectors' pieces. One such dated Thursday 16–Friday 17 June 1887, *For Regulating the Progress of the Train to Convey Her Majesty from Ballater to Windsor, via Aberdeen, Carlisle and Bushey Junction* details every station passed through, times and gradients encountered with noted stops. Much of the royalty of nineteenth-century Europe passed through Ballater railway station on their way to Balmoral. A particularly large crowd assembled at Station Square to see the arrival of Tsar Nicholas II and the Tsarina Alexandra on 22 September 1896. They had been met at Leith from the Imperial yacht *Standart* by the Prince of Wales and his brother Arthur, Duke of Connaught. At Ballater a ceremonial guard of 100 men of the Black Watch awaited them and they were greeted on the platform by the Duke and Duchess of York on behalf of Queen Victoria.

The station at Ballater was closed in 1966 and now houses the Ballater Tourist Information Centre. Restoration has taken place and visitors can now see an exhibition of royal train journeys from Windsor to Ballater. Windsor station itself was opened in 1849 for the convenience of Queen Victoria on her journeys to London and elsewhere. Platforms were decommissioned between 1968–9 and a large part of the old station is now the Windsor Royal Shopping centre.

Although Marlborough House was Albert Edward, Prince of Wales's official residence in London, Queen Victoria and Prince Albert decided that their errant son should have a residence well away from the temptations of louche London society, ostensibly to enjoy 'the country air and way of life'. So many properties were inspected until it was found that The Hon. Charles Spencer Cowper had decided to sell his house and estate at Sandringham, Norfolk. Visiting the late eighteenth-century house in 1862, the Prince of Wales declared it suitable and Queen Victoria agreed to its purchase. Once the house was habitable the Prince of Wales visited the Continent and set in motion his marriage to Princess Alexandra of Denmark. This took place on 10 March 1863 and at the end of the month the prince brought his new bride to Sandringham by rail. The present mansion dates from 1870, with only the conservatory remaining of the old house.

This brought into the public eye a railway station that would earn the title of 'most royal'. In 1862 Wolferton railway station was opened some 2 miles from Sandringham House. Operated by the Great Eastern Railway Co. during 1861–1910, this line was Edward's main means of transport from London as Prince of Wales and king. In time a set of elegant reception rooms were laid out which saw a regular convoy of Edward's guests from prime ministers to fellow royalty, and from mistresses to shady cronies. In 1898 the station was rebuilt in Tudor style. The station closed in 1966 and the whole line was discontinued from 3 May 1969. Subsequently, the buildings have been a museum and private residence.

Over the years the station has been in the news as the starting point for state funerals. Queen Alexandra died on 20 November 1925 and her body was conveyed to London from Wolferton. Again in January 1936 George V's body was processed to Wolferton where it had been lying-in-state at St Mary Magdalene Church, Sandringham. The last monarch's funeral to pass through Wolferton from Sandringham was that of George VI, who died on 6 February 1952.

♦ Where is Scotland's 'forgotten' palace?

Wes nevir in Scotland hand nor sene [fuss nor display]
Sic [such] dansing nor deray [mirth],
Nouthir at Falkland on the green
Nor Pebillis [Peebles] at the Play.

King James I/VI, 'Christis Kirk on the Green'.

During a reception at the Palace of Holyrood, Edinburgh, in June 1923, King George V and Queen Mary met the Provost (the Scottish equivalent of the English mayor) of Auchtermuchty, Fife. Queen Mary asked the dignitary where his town was situated to hear the reply: 'Why Ma'am, only three miles from His Majesty's own Palace of Falkland.' George and Mary were somewhat nonplussed. They were familiar with Holyrood and the historical associations of ruined Linlithgow and Dunfermline palaces where Mary, Queen of Scots and Charles I, respectively, had been born, but Falkland was something of a mystery. Queen Mary decided to pay it a visit during the royal progress into Fife in July/August 1923.

In the reign of Alexander I, King of Scots (r. 1107–24), a castle was constructed to the north of the present site of Falkland Palace, at the foot of the Lomond Hills, Fife. By the fourteenth century it was the residence of the Earls of Fife. The last of the line was Isabel, Countess of Fife, who as her second husband took Walter Stewart, second son of King Robert II; Walter became the first in a long line of Stewarts to inhabit Falkland. The Stewarts were not a happy band with many dying violent deaths. One such was Prince David Stewart, Duke of Rothesay, heir to the throne of Scotland, who was imprisoned at Falkland by his uncle Robert, Duke of Albany. Some say David was poisoned; others that he was starved to death. James I, (r. 1406–37) who was the first Stewart monarch to live at Falkland, was known as 'James of the Fiery Face' because of a large red birthmark, and he started to build a hunting palace on the site as a more comfortable royal residence abutting the fauna-rich Forest of Falkland. Thereafter, a succession of Scottish kings came to Falkland to hunt stags, fly falcons, play tennis and hone up archery skills, or relax in the new gardens where cranes and peacocks strutted. In the evening banquets were held, and cards and chess were played to a background of flute and lute music.

A large part of the palace as seen today was built by James IV (r. 1488–1513) to be beautified by James V (r. 1513–42), who built the real tennis court and chapel royal. Here James died at midnight on 24 December 1542, a few days after the birth of his daughter Mary, Queen of Scots. His widow, Marie de Guise-Lorraine, spent a great deal of her time at Falkland, where her daughter was a regular visitor. On her return from France, Mary, Queen of Scots endeavoured to recreate the atmosphere of the French Court at Falkland, carrying on her father's love of hunting and hawking, a pastime too indulged in by her son James VI. On his marriage to Anne of Denmark in 1589, James conferred the Palace of Falkland on her as part of her dowry. Still today the visitor can see the bullet marks on the gatehouse which was struck in 1593 when the Earl of Bothwell tried an unsuccessful kidnap attempt on James.

After James VI of Scots became James I of England on the death of Queen Elizabeth I, there were only two brief royal visits to Falkland. Charles I stayed there after his Scottish coronation in 1633 and Charles II arrived at the time of his crowning at Scone in 1651. In 1653 the east range of the palace was accidentally burned when the town and palace were occupied by Cromwellian troops. In 1715 the palace appears briefly in history when Jacobite supporters of James Francis Edward Stuart, the 'Old Pretender', rebelled against the Hanoverian George I, and the palace was occupied by Rob Roy MacGregor and his Highlanders; the rising failed and the palace sank into neglect and disrepair.

Over the centuries each of Scotland's royal castles and palaces had their hereditary keepers, once important court prerogatives. In James VI's time the keeper of Falkland was David Murray, Viscount Stormont; in 1787 the keepership was acquired by the Skenes of Pitlour, thence to the Moncrieffes of Myres and subsequently to one Onesiphorous Tyndall Bruce who was advised by Sir Walter Scott to restore it as a 'romantic ruin'. Bruce died in 1855 but, in 1887, John Crichton Stuart, 3rd Marquess of Bute acquired the keepership from the Tyndall Bruce family, and he set about 'a massive and scholarly programme of restoration'. This work was continued by his son Lord Ninian Crichton Stuart and by his grandson Major Michael Crichton Stuart, who in 1952 gave the palace and a deputy keepership to the National Trust of Scotland. 'Details of the arrangements,' records show, 'were communicated to the Queen, for the Palace remains, as it has been for centuries, a Royal property; her Majesty "took note".'

◆ Which Welsh castle has a special royal tradition?

> On 24 April [1284], at Caernarvon, Queen Eleanor of Castile gave birth to a [second] son who was named Edward after his father.
> *The Worcester Annalist,* Chronicles of the Age of Chivalry.

Caernarvon Castle, Gwynedd, remains the largest of Edward I's castles in North Wales. Edward meant it to be a palace as well as a fortress and its building began in 1283. In 1294 the Welsh, under Prince Madog, successfully overran Caernarvon and the damage done meant that a second building phase had to be undertaken; this lasted from 1296–1301.

Tradition has it that Edward I created his second son, the future Edward II, Prince of Wales, at Caernarvon in 1301 when he was 16, and then came to the castle to receive homage. The legend that Edward was created Prince of Wales at his birth in 1284 has long been discredited. Although subsequently the eldest son of every monarch has been given the title of Prince of Wales no investiture took place at Caernarvon for almost 600 years.

On his 16th birthday in 1910 Prince Edward, eldest son of King George V and Queen Mary, had been given the title of Prince of Wales following his father's accession to the throne. In 1911 the king stated that he intended to visit Wales and Lloyd George, Chancellor of the Exchequer and Constable of Caernarvon Castle, considered that the occasion should be made special by the Prince of Wales being formally invested in his title at Caernarvon castle 'in the presence of 10,000 Welsh'. Cynically, some said that 'time-honoured traditions' were 'hurriedly invented'. Caernarvon castle was refurbished and gold quarried from the Merionethshire hills was fashioned into the prince's regalia. A rather pantomime costume 'of white satin breeches and purple velvet surcoat' was tailored for the occasion. Prince Edward was appalled at what he was expected to wear and balked at the idea; he complained, 'what would my Navy friends say if they saw me in this preposterous rig?' Queen Mary persuaded him to wear the outfit and for the occasion Lloyd George taught him some phrases in Welsh to use. To the flowers in Frogmore gardens Edward practised such words as *Mor o gan yw Cymru i gyd* (All Wales is a sea of song). The investiture took place on 1 July and King George wrote in his diary: 'The dear boy did it all remarkably well and looked so nice.'

Some fifty-eight years later, Queen Elizabeth II invested Prince Charles with the insignia of the Prince of Wales, and this time the Constable of the Castle was Lord Snowdon. On this occasion the rig was not considered as 'preposterous' as his great-uncle's and after Charles had paid homage to his mother, he read his address to the people of Wales in Welsh.

♦ Which royal built the most bizarre residence?

...A China view,
Where neither genius, taste, nor fancy dwells:
Monkeys, mandarins, a motley crew,
Bridges, pagodas, swings, and tinking bells.

'Peter Pindar' (John Wolcot, 1738–1819).

Set fire to the Chinese stables, and if it embrace the whole of the
Pavilion, it will rid me of an eyesore.

Sir Walter Scott (1771–1832).

The Pavilion at Brighton is like a collection of stone pumpkins and
pepper-boxes. It seems as if the genius of architecture had the dropsy
and the megrims. Anything more fantastical, with a greater dearth of
invention, was never seen.

William Hazlitt (1778–1830), Travel Notes.

Prince George Augustus Frederick, Prince of Wales, eldest son
of George III and Prince Regent since his father descended into
madness, was self-indulgent, irritatingly thoughtless, inconsistent and
absurdly extravagant. A fine testament to the latter weakness is that
great royal white elephant, partly responsible for the Prince Regent's
huge debts, the Royal Pavilion at Brighton, East Sussex.

George's enthusiasm for Brighton dated back to 1783, the year of
his 21st birthday. At the time he was suffering from glandular fever
and was advised to try sea-bathing for relief. Once the air had filled
his lungs George decided that he must have a house at Brighton.
To this end he took up residence at Grove House on the Steine,
but something would have to be more grand, so George employed
architects, decorators and furnishers to assist his plans. As he had been
prevented from serving in the army alongside his brothers, George
developed his 'aesthetic flair' and 'eclectic connoisseurship' for the
visual arts which were now focused in Brighton.

By 1787 the designs of architect Henry Holland had been
completed to produce 'the conventional Palladian plan of a
central rotunda with flanking wings' that was the Graeco-Roman
Marine Pavilion, with additions in 1801–3 by Holland's pupil
P.G. Robinson. A gift of some Chinese wallpaper gave George a
taste for chinoiserie, so the Marine Pavilion now sported Chinese
designs throughout. By 1808 the cupolad royal stables and the
riding house were added where forty horses were housed and
displayed in buildings which were feats of engineering for their
time. In 1815 the architect John Nash was on site to transform the
appearance of the Pavilion into an Indian style as it appears today.
New 'technologically advanced' kitchens appeared with imposing
state apartments in rapid succession. A dedicated gourmet and

gastronome, George was a regular visitor to the kitchens and employed the finest chefs. The great French chef Antoin Carême worked there and on one occasion, on 15 January 1817, produced a menu of 36 entrées. A special set of three 'confectionary' rooms catered for George's sweet tooth and delighted his guests at dessert. When in residence George gave dinner parties twice a week for some twenty guests, to be entertained afterwards by such as The Regent's Flute Band. George never invited members of the government to the Pavilion, or troublesome relatives like his brother Prince Ernest Augustus, Duke of Cumberland. After the triumph of Waterloo in 1815, George liked to show off to such foreign dignitaries as the Grand Duke Nicholas (heir to the Russian throne) at the Pavilion. After George had pushed his mistress/'wife' Maria Fitzherbert out of the frame, Isabella Marchioness of Hertford often acted as his hostess.

George's mother, Queen Charlotte, was so impressed by what she saw during one visit that she granted her son a payment of £50,000 from her private purse to fund the projects which had been criticised for their extravagance by prominent politicians like Prime Minister, Lord Liverpool and Nicholas Vansittart, the Chancellor of the Exchequer. The country was going through a period of slump following Waterloo and George's extravagance did not go down well in the country. For a while George slowed down the work at Brighton. Over seven years, between 1814–21, the Royal Archives records that £155,000 (in excess of £77.5 million today) was spent on the Pavilion.

One last main touch to the Pavilion in 1822 was the construction of an underground passage from the residence to the stables. Not for secret meetings, but to keep his guests dry as they went to admire his equine exhibits. Even though he was now extremely fat, George had not given up riding and was seen by guests and the public to trot around the Pavilion lawns or in the riding house. George on horseback was an entertainment in itself. As a correspondent of *The Times* noted, guests could marvel as George was hoisted onto his horse by a mechanical contraption:

> An inclined plane was constructed, rising about the height of two feet and a half, at the upper end of which was a platform. His Royal Highness was placed in a chair on rollers, and so moved up the ascent,

and placed on the platform, which was then raised by screws, high enough to pass the horse under; and finally, His Royal Highness was let gently down into the saddle.

George's visits to his bizarre fantasy palace of Brighton Pavilion were a gift to caricaturists; George generally ignored such squibs and cartoons but desisted in using his mounting mechanism when publicly ridiculed.

Although George loved his Pavilion, when he became king in 1820 his visits became less frequent and he last visited it in 1827. His brother William IV did not care for the Pavilion and his niece Queen Victoria was bent on having it demolished. However, it was bought by the municipality of Brighton in 1850 to be developed as a Regency museum. It was later restored through the help of Queen Mary and Queen Elizabeth II and is now a prominent visitor attraction.

♦ Which miser left a queen a fortune from which she built a castle?

...in 1852 she had personally come into a pleasant little fortune.
E.F. Benson (1867–1940), Queen Victoria.

John Camden Neild (*c.*1790–1852) was nominally a barrister but is better known as an 'eccentric old miser' who lived at 5 Cheyne Walk, Chelsea, London. His father James Neild, a prominent philanthropist, had been silversmith to the Prince Regent, and when John Neild died on 30 August 1852 he left his residue fortune of £500,000 to Queen Victoria in his will. At first the queen dismissed the surprise bequest as a joke. Enquiries on the queen's behalf verified the bequest and further examination revealed that Neild had no living relatives, or at least none came forward. So she agreed to accept the bequest personally rather than let it be 'swept into the coffers of the State'. She wrote of her good fortune to her uncle Leopold, King of the Belgians; he sent her this reply from Laeken on 10 September 1852:

...That Mr Neild should have left that great fortune to you delighted me; it gives the possibility of forming a private fortune for the Royal

Family, the necessity of which nobody can deny. Such things only still happen in England, where there exists loyalty and strong affection for Royalty, a feeling unfortunately much diminished on the Continent of Europe, though it did exist there also . . .

After due consideration, reported Sir Sydney Lee, editor of the *Dictionary of National Biography*, 'She increased Neild's bequests to the three executors from £100 to £1,000, provided for her benefactor's servants, [and] gave an annuity of £100 to a woman who had once frustrated his attempt at suicide . . .'

Queen Victoria also arranged, in 1855, for the chancel of North Marston Church, Buckinghamshire, to be rebuilt with a new reredos; this was the neighbourhood in which Neild had held property. She also had a new stained glass window placed in the church in Neild's memory and to express her gratitude to Neild for his largesse 'in the eighteenth year of her reign'.

For some time, since their first visit to Scotland in September 1842, Queen Victoria and Prince Albert were seriously considering establishing a 'Scottish home'. Why did they choose Balmoral? Royal doctor Sir James Clark had leased Balmoral house where his son could convalesce after a long illness. Sir James considered that the area would be a good retreat for the queen to bring relief from her twinges of rheumatism. Prince Albert commissioned a report on the Deeside climate and a series of sketches of the area from Aberdeen artist James Giles. The report and Sir James's comments brought them back to Scotland to see for themselves. On 8 December 1847 the lessee from Lord Aberdeen of Balmoral, Sir Robert Gordon, died, and the royal couple decided to see the area for themselves. So in September 1848 they arrived at Balmoral. Queen Victoria wrote of the visit:

We arrived at Balmoral at a quarter to three. It is a pretty little castle in the old Scottish style. There is a picturesque tower and a garden in front, with a high wooded hill; at the back there is wood down to the Dee; and the hills rise all around.

The royals reviewed the house's history, its estate existing in records from the fifteenth century. The old house had been much improved by Sir Robert Gordon between 1834–9, adding a new deer park.

On 20 May 1848 the trustees assigned the lease of Balmoral to Prince Albert, who began a series of acquisitions in the area. Birkhill was purchased on behalf of the 8-year-old Prince of Wales, and Abergeldie was leased for Queen Victoria's mother, the Duchess of Kent. At first on lease it was not until 22 June 1855 that the Royal Family finally acquired full possession of Balmoral with an outright payment of £31,500. Prince Albert now set about the rebuilding of it and the foundation of a new castle was laid on 28 September 1853 and the Royal Family took possession of the castle on 7 September 1855. Thereafter Balmoral, thanks to the old miser's legacy, became an important part of royal history. Today the estate of Balmoral runs to some 50,000 acres in total, plus 7,000 acres of grouse moor; there are a further 10,000 acres rented from a neighbour, with 190 acres farmed and 272 acres let. The castle itself sleeps in excess of 100 people, attended by fifty-six full-time staff. A further 100 or so work part-time during the visitor season, when some 80,000 people view the castle and its policies.

♦ How many prisons held Mary, Queen of Scots?

But I, the Queen of a' [all] Scotland
Maun [must] lie in prison strang [strong] . . .
And I'm the sovereign of Scotland
And mony [many] a traitor there
Yet here I lay in foreign bands
And never-ending care.

Robert Burns (1759–96), 'Queen Mary's Lament' (1790).

On 24 July 1567, Mary, Queen of Scots, was forced by the confederate lords to abdicate from the Scottish throne in favour of her infant son James, who became James VI. The abdication took place at the first of Mary's prisons, Lochleven Castle on its eponymous loch in Kinross-shire, home of Sir William Douglas. There she miscarried twins by her third husband James Hepburn, Earl of Bothwell, long associated with the murder of her second husband Henry Stewart, Lord Darnley. Mary was desperately ill after the miscarriage, but she regularly received boxes of clothes, sweetmeats and other items to help make her captivity bearable. As her strength grew she walked in the gardens, danced, embroidered and played cards. Much worse was to come.

Mary's chief jailor was Margaret Erskine, who was the mother of Mary's half-brother James Stewart, Earl of Moray, the bastard son of James V, now Regent of Scotland. As Mary had abdicated there had to be a serious reason why she was to be kept a prisoner. So the confederate lords emphasised that Mary was 'privy, art and part of the actual devise and deed of the forenamed murder of the King her lawful [second] husband'. Thus her chances of release were pretty slim.

As time passed Mary was able to smuggle letters out of the castle to France appealing for aid to escape. She also wrote to Queen Elizabeth I of England for help to end *la langueur du temps de mon ennuieuse prison*. Yet within hours of sending the appeal Mary was able to escape from Lochleven with the help of George Douglas who had quarrelled with his brother Sir William, and an orphaned cousin Willie Douglas. Dressed as a countrywoman Mary was spirited out of the castle to a boat secured by Willie Douglas. Once on the mainland they made for the castle of Niddry, the home of loyal Lord Seton of Riccarton at Winchburgh. It was 2 May 1568 and Mary had been a prisoner for ten and a half months on the tiny island.

Mary was now joined by some 6,000 Roman Catholic supporters who on 13 May met the lesser forces of the Regent Moray at Langside, near Glasgow. Mary's supporters were routed and she fled first to Dumfries, and at Lord Maxwell's castle of Terregles she decided to throw herself on the mercy of Elizabeth I whose 'siren song of friendship' now greatly appealed. The flight has become woven into the history of courage and romance, but the decision was unwise in the extreme.

In borrowed clothes Mary and her party made for the twelfth-century Cistercian Abbey of Dundrennan and on the afternoon of Sunday 16 May 1568 she sailed from the Abbey Burn across the Solway Firth to England, never to return to the land of her birth.

Via Workington Hall and Cockermouth, Mary was now joined by Richard Lowther, deputy governor of Carlisle. By 18 May Lowther installed her at Carlisle Castle in semi-captivity. Queen Mary's Tower at the castle is still pointed out to visitors. In London there was consternation on the appearance of Mary in England. The abdicated Scottish queen was a dangerous nuisance: Had she not repeatedly said she was the rightful Queen of England? Certainly Elizabeth I could not send an army to impose a Roman Catholic queen on a Protestant Scotland. The answer was to dissemble until such time as Mary's possible involvement in her second husband's death was cleared up. To Carlisle Elizabeth sent Sir Francis Knollys, vice-chamberlain, a Puritan gentleman of undisputed loyalty to the Crown, and Lord Scrope as emissaries to exchange civilities. In the meantime Mary would be closely watched, suitably clothed and given as much comfort as possible. She would be allowed out of Carlisle Castle to ride for exercise but she would be accompanied by 100 horsemen. Elizabeth's chief minister William Cecil emphasised that Carlisle Castle was very near to the Scottish border so it was decided to move Mary further into England. Bolton Castle in the North Riding of Yorkshire was chosen. Mary would be here from July 1568 to January 1569. The castle belonged to the Scropes of Wensleydale, but was scant of comfort for Mary's incarceration. Tapestries were sent by Sir George Bowes and the Earl of Northumberland sent venison, while clothes reached Mary from Scotland. (Bolton Castle is now a ruin.)

Conferences held at York – wherein the evidence of the Casket Letters was produced – and at Westminster and Hampton Court were all unable to prove the case of murderess against Mary. But it was decided to move Mary to the more secure prison of the already part-ruined Tutbury Castle, Staffordshire, under the care of Sir Francis Knollys. Mary would be here at various times during 1569 and 1585. Of it she wrote: 'I am in a walled enclosure, on top of a hill, exposed to all the winds and inclemencies of heaven.' Until Mary's imprisonment the castle had been the headquarters of the administration of the Duchy of Lancaster and was in a cold and dilapidated condition. The tower where Mary spent most of her time is also still pointed out. Her chief jailor was Sir Ralph Sadler, then replaced by George Talbot, Earl of Shrewsbury for some fifteen years, along with his wife Bess of Hardwick. During the period April 1569 to 1584 Mary would be imprisoned in various places: South Wingfield Manor, owned by the Earl of Shrewsbury. Now ruined, the house was the gateway to the Peak District and Sir Anthony Babington planned Mary's escape from here. At Buxton Baths Mary was allowed to bathe for the sake of her health. Prisons came and went: 'Queen Mary's Bower' at Chatsworth; long vanished Sheffield

Castle and Tixall Manor Park, Northamptonshire were all in the frame as was the now ruined Sir Walter Aston's Chartley Manor, Staffordshire. Mary was here from December 1585 to September 1586. Here letters were intercepted which implicated Mary in the Babington Plot.

Mary was eventually back at Tutbury Castle, her most hated prison under the jailorship of Sir Amyas Paulet. As Roman Catholic intrigues to release Mary, murder Elizabeth I and put Mary on the throne continued, Mary was put under even stricter confinement. Ill and dispirited, on 25 September 1586 Mary made her final move to Fotheringay Castle, some 20 miles south-west of Peterborough, Northamptonshire. Pressure built on Queen Elizabeth to make a decisive choice on what to do with Mary. She dared not let her go to France for fear of stimulating a French invasion. And restoring her to the Scottish throne still remained unthinkable. The plan adopted was to keep Mary in England. In the event this made Mary the focal point of continuing Roman Catholic plots. Thus Mary continued as a source of danger to Elizabeth. By the ideas of the time Elizabeth was justified in authorising the execution of Mary. However heinous the execution of a anointed sovereign might be, Elizabeth had to protect the integrity of her realm and people. Vacillation and guilt undermined Elizabeth's actions. Elizabeth signed the death warrant, the Council sent it and delivery was as necessary as a signature. The responsibility was thus shared between Elizabeth and the Council; she showed great cowardice though in endeavouring to avoid all responsibility and in punishing her faithful servants, William Cecil and William Davison, for carrying out her orders.

Mary was executed on 8 February 1587 in the Great Hall of her tenth prison of Fotheringay. James I/VI had his mother's final prison demolished after he had acceded to the throne of the united kingdoms in 1603.

♦ Which homes and locations in Britain were sanctuaries for exiled royalty?

O palais, sois béni! soyez bénie, ô ruine!
Qu'une auguste auréole à jamais t'illumine!
Devant tes noirs créneaux, pieux, nous nous courbons,
Car le vieux roi de France a trouvé ton ombre
Cette hospitalité mélancolique et sombre
Qu'on reçoit et qu'on rend de Stuarts à Bourbons!
Victor Marie Hugo (1802–25), 'Les Rayons et Les Ombres' (1839), remembering a visit to Charles X, 7 August 1829.

On the outbreak of the French Revolution, with the taking of the Bastille in Paris in 1789, King Louis XVI of France was required to 'assent to the exile' of those at his court who the revolutionaries thought were 'evil counsellors'. The chief of those singled out was his younger brother Charles Philippe, Comte d'Artois (1757–1836), known in court circles as 'Monsieur'. At first Charles fled to Switzerland and Italy. On the execution of his brother Louis XVI at Paris on 21 January 1793 he went to Russia to plead the royalist cause with Empress Catherine II. By 1795 Queen Marie Antoinette, her son the Dauphin (proclaimed Louis XVII by royalists) and her sister-in-law Elizabeth, were all dead and Charles now decided to seek exile in Britain. In due course Charles, heir presumptive to the French throne, was offered, through the Duc d'Harcourt, refuge at the palace of Holyrood House, Edinburgh, by George III.

At the time the palace was in bad repair, damp and rat-infested, and was already inhabited by several aristocrats like the Duke of Hamilton, Hereditary Keeper of the Abbey and Palace of Holyrood. Charles and his suite arrived at Leith aboard the *Jason* on 6 January 1796 to be met on behalf of George III (who never visited his northern realm) by Lord Adam Gordon. Welcomed with due ceremonial, Charles held a levée at the palace the next day to greet Scotland's nobility. He was to stay four years. Thus began the story of the exiled Bourbons in Scotland, and of exiled royalty in Great Britain.

A prominent reason why Charles had sought exile in Britain was to escape his creditors. Thus the Comte could not leave the palace and park during weekdays, only on Sundays, '*dies non* on which no arrests for debt could legally be made'. On Sundays Charles went out to hear Mass at the Roman Catholic Chapel of St Andrew, Blackfriars Wynd. In time he established a chapel at Holyrood, where Mass was celebrated for the first time since the days of Mary, Queen of Scots. Even though the British government allowed Charles £6,000 a year, all went on the expenses of himself, his suite of hangers-on and the political schemes of his brother, now dubbed Louis XVIII, himself exiled in Brunswick. On 21 January 1796 Charles was joined by his son Louis, Duc d'Angoulême (1775–1844). Unencumbered by his father's debts, Louis was free to cut a dash any time in Edinburgh society.

Soon other emigrés joined Charles and Louis to inhabit the environs of Holyrood and eventually the royal princes were joined by Charles's other son Charles, Duc de Berri (1778–1820). Until his restoration to the French throne in 1814–15, Louis XVIII declined exile at Holyrood and preferred to take up his abode at Hartwell House, Aylesbury, Buckinghamshire in 1807.

In time Charles Philippe became King of France with the title of Charles X. Three other members of the French Royal Family took up residence with him once more at Holyrood in 1831 after the revolution of 1830 deposed him and replaced him with Louis-Philippe. They were Caroline of the two Sicilies, Duchess de Berri (1798–1870), Henry, titular Henry V of France, Charles Philippe's grandson, Duc de Bordeaux, Comte de Chambord (1820–83), and granddaughter Louise (1819–64), dubbed 'Mademoiselle' who married the Duke of Parma. At first the Duc and Duchess d'Angoulême lodged at Regent Terrace and then moved to Holyrood.

Charles Philippe, free to travel in Scotland where he would, indulged with his son their passion for hunting and shooting. They became popular names on the guest lists of Scotland's gentry and were guests at such places as Fordel Castle, Fife, and Gosford House, the seat of Lord Wemyss. Another favourite shooting site was Hunter's Bog. As his carriage swept out of the gates of Holyrood on such an expedition, the Canongate urchins chanted: 'Frenchy. Frenchy, dinna shoot the speugs [sparrows].' The French Royal Family still worshipped regularly at St Mary's, where a royal pew had been filled up for them. Charles Philippe also gave generously to the poor folk of Edinburgh, with a daily dole to debtors and free medical treatment from his own physician Dr Burgon.

The Duc and Duchesse d'Angoulême were well known faces in Edinburgh strolling the streets in their shabby clothes. They also made incognito trips in the Highlands as the 'Comte and Comtesse Marness'.

Although he was deposed Charles Philippe still thought of himself as King of France, but Bourbon supporters considered his grandson Henry to be King Henry V. Both of course were not monarchs and Charles Philippe said that he would like to spend the rest of his life at Holyrood. This was not to be.

The Duchesse de Berri hated Edinburgh and wanted to return to France and have her son Henry restored as king. She began to stir up trouble in France to this end and eventually the French government complained of her machinations to the British government. Charles Philippe and his entourage's presence in Scotland began to be a political embarrassment. So on 20 September he and the French Royal Family left Leith aboard the steamship *United Kingdom* for Hamburg. Four more years of exile followed until news came to the British Court that Charles Philippe had died of cholera on 6 November 1836.

Purists could argue that another royal exile to reside at Holyrood should be mentioned. This was Prince Charles Edward Stuart during his fateful attempt in 1745 to wrest the throne of Great Britain from the Hanoverians in favour of the Stuarts and restore his father as James III/VIII. On 16 September Charles and his Jacobite army entered Edinburgh and he took up residence at Holyrood. There he proclaimed his father king and launched a successful attack on the Hanoverian army at nearby Prestonpans. Charles stayed at Holyrood from 22 September to 31 October gathering supporters around him and delighting the populace. Here is a contemporary description of the scene:

> The Prince lived in Edinburgh with Great Splendour and Magnificence, had every morning a numerous Court of his officers. After he had held a Council, he dined with his principal officers in public, where there was always a crowd of all sorts of people to see him dine. After dinner he rode out attended by his Life Guards and reviewed his army, where there was always a great number of spectators in coaches and on horseback. After the review, he came to [Holyrood] Abbey, where he received the ladies of fashion that came to his drawing-room. Then he sup'd in public and generally there was music at supper, and a Ball afterwards.

The fateful decision was made to leave Edinburgh, march into England and seize the throne. It did not work out that way as his army eventually retreated to Culloden where it was slaughtered by his cousin the Duke of Cumberland on 16 April 1746. From here Charles fled into exile once more.

It is interesting to note that Charles Edward Stuart made a secret visit to London in 1750 to see how the land lay should George II die. He met a group of Jacobites at a house in the city's Pall Mall and informed them that he could, with foreign help, seize the throne of Great Britain with an army of only 4,000. The possibilities of such a coup were discussed, but the prince soon realised that there was no political will for him to be successful and he returned to the Continent six days after his arrival at Dover.

Louis-Philippe, King of France 1830–48, abdicated the throne during the February Revolution. He escaped as 'Mr Smith' and was smuggled across the Channel by the British Consul at Le Havre. Lord Palmerston advised Queen Victoria 'she must be careful about harbouring ejected Royalties or the country would not like it'. Nevertheless, he arranged a grant of £1,000 for Louis-Philippe 'from secret service funds'. Louis-Philippe died at Claremont House, Surrey, in 1850 after a two-year exile.

Charles Louis Napoleon Bonaparte (b.1808), was nephew of Napoleon I. As Napoleon III he became emperor of the Second Empire in 1852. In 1870 France was involved in the disastrous Franco-Prussian War; after leading his troops into the fatal Battle of Sedan, he surrendered to be deposed as emperor. He and his empress Eugenia del Montijo (Eugénie to the French), a former Spanish countess, fled to England with their son 'Napoleon Eugène', the Prince Imperial.

They took up residence in 1871, with Queen Victoria's blessing, at the twenty-roomed Camden Place, Chislehurst, Kent, with a suite of thirty-two ladies and gentlemen and twenty-three servants. Both Queen Victoria and the Prince of Wales visited the French Royal Family early on and all the French royals entered London society with enthusiasm, paying visits to Scotland and English locations. Napoleon III's health deteriorated and on 2 January 1873 he was operated on by Sir Henry Thompson for kidney stones; in total, four operations were carried out; he died at 10.45 a.m. on 9 January 1873. On 15 January he was buried at St Mary's Roman Catholic Church, Chislehurst.

During the British government's expedition in 1879 'to conquer the troublesome African tribes in Zululand', the Prince Imperial, who was there as a 'distinguished visitor attached to the General Staff', was killed by Zulu assagais. His grieving mother lived on until 11 July 1920, dying at Madrid aged about 94. In 1879 Eugénie had bought Farnborough Hill, Farnborough, Hampshire, and she was buried in the crypt of Farnborough Abbey; her tomb is adjacent to those of Napoleon III and the Prince Imperial whose coffins had been moved there in 1888.

Following the murders of Tsar Nicholas II, his Tsarina Alexandra Feodorovna, and their five children at Ekaterinburg on 16 July 1918, the roster of members of the Russian imperial family in exile was headed by the Tsar's mother. She was the former Princess Dagmar (b. 1847), second daughter of Christian IX, King of Denmark, and sister of Queen Alexandra, wife of Edward VII. Dagmar, baptised into the Russian Orthodox faith as Marie Feodorovna, was married at St Petersburg to Tsarevich Alexander in 1866. On the death of his father Alexander II in 1881, the Tsarevich became emperor Alexander III; he died at Livadia on 20 October 1894 and his widow became the Dowager Empress Marie.

In 1919, as the Bolshevik army approached the Crimea, the 72-year-old Dowager Empress left for exile aboard the battleship HMS *Marlborough* at the insistence of Queen Alexandra and her son George V. She arrived at Portsmouth via Malta and was taken to Marlborough House. Resentful of her loss of power, the British Royal Family's 'Aunt Minny' was further annoyed by their indifference to Russian aristocratic refugees, lapses of protocol and a myriad of other niggles; she then left for Denmark. She died at Copenhagen in October 1928. In 2006 her body was re-interred at the royal crypt of St Petersburg's Peter and Paul Fortress. Her daughter Grand Duchess Xenia had also left Russia aboard the British warship. For twenty-five years she lived in a grace-and-favour mansion called Wilderness House, Hampton Court provided by George V, who also loaned her the use of Frogmore Cottage and settled a pension on her of £2,400. Sister of Tsar Nicholas II, Xenia married her cousin Alexander; her grandson Prince Rostislav Romanov III (b. 1936), thus the great-nephew of the murdered Nicholas II, became a London banker. He died in 1999.

Assorted Romanovs came and went through the capitals of Europe. Another who was exiled in Britain was Prince Vsevolode, who worked for United Lubricants at Notting Hill Gate, London, as 'Mr Romanov'. He was born in 1914, a grandson of Grand Duke Constantine, brother of Alexander II. He was smuggled out of Russia with his sister by his English governess Miss Irwin of Cheltenham. He was educated at Eton and Oxford to later reside in Kensington.

King Ferdinand of Romania succeeded his father to the throne of the kingdom which had been so declared in 1881. His queen was a granddaughter of Queen Victoria, the daughter of her second son Alfred, Duke of Edinburgh. In 1927 Ferdinand was succeeded by his grandson Michael, then 6 years old. Michael was deposed in 1930 by his father, Carol II, who had been removed from the succession by Ferdinand because of his scandalous private life. Carol II abdicated in 1940 in favour of Michael, who abdicated on 30 December 1947, when the Romanian government did not approve of his marriage in 1948 to Princess Anne of Bourbon-Parma. Living peripatetically in Florence and Copenhagen, Michael, with his wife and five daughters rented a house in Ayot St Lawrence and Michael ran a market garden. Holidays were spent from time to time at Balmoral. Michael then moved his family to Switzerland to work as a test pilot, but regular visits were made to his Windsor cousins.

The Greek Royal Family have always been prominent royal exiles in Britain, since the flight from Greece by King Constantine II following the coup of 1967. Princess Alice, daughter of Queen Victoria's younger daughter Princess Beatrice and Prince Louis of Battenburg, was born at Windsor Castle in 1885. She married Prince Andrew of Greece in 1903 and gave birth to Prince Philip, Duke of Edinburgh as her fifth child in 1921. Her life was overshadowed by wars, revolutions and enforced exile and time spent in sanatoriums. In later life she took to wearing the habit of a nun. Following the flight of Constantine II, Princess Alice took up permanent residence at Buckingham Palace. She died on 5 December 1969.

♦ Which royal foundation commemorates a significant battle victory?

As the Duke left his vessel to set foot on land
He stumbled and fell with his hands on the sand.
All those who stood near him upraised a great cry,

Struck with fear at so evil an Augury.
But the Duke he exclaimed
'By the spleandour of God
I thus with both hands lay my grasp on this Sod
Prise without challenging – no man can make
So thus of all around us due seizin' I take.
We shall see who are brave.'

Canon Robert Wace, 'Roman de Rou et des Duc de Normandie'.

The year 1066 marked the last true invasion of England. On Saturday 14 October, Harold II, King of the English, encountered William the Bastard, Duke of Normandy, on Senlac Hill, near Hastings, Sussex. The two armies fought for some ten hours in what is one of the longest battles in early medieval history. The victory by William's Normans is a well-known defining moment of English history, and to mark it William sought to express his gratitude to a helpful deity in stone.

William had two main secular motives in building the Abbey of St Martin de Bello (soon known as Battle Abbey) in 1067. One was to hallow the site of the battle and the other to provide prayers for the fallen. It was colonised by Benedictine monks from Marmoutier in Touraine. Tradition has it that William ordered the high altar to be sited on the exact spot where King Harold fell. As the original high altar stood on the highest elevation of the site (a likely spot for Harold to have his battle stance), the tradition was backed up by archaeological excavation in 1929.

Today the church and chapter house survive as a low wall, with the greater part remaining buried. The east and west cloister ranges remain, with the west range, now a private school, made up of the Abbot's House. To the south is the basement of the monastic guest house, and the site is partially enclosed by a well-preserved wall incorporating a twelfth- to fourteenth-century gatehouse. For the whole of his life William was a *confratre*, that is honorary chapter member of Battle Abbey.

The abbey was suppressed at the Dissolution of the Monasteries in May 1538. Abbot Hammond, the last superior, was pensioned off and the abbey was given to the court favourite Sir Anthony Browne, 1st Viscount Montague. Browne dismantled the abbey and built a mansion on the site. After a series of private ownerships the mansion became the core of a private school in 1922.

RUMOUR AND SCANDAL

♦ Which monarch topped the list for siring royal
bastards?

> [The Duke of Clarence had] spread the falsest and most unnatural
> coloured pretence that man might imagine, that the King our most
> sovereign lord was a bastard, and not begotten to reign upon us.
> *Indictment against George, Duke of Clarence for slandering his brother King*
> *Edward IV (1478).*

Royal illegitimacy has been the stuff of 'skeletons in the royal
cupboard' for generations, with people popping up all over the
place to be 'royal bastards'. In 1981 the *Miami Herald* noted the
death of Irene Victoria Alexandra Louise Isabel Bush. Her claim
to royal ancestry was her assertion that she had been born in
Ireland at Carton, County Kildare on 28 February 1899, as Lady
Irene Fitzgerald Coburg, the daughter of one Mabel Fitzgerald
and HRH Prince Alfred of Edinburgh and Saxe-Coburg
(1874–99), the son of Queen Victoria's second son Prince Alfred
('Affie'), 5th Duke of Edinburgh and Saxe Coburg, and his wife
Marie Alexandrovna, Grand Duchess of Russia. Young Alfred was
destined to the Duchy of Saxe-Coburg and was given 'a thorough
German education'. During his service in the 1st Regiment of
Prussia Guards he had led a dissipated life, which was a kind
of solace for his troubled childhood and youth wherein he had
endured 'a frequently absent father', an 'unsympathetic mother'
and a martinet of a German tutor in Dr Wilhelm Rolfs. Around
1899 it appears that Alfred had married Mabel Fitzgerald, an Irish
commoner, totally against the Royal Marriage Act of 1772. In
1899 Alfred, in a bout of severe depression, and suffering from

venereal disease, shot himself at Meran in the Austrian Tyrol. However, he lasted a few days to die at Schloss Rosenau, Coburg on 10 February 1899. For decades Prince Alfred's demise was glossed over as was his liaison with Mabel Fitzgerald and his putative daughter. Then in 1924 Walburga, Lady Paget, wrote of Prince Alfred's attempted suicide in her memoir *In My Tower* giving the lie that he had died of 'phthisis' (tuberculosis). His father's biographers John Van der Kiste and Bee Jordaan noted in 1984, 'The Royal Archives at Windsor . . . have intimated that the facts do not apply [*sic*]'.

Still assertions go on. In 2006 a Jersey accountant Robert Brown, made the bizarre claim that he was the illegitimate nephew of Queen Elizabeth II, being the 'love child' of the late Princess Margaret, Countess of Snowdon. Brown averred that he was born in 1955 following an affair between Princess Margaret and the man she was once in love with Group Captain Peter Townsend or, said Brown, from her well-publicised affair with the late Robin Douglas-Home. His claim received only publicity in the press.

Royal illegitimacy is a matter of state record since at least the eleventh century, with William the Conqueror – William the Bastard – the illegitimate son of Robert I of Normandy by Herleve, a girl from Falaise where Robert had a castle, being one of the most famous royal illegitimates in history. Yet what do royal records show about other royal bastards?

House of Normandy
HENRY I (r. 1100–35):
Purported to have twenty-five illegitimate children by six known women and others unknown. Four children paternity uncertain.

He had six children by Sybilla Corbet of Alcester:
Robert, Earl of Gloucester, married Mabel Fitzhamon. Issue. d. 1147.
Reginald, Earl of Cornwall, married Beatrice Fitzrichard. Issue. d. 1175.
William, married Alice. Issue not known. d. *c*. 1187.
Sybilla, married Alexander I, King of Scots. No issue. d. 1122.
Gundrada. Background not known.
Rohese married Henry de la Pomerai. Issue. d. *c*. 1176.

He had three children by Ansfrida widow of Anskill, a knight:
Richard of Lincoln. Died on 25 November 1120 in the White Ship
disaster.
Brother Fulk, a monk. (Name of several Counts of Anjou.)
Juliana, married Eustace de Pacy, Lord of Bréteuil. Issue. d. 1136, a nun.

By Nest, daughter of Rhys ap Tewdwr, King of Deheubarth, SW
Wales, one son:
Henry Fitzhenry. Issue. d. 1157 in battle.

By Edith Sigulfson of Greystoke, one son:
Robert Fitzedith, Baron of Okehampton, married Maud d'Avranches.
Issue. d. 1172.

By Isabel de Beaumont, daughter of the Earl of Leicester, two
daughters:
Isabella who died unmarried *c.* 1120, and Matilda, Abbess of
Montivilliers.

By Edith, one daughter:
Matilda, who died in the White Ship disaster. She married Rotrou II,
Count of Perche. Issue.

STEPHEN (r. 1135–54):
At least five illegitimates including Gervase, Abbot of Westminster.
Children by mothers unknown:
Gilbert. d. *c.* 1142.
William de Tracy. Issue. d. *c.* 1136.
Matilda, married Conan II, Duke of Brittany. Issue.
Constance, married Roscelin de Beaumont. Issue; a granddaughter,
Ermengarde married William I, The Lion, King of Scots and had
four children including King Alexander II.
Eustacia, married William Gouet III, Lord of Montmireil. Issue.
Alice, married Mathew de Montmorenci, Constable of France. Issue.
(There is a record that an unknown daughter was betrothed to
William de Warenne; but never married.)

Records show four more of uncertain paternity:
Joan, married Fergus of Galloway. Issue.

Emma, married Guy de Laval. Issue.
Sybilla, married Baldwin de Boullers.
(Records show an unknown daughter betrothed to Hugh Fitzgervais;
never married.)

House of Anjou
HENRY II (r. 1154–89):
He had twelve illegitimates by five or more mothers.
Geoffrey Plantagenet, Bishop-elect of Lincoln (1173), Royal Chancellor.
William Longsword.

RICHARD I (r. 1189–99):
Possibly two illegitimates.

JOHN (r. 1199–1216):
He had at least twelve illegitimates.
Geoffrey.
Joan, married Llewelyn ap Ioworth, mother Clementina.
Oliver.
Richard.
Osbert.

EDWARD I (r. 1272–1307):
He had one disputed illegitimate.

EDWARD II (r. 1307–27):
He had one known illegitimate, Adam.

EDWARD III (r. 1327–77):
He had possibly three illegitimates by his mistress Alice Perrers
(*c.* 1348–1400), maid of Queen Philippa's Bedchamber. Jane and Joan
are known names.

House of York
EDWARD IV (r. 1461–70):
He had two known illegitimates.
Arthur Plantagenet, Viscount Lisle by Elizabeth Lucy, and one
daughter of whom little is known.

RICHARD III (r. 1483–85):
He had four known illegitimates of which two are prominent.
John of Gloucester, titular Captain of Calais. No issue.
Katherine Plantagenet, married in 1484 to the Earl of Huntingdon.
No issue.

House of Tudor
HENRY VII (r. 1485–1509):
He had one disputed illegitimate.

HENRY VIII (r. 1509–47):
He had two recorded illegitimates.
During the festivities of New Year 1514, Henry's eye was caught by
one of Queen Catherine of Aragon's ladies-in-waiting, Elizabeth
'Bessie' Blount, cousin of William Blount, 4th Baron Mountjoy. She
became Henry's 'official' mistress and bore him a son in June 1519,
Henry Fitzroy, Duke of Richmond and Somerset (so created in 1525),
Earl of Nottingham, Lord High Admiral, Lt Gen North of the Trent,
Warden of All the Marches up to Scotland. When it was clear that
Catherine of Aragon was incapable of bearing King Henry a son it is
thought that he had a mind to make Henry Fitzroy his legitimate heir
and talked of making him King of Ireland. This came to naught. Bessie
Blount was 'packed off to the country' in 1522 with one of Cardinal
Wolsey's protégé's Gilbert Tallboys; Henry gave the young couple the
Manor of Rokeby to live their lives henceforth in obscurity.

Although it was once proposed that Henry Fitzroy marry his half-
sister Princess Mary Tudor (even though this was against canon law)
he married Mary Howard, daughter of the Duke of Norfolk, sister of
his childhood playmate Henry Howard, Earl of Surrey. Henry Fitzroy
died in 1536; rumour had it that he was poisoned by King Henry's
second wife Anne Boleyn, but modern historians log his demise as
being from tuberculosis; he was childless. Mary died in 1557.

House of Stuart
CHARLES II (r. 1650–85):
He had sixteen illegitimates by eight mistresses.
By Lucy Walter of Haverfordwest (c. 1630–58):

How Fat was Henry VIII?

James, Duke of Monmouth, married Anne Scott of Buccleuch (1651–1732). Issue. d. 1685.

By Elizabeth Killigrew, later Lady Shannon:
Charlotte Fitzroy, married William, Earl of Yarmouth. Issue. d. 1684.

By Barbara Villiers (1641–1709), later Duchess of Cleveland:
Anne Fitzroy, married Henry Lennard, Earl of Sussex. No issue. d. 1722.
Charles Fitzroy, Duke of Southampton and Cleveland, married (2) Anne Poultney (1663–1745). Issue. d. 1730.
Henry Fitzroy, Duke of Grafton married Isabella Bennett (d. 1723). Issue. d. 1690.
George Fitzroy, Duke of Northumberland, twice married. No issue. d. 1716.
Barbara Benedicte, Prioress. Some historians suggest that she was the daughter of John Churchill, Duke of Marlborough.

By Nell Gwynne (1650–87):
Charles Beauclerk, Duke of St Albans, married Diane de Vere (d. 1742). Issue. d. 1726.
James Beauclerk. d. 1680.

By Louise de Kéroüaille (1649–1734), Duchess of Portsmouth:
Charles Lennox, Duke of Richmond and Duke of Aubigny, married Anne Brudenell. Issue. d. 1723.
Mary 'Moll' Davies.
Mary Tudor. d. 1726. Mary was married three times, but by her second and third husbands, Henry Graham of Levens and James Rooke, respectively, she had no children. By her first husband, Edward, Earl of Derwentwater (d.1705), she had children who became significant in Jacobite history. James (1689–1716) was executed for his part in the Jacobite rebellion of 1715; Charles (1693–1746) became private secretary to Prince Charles Edward Stuart and was executed for his part in the Jacobite rebellion of 1745.

The current dukes of Buccleuch and Queensberry, Grafton, St Albans, Richmond and Gordon are all direct descendants of Charles II's illegitimate children. Other connections can be made through the convolutions of family tree branches. For instance, Ralph George

Algenon Percy, 12th Duke of Northumberland (b. 1956), although nothing to do with the title created for Barbara Villiers's second son, is related to Charles II and Louise de Kéroüalle, and to Charles II and Lucy Walter as his mother was a daughter of the 8th Duke of Buccleuch and his grandmother a daughter of the 7th Duke of Richmond.

JAMES II/VII (r .1685–88):

He had seven illegitimates by two mothers.

One significant offspring of four was by Arabella Churchill (1648–1730), maid-in-waiting to Queen Anne Hyde, sister of John Churchill, Duke of Marlborough:

James Fitzjames, Duke of Berwick, Marshal of France. d. 1734.

House of Hanover
GEORGE I (r. 1714–27):

He had three illegitimates by his German *maîtress en titre* the 'tall and lean of stature' Ehrengard Melusina von der Schulenberg (1667–1747), Duchess of Kendal, nicknamed 'The Maypole'. (There were persistent rumours that George had married her 'with his left hand' according to the Continental custom of kings marrying commoners.)

GEORGE II (r. 1727–60):
He had one recorded illegitimate.

GEORGE IV (r. 1820–30):

He had some six possible illegitimates, including Lord Albert, by his mistress Elizabeth, Marchioness of Conyngham, and of which three are considered 'most certain'.

By Grace Eliot:

Georgina Augusta Frederica Seymour, b. 30 March 1782, married Lord Charles Bentinck, 1808.

By Elizabeth Fox (Mrs Crole):

George, b. 23 August 1799, followed a privileged military career.

By Lucy Howard:
George Howard (*c.* 1818–20)

WILLIAM IV (r. 1830–37):

He had ten illegitimates with his mistress, comedy actress Dorothy Jordan (Bland), (1761–1816).

George Augustus Frederick Fitzclarence, 1st Earl of Munster. Born on 29 January 1794. Married Mary Wyndham Fox, daughter of the Earl of Egremont. Committed suicide, 20 March 1842.

Sophia Fitzclarence. Born on 4 March 1795. Married Philip, 1st Baron De L'Isle and Dudley. Died on 10 April 1837 in childbirth.

Henry Edward Fitzclarence. Born on 8 March 1797. Died on 3 September 1817.

Mary Fitzclarence. Born on 19 December 1798. Married Charles Fox, illegitimate son of Henry, Baron Holland and Elizabeth Vassall. Died on 13 July 1864.

Frederick Fitzclarence. Born on 9 December 1799. Married Lady Augusta Boyle, daughter of George, Earl of Glasgow. Died on 30 October 1854.

Elizabeth Fitzclarence. Born on 17 January 1801. Married William Hay, Earl of Erroll, 16 January 1856. Their daughter Lady Agnes was mother-in-law to Louise, Princess Royal, eldest daughter of Edward VII.

Adolphus Fitzclarence. Born on 17 February 1802. Died on 17 May 1856, unmarried.

Augusta Fitzclarence. Born on 17 November 1803. Married (1) John Kennedy-Erskine of Dun, second son of the 1st Marquis of Alisa (d. 1831); (2) Lord Frederick Gordon, son of the 9th Marquis of Huntly. (d. 1878). Issue by first marriage. Died on 8 December 1865.

Revd Augustus Fitzclarence. Born on 1 March 1805. Married Sarah Elizabeth Gordon, eldest daughter of Lord Henry Gordon, fourth son of the Marquis of Huntly. Rector of Mapledurham, Oxfordshire. Died on 14 June 1854.

Amelia Fitzclarence. Born on 21 March 1807. Married Lucius Bentinck Cary, 10th Viscount Falkland. Died on 2 July 1858.

So by extant records Henry I, with twenty-five purported illegitimates, tops the list of siring royal bastards. But what of the monarchs of Scotland ?

WILLIAM I, THE LION (r. 1165–1214):

He had nine purported illegitimates.

ALEXANDER II (r. 1214–49):
He had one illegitimate daughter.

ROBERT II (r. 1371–98):
He had at least eight illegitimates.

ROBERT III (r. 1390–1406):
He had one illegitimate child.

JAMES II (r. 1437–60):
He had one illegitimate child.

JAMES IV (r. 1488–1513):
He had at least seven illegitimates. His most prominent were:
By Mariot Boyd, daughter of Archibald Boyd, Laird of Bonshaw:
Alexander Stewart, b. 1493. Archdeacon of St Andrews aged 9;
Archbishop of St Andrews aged 11; Chancellor of the University of
St Andrews, founder of St Leonard's College, 1512. Died with his
father at the Battle of Flodden, 9 September 1513.
Mariot Boyd also bore James a daughter, Catherine, b. 1494.

By Janet Kennedy, daughter of John, Lord Kennedy:
James Stewart, Earl of Moray, created 1501.

By Isabel Stuart, daughter of James, Earl of Buchan, a child, details
unknown.

JAMES V (r. 1513–42):
He had at least nine illegitimates, of which the most prominent
in history was by Margaret Erskine, wife of Robert Douglas of
Lochleven:
James Stewart, Earl of Moray. b. 1531. Commendator of St Andrews
Priory aged 7. He became the chief minister of his half-sister Mary,
Queen of Scots, thereafter Regent of Scotland on her abdication. He
was murdered by James Hamilton of Bothwellhaugh at Linlithgow
on 23 January 1570.

◆ Which British monarchs were put in prison or appeared in court?

> King Henry VI was a very ignorant and almost simple man and,
> unless I have been deceived, immediately after the battle the Duke of
> Gloucester, Edward's brother, who later became King Richard killed
> this good man with his own hand or at least had him killed in his
> presence in some obscure place.
>
> *Philippe de Commynes,* Memoirs, *(c. 1498).*

Like Henry VI who ended his life at the Tower of London, many of
royal birth have spent years in prison, quite often because they were
in the way of others who wished to succeed to the throne. One such
was Edward Plantagenet, nephew of Edward IV and Richard III. He
was imprisoned both by Richard III and Henry VII. In prison since
childhood, Edward was executed on a 'trumped-up charge' of treason
in November 1499; he had been in prison for fifteen and a half years.
In Scotland David, Duke of Rothesay (b. 1378), heir apparent to
Robert III, was imprisoned at Falkland Castle in 1402 on the urgings
of his uncle the Duke of Albany and his father-in-law the Earl of
Douglas, to die in obscure circumstances a few months later.

Undoubtedly the most romantic prisoner was Mary, Queen of
Scots, who spent nineteen years, seven months and ten days as a
prisoner of Queen Elizabeth I, until her execution at Fotheringay on
8 February 1587. Again, two royal prisoners whose story is steeped
in mystery and pity are the 12-year-old Edward V and his 9-year-old
brother Richard, Duke of York, the famous 'Princes in the Tower'
who 'disappeared' some time after 1483. Charles I also suffered trial
and imprisonment. He surrendered to the Scots about a year after the
Battle of Naseby on 14 July 1645, to be imprisoned at Newcastle and
Hampton Court (from which he escaped) and Carisbrooke Castle.
In January 1649 he was brought to trial for treason at a court he
did not recognise as legal; he was found guilty of the charge that he
had fought against his subjects and was executed at Whitehall Palace,
30 January 1649.

Queen Consorts fared little better. For thirty-nine years Eleanor
of Brittany, niece of Kings Richard I and John, was imprisoned
because of her superior claims to rule England over King John. She
died at Bristol Castle, 10 August 1241. Isabella of France, daughter

of Philippe IV of France, queen of Edward II was imprisoned for just over twenty-eight years. With her lover Roger Mortimer, she plotted the overthrowal and death of Edward II. Her imprisonment at Castle Rising, Norfolk, lasted from April 1330 until her death on 22 August 1358. Other kings died in incarceration. Edward II was murdered at Berkley Castle, Gloucestershire, on 21 September 1327; and Richard II was starved to death at Pontefract Castle to die around 14 February 1400.

Three Scottish kings stand out as royal prisoners. Duncan II (d. 1094), son of Malcolm III and his first wife, Ingibjord, were taken as hostage by William I, the Conqueror, during one of his father's five fruitless raids into Norman suzerainty in England. Historians believe that Malcolm favoured as his heirs his children by his second wife Margaret, granddaughter of Edmund II of England, with possible disinheritance. Duncan spent fifteen years in Norman captivity. Duncan was killed in battle in 1094 after his invasion of Scotland to win his throne from Donald III who had usurped it on Malcolm's death in 1093.

David II (r. 1329–32; 1332–3; 1336–71), son of Robert I, The Bruce, and Elizabeth de Burgh, was taken prisoner after he had invaded England at the Battle of Neville's Cross, near Durham, on 17 October 1346. He was released under the terms of the Treaty of Berwick of October 1357 for a ransom of 100,000 marks of which the balance was never paid. David was thus in what has been described as 'agreeable captivity' in London and Hampshire for just under eleven years.

James I (r. 1406–37), son of Robert III and Annabella Drummond, tops the list of royal prisoners who were held in custody while still reigning. At the age of 11 James was captured at sea while on his way to safety in France from lawless Scotland. He was handed over by pirates to Henry IV to be confined first at the Tower of London and then Nottingham Castle. He was allowed to vacillate at the English court, and eventually married in 1424 Lady Joan Beaufort, great-granddaughter of Edward III; this was the year of his coronation in Scotland, his release coming after the death of Henry IV in 1422. James was assassinated at Perth, 21 February 1437. In all, James had been in confinement for almost eighteen years.

A number of British royals appeared in law courts for various reasons from Cardinal Wolsey's opening of the 'Secret Trial of the

King's Marriage' on 17 May 1527, concerning Henry's divorce of Queen Catherine of Aragon, to the proceedings against Queen Caroline, wife of George IV during August–November 1820, when she appeared in the House of Lords on charges of immorality. Only one subsequent British monarch appeared in a civil court.

As Prince of Wales, Edward VII appeared in court as a witness, twice. In 1890 he was called to the civil court in what is known to historians as the 'Royal Baccarat Scandal' but twenty years earlier he appeared in more serious circumstances, for since the reign of Henry IV no Prince of Wales had ever stood before a Court of Justice.

Albert Edward, Prince of Wales, was drawn into the 'Mordaunt Case' because of his vigorous and hectic social life. Lady Harriet Mordaunt (d.1906), one of the daughters of Sir Thomas Moncrieffe, was an attractive 21-year-old who appeared regularly at Edward's parties from Abergeldie near Balmoral to Marlborough House, London. Her husband Sir Charles Mordaunt (1836–97) was Tory MP for South Warwickshire and was many years her senior. To all in society Harriet appeared 'excitable and highly strung'. Following the birth of her first child Violet (later Marchioness of Bath) in 1869, the premature infant was diagnosed with what Harriet interpreted as threatened blindness. This she told people was caused by a 'fearful disease' (i.e. venereal contagion). As time passed Harriet exhibited postpartum depression leading to increased eccentricity of behaviour. She told her husband that the child was not his and that she had committed adultery 'often and in open day' with Lowry Egerton, Lord Cole, Sir Frederick Johnstone and the Prince of Wales among others. She identified Lord Cole as the father of Violet. Instead of dismissing the confession as nonsense, Mordaunt chose to believe his wife. The child was soon cured of a mild eye infection and there were no traces of venereal infection in either Harriet or her infant.

Incensed by her confession Mordaunt forced open her private desk and removed a diary and correspondence Harriet had had with the Prince of Wales and others. Although Edward had sent her a valentine card as well, the eleven extant letters from him were innocuous social gossip, but Mordaunt filed for divorce. Edward strongly voiced his innocence, and the Lord Chancellor, Lord Hatherley, pronounced the letters to Harriet as 'unexceptional in every way', and the Lord Chief Justice, Sir Alexander Cockburn, advised Edward of what would happen in court. Yes, Edward had written to Harriet; yes, he had visited her on several occasions; but, no, he had not had sexual intimacy with her. Alexandra, Princess of Wales, believed her husband and publicly supported him. When the facts were communicated to an aghast Queen Victoria she telegraphed her support for her son, adding that he should be more circumspect in future when dealing with young married women. The anti-royal press, like the *Reynolds's Newspaper*, had a field day stirring up wide public interest in the trial which was heard before Lord Penzance in the Court for Divorce and Matrimonial Causes in Westminster Hall, and before a special jury on 23 February 1870 (postponed from the 16th).

Edward was not cited as a co-respondent, a counter-petition having been filed by Sir Thomas Moncrieffe on his daughter's behalf to the effect that Harriet was clinically insane; at that time she was already in an asylum. Edward was only subpoenaed by Harriet's counsel Dr Francis Deane as a witness. The prince, who had shown great nervousness at the thought of appearing in court, was confident in the witness box. It appears that Sir Charles Mordaunt had suspected his wife of illicit liaisons for some time but had kept quiet. Yet, on returning home to Walton Hall (his country house in Warwickshire) he found Harriet showing off her driving skills to the Prince of Wales. When Edward had gone Sir Charles had the ponies he had given to her shot before her eyes. The testimony further heard by the jury shed public light on Edward's social habits of visiting attractive married women when their husbands were out. They heard from Mordaunt's butler and a ladies' maid how the prince had visited Harriet in 1867 and 1868 several times. The butler said: 'Lady Mordaunt gave me directions that when the Prince called no one was to be admitted.' Occasionally Edward would arrive in a hansom cab. Then came the blunt question from Mordaunt's counsel, Mr Serjeant Thomas Ballantyne: 'Has there ever been any improper familiarity or criminal act between yourself and Lady Mordaunt?'

'There has not,' replied the prince, to much applause from spectators in the public gallery (admonished by Lord Penzance). There was no cross-examination and Edward's 'ordeal' only lasted seven minutes. Sir Charles Mordaunt's petition for divorce was dismissed on the grounds that Harriet Mordaunt was clearly insane and 'could not be a party to the suit'. Much litigation followed the case, yet on 11 March 1875, Mordaunt was granted his divorce. Before setting off to dine with Prime Minister W.E. Gladstone, that night the Prince of Wales wrote this to Queen Victoria:

> I trust by what I have said today that the public at large will be satisfied that the gross imputations which have been so wantonly cast upon me are now cleared up.

The Prince of Wales had not been on trial, but the public found him guilty. *Reynolds's Newspaper* voiced the widespread public disapproval of the Prince of Wales's conduct and hoped that Queen Victoria's health would be robust to defer the Prince of Wales's accession to the throne; within days of the trial he was publicly booed at the theatre and at Epsom races. Queen Victoria said she believed that the Prince of Wales's conduct in public did 'damage him in the eyes of the middle and lower classes' and that he should spend less time in the company of the 'frivolous, selfish and pleasure-seeking rich'. The Prince of Wales ignored her.

◆ Was there a case of incest in the Royal Family?

> … a very delicate subject [arises] – the cruelty of a fabricated and most scandalous and base report concerning P.S. [Princess Sophia].
> *Letter of March 1801 from Princess Elizabeth to Dr Thomas Willis.*

Princess Sophia was born at Queen's House, Kensington, on 3 November 1777, the fifth daughter and eleventh child (of fifteen) of George III and Queen Charlotte. Beloved of her siblings, Sophia never married; she died in 1848 blind like her father and, according to the backbiting of the time, she had an illegitimate baby. By the 'cackle of gossip' and the 'savagery of politics', the affair was reinvented as an incestuous illegitimacy with her brother Prince Ernest, Duke of Cumberland, later King of Hanover.

Never of robust health Sophia was kept mainly at Windsor along with her sisters, in a close confinement by the orders and presence of Queen Charlotte. Sophia was seriously ill at Weymouth during January–October 1800, to be attended by Physician to the Royal Household (later Sir) Francis Milman. According to his records the princess was suffering from 'spasms', but somehow gossip was developed that the 'spasms' were actually a cover-up for pregnancy. By the end of 1800 it is clear that Sophia knew what was being said about her. She wrote this to Elizabeth, Countess Harcourt: 'It is grievous to think what a little trifle will slur a young woman's character for ever.' Could she really have considered pregnancy 'a little trifle', later historians wondered?

Who initiated the pregnancy story? Historians believe that it was 'fostered' and 'embellished ... with its malignant horror' by Princess Caroline of Brunswick (1768–1821), wife of Sophia's brother George, Prince of Wales. Caroline was a poisonous member of the Royal Family, who constantly sought revenge for the 'humiliation of her marriage' (George parted from Caroline for ever after the birth of their daughter in 1796). Caroline's gossiping concerned many of the Royal Family, from George III who she said had 'freedoms with her of the grossest nature' to anecdotes about changeling infants and incestuous relationships. All were laughed off by family and courtiers alike. But why did the gossip about Princess Sophia remain for generations?

Writing in 1977 in *Society Scandals* the historian Sir Roger Thomas Baldwin Fulford (1902–83), set out a theory of how Princess Sophia was so accused. He identifies the lawyer-turned-politician Sylvester Douglas, Lord Glenbervie (1743–1823) as a diarist who married the elder daughter of Prime Minister Lord North. She was lady-in-waiting to the Princess of Wales and, through her, titbits of gossip about Princess Sophia appeared in his diary. Glenbervie wrote on 25 March 1801:

> I heard yesterday a recapitulation of many of the circumstances of the Princess Sophia's extraordinary illness last autumn at Weymouth. . . . They are too delicate a nature for me to commit them ... even to this safe repository. But they are such as leave scarce a doubt in my mind.

He later noted that the 'extraordinary illness' was a pregnancy and that the child's father was General Thomas Garth (1774–1829) equerry to George III. Glenbervie went on to say that 'the Weymouth foundling' was christened Thomas and was lodged at the house in Weymouth of Col Herbert Taylor, George III's private secretary. Garth was a long-trusted friend of the Royal Family and a prominent courtier. Fulford dismisses Glenbervie's accusations with: 'would they [the princess's siblings] have allowed one who had behaved in this way to their favourite sister to remain in the Court circle?' Fulford further quotes the diarist Charles Greville who said of Garth:'he is a hideous old Devil, old enough to be [Sophia's] father, and with a great claret mark on his face.'

Thus Fulford dismisses Garth as being an improbable lover and says that the 'scandalmongers' were made to 'dig deeper'. So he identifies Glenbervie as saying:'the Duke of Kent [Prince Edward] tells the Princess [of Wales] that the father is not Garth but the Duke of Cumberland. How horrid!' A womanising blackguard, Cumberland was a popular target for invective and the incest story would have had willing listeners who believed, as Christopher Hibbert put it, that '[Cumberland's] watchful affection for [Sophia] was certainly felt to be unnatural'. Fulford dismisses the stories of Princess Sophia's pregnancy and quotes Henry Petty-Fitzmaurice, Marquis of Landsdowne on Princess Sophia's death:'Her Royal Highness has passed a long life of virtue, charity and excellence in every position, public and private, in which she was placed.' Other historians have had a different opinion.

In 1882 Percy Fitzgerald noted that 'there was a secret morganatic marriage between General Garth and Sophia', and others, like Anthony Bird, attested that she gave birth to the offspring Thomas Garth Jr who was 'a thoroughly unpleasant and unprincipled young man'. Fitzgerald went on:'there seems to have been no doubt in the [Royal] Family about his parentage'. During one illness which was deemed terminal, General Garth entrusted to his son 'very incriminating papers' about the illegitimacy. Garth Jr promptly attempted to blackmail the Royal Family.

In her reassessment of the six daughters of George III in 2004, Flora Fraser added that a child (purporting to be Sophia's) was baptised at Weymouth on 11 August 1800. Born on the 5 August the child, 'Thomas Ward, stranger' (or foundling) was 'adopted by Samuel and Charlotte Sharland'. Was this child's entry a royal cover-up? We shall probably never know, but the charge of incest against Cumberland is summed up by his biographer Anthony Bird:

> The canard that Cumberland added incest to his crimes became accepted as an article of faith and is believed to this day [1966] – for the vilification of his character continues.

♦ Which reigning English, Scottish and British monarchs were rumoured to be homosexual?

[King James] loved young men, his favourites, better than women, loving them beyond the love of men to women.

Sir John Oglander (1585–1655), Diary.

Dating from the succession of the houses of Normandy, Atholl and the United Kingdom, four English, one Scottish and four British monarchs have been identified as being, or rumoured to be, homosexual.

William II, by-named Rufus (r. 1087–1100), is the first to be so called after the Norman Conquest of 1066. Victorian historians, like Edward Augustus Freeman (d. 1892), followed monastic chroniclers in charging William II with 'sexual depravity and irreligion'. What did the early chroniclers say of William in this connection? He was noted as having a love of dressing up as a Roman emperor – his coat was described as being like that of Emperor Caligula – and male courtiers were encouraged by the king to go nude or dress effeminately and act in a camp manner. William never married so there was no element of female decorum at court. William of Malmesbury in his *Gesta Regum Anglorum* noted that his knights were prone to 'rob and rape', wherein their high testosterone levels also led to uninhibited behaviour at court. Others like the secular cleric Wace, in his *The Roman de Rou* averred that William was bisexual, but all chroniclers failed to identify any of William's male (or female) lovers.

Richard I (r. 1189–99), Coeur de Lion, while being married to Berengaria, daughter of Sancho VI, King of Navarre, with possibly two illegitimate children, has also been identified as homosexual. His fame is international as a warrior-king, a crusading knight and a prince of troubadours, so where has the allegation come from?

It is believed that Richard's marriage was never consummated; the match had been made by Richard's mother Eleanor of Aquitaine, who attempted to lessen her son's homosexual desires. Throughout his reign clerics fulminated at him 'to beware the fate of Sodom'. In July 1190 Richard set off on crusade with Philippe of France with whom he was to have an 'intense friendship'. Alarm was expressed that they were said 'to eat at the same table, share the same dish and sleep in the same bed'.

Edward II (r.1307–27), caused a great scandal at court over his infatuation with Piers Gaveston. Edward I believed that his son was having homosexual relations with his childhood friend Gaveston and banished the latter from court. On Edward I's death in 1307, Gaveston was called back and Edward II made him Earl of Cornwall, to the disgust of his courtiers, as the title was usually given to a son of the monarch. Edward also married Gaveston off to his niece Margaret. In 1308 Edward married Isabella, daughter of Philippe IV of France. Gaveston organised Edward's coronation in the same year and totally disgraced himself at the coronation celebrations by his amatory display of affection for Edward. Queen Isabella was greatly distressed. In time Gaveston was forced into permanent exile by the English barons, but he returned and continued his arrogant and obnoxious behaviour driving the barons to arrest him; he was executed in 1312. On 21 February 1327 Edward himself was murdered at Berkley Castle, Gloucestershire. Cynically, because of his homosexuality, commentators said the manner of Edward's demise was fitting. Here it is described by John Capgrove in his *Chronicle*:

> In this same year [1327] was this old Edward slain with a hot spit put into his body, which could not be spied when he was dead for they put a horn into his tewhel [rectum] and the spit through the horn that there should be no burning appear outside. This was by the ordinance as was said of Sir John Maltravers and Thomas Gournay, which laid a great door upon him while they did their work.

Edward II's great-grandson Richard II (r.1377–99) was another candidate for the charge of homosexuality. He was married twice, first to Anne (d.1394), daughter of Charles IV, the Holy Roman Emperor and King of Bohemia, and then to Isabella, daughter of Charles VI of France. There were no children of the unions. History often identifies Richard's foppish dress, supposed effeminacy and a listing of court favourites as proof of Richard's sexual proclivities but there is no firm evidence of infatuations with males. Richard abdicated in 1399 in favour of Henry IV, and died (of starvation) at Pontefract Castle in 1400; there was no hint of murder.

In Scotland, Malcolm IV (r.1153–65) was dubbed 'The Maiden', because of his girlish looks, chroniclers said. He never married, was largely a poor ruler, and raised in the company of women, his effeminacy has been construed as homosexuality, apparent or repressed. Some chroniclers say that he was a confirmed celibate and his nickname came from him being a virgin; rumour thinks otherwise.

In 1603 the kingdoms of Scotland and England were united under James VI of Scotland, who now became James I of England, and who ruled the joint kingdoms until his death in 1625. James Stuart, born in 1566, was one year old when he ascended the throne of Scotland on the forced abdication of his mother, Mary, Queen of Scots. Biographers have noted that like Edward II and Richard II, he was 'starved of affection' as a child and in a male-dominated court sought love and comfort from males. As D. Harries Willson wrote:

> As [James] grew into a youth he showed no interest in young women and held them in contempt. Indeed, through all his life he entertained most lofty views of the superiority of the male, views first inculcated by the boorish [George] Buchanan [tutor to James], a bachelor, who thought that women did nothing but cause trouble and make cuckolds of their husbands.

Writing her biography of James in 1974, Antonia Fraser gave the opinion that had an 'attractive woman' appeared in James's life at the moment he needed 'to be loved in the romantic sense' that 'the homosexual inclinations of King James might never have been aroused'.

If the numerous biographies of James I/VI are to be believed, both as prince and king, James had many male lovers, but three in particular have been identified: First, his adolescent love for his cousin Esmé Stuart, Sieur d'Aubigny (*c.*1542–83), whom James created 1st Duke of Lennox and Chamberlain. When a party of ultra-Protestant nobles seized James in the Ruthven Raid in 1582, he was separated from Lennox who was deemed a Roman Catholic intriguer. Lennox was ordered to leave Scotland and a broken-hearted James never saw him again.

Next to be particularly mentioned as a lover of King James was Robert Carr (d.1645), Viscount Rochester and Earl of Somerset. He accompanied James to England in 1603 as a page and advanced to be private secretary in 1612. Carr fell from grace after quarrelling with James, wherein Carr was accused of poisoning the poet, and target of court intrigue, Sir Thomas Overbury in 1615. Carr was replaced in James's affections by George Villiers (1592–1628), 1st Duke of Buckingham. Neither dalliance brought James happiness.

Two female sovereigns have been identified as possible lesbians: Mary II (ruled jointly with William III, 1689–94) and Queen Anne. Although joint monarchs, Mary and William were not particularly compatible as their marriage was diplomatic, celebrated when Mary was only 15. However, a certain 'devotion' grew between them, threatened only in 1685 when news of William's relationship with his mistress Elizabeth Villiers (later Countess of Orkney) was publicised by Jacobite agents. Mary and William were reconciled. In her youth Mary's main companions were the six daughters of her governess Lady Frances Villiers. Yet her greatest affection was for Frances Apsley, nine years her senior.

Mary's letters to Frances, whom she called 'Aurelia', have been cited as proof of lesbian tendencies. Ill-written, effusively sentimental and passionate, the letters call Frances Mary's 'Husband', and therein Mary described herself as '[Frances's] humble servant to kiss the ground where you go, to be your dog on a string, your fish in a net, your bird in a cage, your humble trout'. Mary's father James II and step-mother Mary of Modena were appalled at the sentiment of the letters. Mary's biographer John Miller assessed the letters with the comment: 'but they were really only the outpourings of a warm and loving adolescent, seeking an outlet for her emotions within an all-female environment.'

On Mary's death in 1694, William put aside his mistress Elizabeth Villiers and took up with Arnold Joost van Keppel, one of his pages, who was later elevated to the earldom of Albemarle. Keppel's effeminate good looks gave rise to rumour that his relationship with William was homosexual. William knew about the rumours and said: 'It seems to me very extraordinary that it should be impossible to have esteem and regard for a young man without it being criminal.' One who was never convinced that William was not homosexual was Dean Jonathan Swift. He made public his opinion that William had covered up his homosexuality to his wife Mary by taking his mistress Elizabeth Villiers, who later married Lord George Hamilton.

♦ Did Edward VII have a 'secret family'?

> If you were to try and deny it [that Edward had fathered an illegitimate
> child], she [Nellie Clifton] can drag you into a court of law to force
> you to own it & there with you in the witness box, she will be able
> to give before a greedy Multitude disgusting details of your profligacy
> for the sake of convincing the Jury; yourself crossexamined by a
> railing indecent attorney and hooted and yelled at by a Lawless Mob!!
> Oh horrible prospect, which this person has in her power, any day to
> realise! and to break your poor parents' hearts!
>
> *Albert Consort, to Edward, Prince of Wales on discovering that Edward had
> had sexual relations with Nellie Clifton while on military service at The
> Curragh, Ireland.*

When King Edward VII breathed his last at 11.45 p.m. on 6 May 1910
at Buckingham Palace, surrounded by Queen Alexandra, George and
Mary, the Prince and Princess of Wales, Louise, the Princess Royal,
Duchess of Fife, daughter of Princess Victoria and sister Princess
Louise, Duchess of Argyll, the international press rushed into print
with eulogies on Edward as the 'Uncle of Europe' and his devoted
family. None mentioned his 'secret family' of supposed children,
products of decades of philandering in and out of the boudoirs of
some of society's beauties.

Leonie Blanche Jerome (1859–1943), wife of Col (later Sir) John
Leslie (1857–1944) and sister of Jennie, Lady Randolph Churchill,
had in her possession at Castle Leslie, Co. Monaghan, Ireland a photo
album, one of its pages containing an intriguing picture. It showed
the image of one Baroness de Meyer and, said writer Anita Leslie,
'lightly pencilled under the name [was the caption] "daughter of
Edward VII"'.

The Baroness was the daughter of Blanche, Duchesse de Caracciolo,
who seems to have separated from her husband on her wedding
day to return for a while to her philandering lover, Prince Josef
Poniatowski, a current equerry to Emperor Napoleon III. During
the late 1860s, Edward, Prince of Wales, met her and when she fell
pregnant around 1868 arranged for her to live with his supposed baby
daughter, Alberta Olga Caracciolo at a cliff-top villa at Dieppe, where
he visited her when passing in a borrowed yacht. The house became
the Villa Olga and was dubbed *La Villa Mystère* by locals, and Edward's

visits were well known among the resident English elite. Lee Jortin, the local English consul, monitored Edward's visits. Blanche later recalled: 'When the august parent of [Alberta] Olga came incognito we were supposed not to know, although plain-clothes policemen paraded our quarter in relays day and night.' Edward stood godfather to baby Alberta Olga. In later life the pretty girl would be drawn and painted by Sickert, Whistler, Boldini, Helleu and Jacques-Emile Blanche in 1887. In due course Alberta Olga married the society photographer Adolphe de Meyer and Edward prevailed upon Albert, the Wettin King of Saxony to confer a Saxon barony on de Meyer so that Alberta Olga could attend his coronation in 1902 as a baroness. The de Meyers were regular guests of members of the louche (the Prince of Wales's) circle, for instance enjoying the after Ascot week with the Ernest Becketts, he who fathered Edward's mistress The Hon. Mrs George Keppel's daughter Violet.

In September 1871 the Prince of Wales received a letter while at Abergeldie containing these words: 'Without any funds to meet the necessary expenses and to buy the discretion of servants, it is impossible to keep this sad secret.' The letter had come from a Mrs Harriet Whatman, a friend of his mistress since 1867 Lady Susan Pelham-Clinton, and announced the impending birth of his child. Lady Susan Charlotte Catherine was the daughter of Henry Pelham-Clinton, 5th Duke of Newcastle, a mentor to the Prince of Wales and a great friend of Queen Victoria and Prince Albert; Lady Susan had been a bridesmaid to the Princess Royal in 1858. On 23 April 1860 she married against parental wishes the clinically insane Lt Col Adolphus Vane-Tempest (b. 1825), third son of Charles Stewart, 3rd Marquis of Londonderry. He died in 1864 having had some kind of 'struggle' with his keepers.

Edward was annoyed that Lady Susan had not informed him concerning the pregnancy. She said that she had done so to protect one she 'loved and honoured', and she had contemplated an abortion. Only when her financial situation worsened did she contact Edward, who she had not seen for some time. Through Edward's private secretary Francis Knollys, Lady Susan was given instructions to see Edward's 'confidential practitioner' Dr (later Sir) Oscar Clayton. But history does not show whether or not an abortion took place; certainly the fate of the child is not known. Lady Susan was still too ill in 1872 to attend the service of thanksgiving for the recovery of Edward from typhoid, although he sent her tickets. Lady Susan died on 6 September 1875, still in her thirties. Years later it was discovered that Edward had kept all her love letters enabling historians to add detail to the story of one of Edward's best attested illegitimate children.

Servants' gossip was always a good source of material for stories about the Prince of Wales's being 'susceptible to feminine charms'. When the little daughter of an employee on the Eaton Hall estate in Cheshire of Hugh Grosvenor, 1st Duke of Westminster reported to her father that she had seen Edward 'lying on top of 'Mrs Cornwallis-West in the woods, she was hit with 'a violent blow and told she'd be killed if she repeated the story'. Mary ('Patsy') Cornwallis-West was born Mary Fitzpatrick in 1858 and when she was 17 she married Col William Cornwallis-West of the 1st Volunteer Battalion, Royal Welsh Guards and of Ruthin Castle, Wales. Patsy was the kind of woman the Prince of Wales liked; she was flirty, sexy and fun – her favourite party trick was to slide down the stairs on a tea-tray. In 1874 Patsy gave birth to George to whom Edward became godfather. In his autobiography *Edwardian Hey-Days* George wrote:

> The Prince of Wales often came [to the Cornwallis-West London home at 49 Eaton Square] and was invariably kind to me and always asked to see me. Never a Christmas passed without his sending me some little gift in the shape of a card or a toy.

In 1900 George married Jennie, Lady Randolph Churchill (against Edward's advice); they divorced in 1913. In all Patsy had three children to include Daisy and Constance. The Prince of Wales monitored George's career in the army carefully using his influence when necessary.

It was widely believed that Edward was George's father. Writing in 2003, biographer Tim Coates said that Edward 'was a lover of many women and father of many children, including possibly all of Patsy's'. Patsy's two daughters also rose high in society. Daisy (d. 1943) married Prince Hans of Pless, and Constance (known as Shelagh, d. 1970) married Bendor, 2nd Duke of Westminster, and George married for a second time the actress Stella Patrick Campbell (d. 1940). Patsy Cornwallis-West died on 21 July 1920 at Arnewood, Near Newlands, in the New Forest.

The Prince of Wales was further rumoured to have fathered a child with the Princesse Jeanne-Marguerite Seillière de Sagan, wife of the Duc de Talleyrand-Périgord, whom he had first met during his visit to Louis Napoleon at Fontainebleau in 1862. Whenever he was in France Edward made efforts to meet her and visited her mostly at her home at the Château de Mello, south of Paris. There, a well-attested incident took place. Her eldest son, on being curious why his mother lunched alone in her boudoir with Edward, crept into the room to find the Prince of Wales's clothes spread over a chair. Gathering them up he threw them all out of the window to flutter down into a fountain in the gardens below. When Edward emerged from the princess's bedroom his sodden clothes were being fished out of the fountain. He had to return to Paris in borrowed clothes which did not fit him. It is said by French historians that the princess's second son, Prince Hélie de Sagan, was Edward's child. Aristocratic gossips further inferred that Chief Constable of Edinburgh Roderick Ross was also a child of Edward, as was Sir Stewart Graham Menzies, 'C' of the British Intelligence Service MI6.

In more recent times the art collector Edward James (1907–84) said that his mother, Evelyn 'Evie' Elizabeth James (1869–1930), was the illegitimate daughter of the Prince of Wales. She was officially the eldest daughter of Sir Charles Forbes, fourth baronet of Castle Newe, not far from Balmoral; her mother being Helen Moncrieff. Evie, noted James's biographer John Lowe, was 'the result of an indiscreet romp in the Highland heather between the young Prince of Wales and Helen ...' It is said that the union was well known in aristocratic circles and Evie was a regular visitor to Balmoral as a child. Evie married William Dodge James who bought in 1891 West Dean Park, West Sussex, which became a place of royal visits. At West Dean Park a collection of royal letters was found on Evie's death which Edward James cited as proof of his mother's parentage.

Edward VII had six legitimate children with his wife Alexandra of Denmark and, considering Edward's life of serial adultery, perhaps several more from the wrong side of the blanket. Today there are still many in aristocratic families who believe that in their family trees are members of Edward's 'secret family'.

A MISTRESS'S HYSTERICS AND A MYSTERY CHILD?

For the last twelve years of his life Edward VII had a deep affection for Alice, The Hon. Mrs George Keppel, remembered today as the great-grandmother of Camilla, Duchess of Cornwall and Rothesay. Born Alice Frederica Edmonstone on 29 April 1868, in 1891 she married The Hon. George Keppel (1865–1947), third son of William Keppel, 7th Earl of Albemarle. Tradition has it that she gave birth to a daughter by Ernest William Beckett (later Baron Grimthorp) in 1894, called Violet (d. 1972). Violet married Derek Trefusis in 1919 and scandalised society with a very public lesbian affair with the writer Vita Sackville-West. In 1898 Alice met Edward VII – then Prince of Wales – and in 1900 Alice gave birth to Sonia Rosemary (d. 1980), who society gossips said was the prince's child. This assertion has been denied by relatives.

From 1898 Alice Keppel devoted her social life to the prince and thereafter when Edward became king in 1901. He used his financial contacts to help make her money to pay for the great expense of being *maîtresse en titre*. By 1901 Alice was the king's regular companion, as his wife Queen Alexandra's worsening deafness kept her increasingly out of society.

In 1910 Alice accompanied the king on his last holiday to Biarritz. It was clear that the monarch was becoming increasingly ill. On their return Alice became more and more agitated at the king's declining health and asked to be with him at Buckingham Palace. Queen Alexandra did not send for her. This prompted Alice to play what she considered a trump card. At the time of his appendix operation in 1902 Edward had sent Alice a letter in which he said if he was dangerously ill he was certain that the queen would allow Alice to come to him. On being shown the letter Queen Alexandra relented.

In due time Alice told her friends a story of what allegedly happened at the king's deathbed: When she arrived at Buckingham Palace she remembered in her highly emotional state to curtsey to the queen and her daughter Princess Victoria. The king then called her over to sit beside him. He stroked her hand and told her to dry her tears. Then he called to the queen who was standing by the window to come over and kiss Alice. This, according to Alice, the queen did and she sat with the royal lovers by the bed. The king, continued Alice, then slumped back into one of his phases of unconsciousness and Alice left with the queen sobbing on her arm and promising that the Royal Family would care for her.

When courtiers heard of Alice's version they were incensed. Lord Esher noted: 'Mrs Keppel has lied about the whole affair ever since, and describes quite falsely, her reception by the queen.' Esher added this in his journal:

> The queen did not kiss her, or say that the royal family would 'look after her'. The queen shook hands, and said something to the effect, 'I am sure you always had a good influence over him', and walked to the window. The nurses remained close to the king, who did not recognise Mrs K and kept falling forward in his chair. Then she [Alice] left the room with Princess Victoria, almost shrieking, and before the pages and footmen in the passage, kept repeating, 'I never did any harm, there was nothing wrong between us', and then, 'What is to become of me?' Princess Victoria tried to quiet her, but she then fell into a wild fit of hysterics, and had to be carried to Freddy's [Sir Frederick Ponsonby, Private Secretary to the King] room where she remained for some hours. Altogether it was a painful and rather theatrical exhibition, and ought never to have happened.

Cynical folk said that Alice's hysterics were caused by the fact that royal court doors had been slammed shut on her and she could no longer parade as the king's mistress. Others said, as mother of the king's child, her feeling of being spurned had tipped her into hysterics. After a period of personal mourning Alice Keppel re-invented herself in society, but maintained a discreet silence on whatever her relationship with Edward VII had been. She died at Florence on 11 September 1947, aged 79.

◆ Were some of Queen Victoria's great-grandchildren supporters of Adolf Hitler's National Socialists?

I never thought Hitler was such a bad chap.
Prince Edward, Duke of Windsor, during an interview in 1970. (Richard Woods, Sunday Times, 16 January 2005).

In a radio address from Windsor Castle on the evening of 11 December 1936, Edward VIII endeavoured to explain to the British Nation and Commonwealth why he had shocked them by abdicating his role as monarch. He said: 'I have found it impossible to carry the heavy burden of responsibility and to discharge my duties as King as I would wish to do without the help and support of the woman I love ...' That woman was Mrs Wallis Warfield Simpson (1896–1986), the twice-divorced native of Baltimore, Maryland, and he Edward Albert Christian George Andrew Patrick David (1894–1972), eldest son of George V and Queen Mary, and great-grandson of Queen Victoria. Edward and Wallis were married in the salon at the Château de Candé in the Loire Valley, France, on 3 June 1937 and lived the rest of their lives in exile as the Duke and Duchess of Windsor. Later that year the Duke and Duchess embarked on a visit that enraged sections of public opinion in Britain, caused the new King George VI to call it 'a bombshell and a bad one', and historians to ask: 'What was behind the Duke of Windsor's purported flirtation with Adolf Hitler?'

Despite such legislation as the promulgation of the racist Nuremberg laws of 1935 and the clear evidence that National Socialist Germany was rearming in violation of the Versailles Agreement of 1919, the Duke and Duchess of Windsor met the Führer of the Third German Reich, Adolf Hitler on 22 October 1937, at his mountaintop villa, the Berghof, above Berchtesgaden. While in Germany they met deputy leader and Reich Minister Rudolf Hess and the flamboyant Reichsmarschall Herman Göring.

Why were the Windsors there at all? The visit had been arranged by Charles Eugene Bedaux – who had lent them his house for their wedding – a French businessman who had major deals with German companies. Of dubious security background – he was suspected of spying for Germany in the First World War – Bedaux was trying to ingratiate himself with Hitler who could open German markets to him by arranging a meeting with a man Hitler had always wanted to meet. The Duke of Windsor's publicly announced reason for going to Germany was to study 'housing and working conditions', a subject that had always interested him as Prince of Wales and king, emphasised by his visit to South Wales in 1936. Edward's total disregard for British governmental and public opinion against the visit is likely to have come about because he was prevented from having a morganatic marriage, and because of the way his family treated his new wife denying her royal status.

Several books have been written on the Duke of Windsor's supposed 'treachery' against king and country through his Nazi sympathies and the 'constant contact' the duchess had 'during Britain's dark hours' with Hitler's Foreign Minister Joachim von Ribbentrop (with the suggestion that the duchess had an affair with him). Moreover, Edward's reluctance to leave Paris in 1940 was interpreted in some quarters as Edward having knowledge of a German invasion of France and wherein he could have a base to negotiate peace between Hitler and Britain. While Edward was in Paris he presented a security risk; however, he then went to fascist Spain where his blatant passing of information to Hitler's diplomats in Madrid after the war had begun adding to negative public opinion. It was widely believed that Hitler thought that when (not if) he conquered the United Kingdom he could put a compliant Duke of Windsor back on the throne as a puppet king. The German blood of the British Royal Family had been greatly researched by the National Socialists. To get the Windsors out of the way, and to stop them doing any diplomatic harm, on 9 July 1940, the wartime government of Prime Minister Winston Churchill appointed a reluctant Duke of Windsor as Governor of the Bahamas.

Despite the books denouncing the Duke of Windsor as 'a dangerous enemy of Great Britain', Francis Edward, 8th Baron Thurlow, Governor and C-in-C of the Bahamas 1968–72, speaking in 1999, summed up what many people thought about the Duke of Windsor and Germany:

> [Windosr] was basically taken for a ride. I don't accept at all that there was anything more than poor judgement [concerning his visit to Germany]: he was suckered into this situation, and he had nobody to advise him – no official staff at all.
>
> And [Windsor] enjoyed being made a fuss of: it's very difficult, if you've been made a fuss of all your life and then suddenly find that nobody is interested in you, so it's rather nice to be made a fuss of [as Windsor was by Hitler and his followers].

In the event of Hitler being successful in his conquering of the United Kingdom it is a matter of speculation whether or not the Duke of Windsor would have agreed to cooperate in the governance of his occupied birthplace, let alone agree to be its puppet king. Some four decades after his death the jury is still out.

The appearance of Prince Henry of Wales ('Harry') dressed as a Nazi soldier at a fancy-dress party in 2004 raked up memories and suspicions in the press concerning the House of Windsor's links to Hitler and their German background.

One of the most interesting of these links was HRH Prince Leopold Charles Edward, 2nd Duke of Albany, Earl of Clarence and Baron Arklow, born at Claremont House, Surrey on 19 July 1884. His parents were Prince Leopold, fourth son of Queen Victoria and Princess Helen of Waldeck-Pyrmont. Considered to be 'Queen Victoria's favourite grandson', he was educated at Eton. Yet his devoted grandmother dealt him a card that would seal his fate for ever. She decreed that he should succeed to the duchy of Saxe-Coburg and Gotha, from which German principality his grandfather Prince Albert had come.

So, aged 16, Charles Edward (now Karl Eduard) became duke of thousands of hectares of land in Bavaria and thirteen castles. Charles Edward was enrolled in the German army (at the insistence of his overlord and cousin Kaiser Wilhelm II); the Kaiser then married him off to his own niece Victoria. When war was declared in 1914 Charles Edward had the nightmare situation of fighting for the Kaiser against the country of his birth.

By the end of the war in 1918 Charles Edward was declared a 'traitor' by his family in Britain and was stripped of his British titles. In his fear that Germany, now a republic after the deposition of the Kaiser, would fall to the communists, Charles Edward allied himself with Hitler and his National Socialists. Over the years he tried to develop good relations with Britain in the Anglo-German Fellowship, hoping that his cousin Edward VIII would develop his pro-German inclinations. All this came to an end on Edward VIII's abdication, and when George VI came to the throne relationships with Britain became icy for Charles Edward.

Under Adolf Hitler, Charles Edward accepted certain official positions. He was president of the German Red Cross, thus he presided over the programme of enforced euthanasia of around 100,000 disabled men, women and children all deemed by the Nazis to be a drain on resources. Still today the extent of Charles Edward's involvement is not clear. He turned up at George V's funeral in 1936 in military uniform, steel helmet and swastika armband. Again, war broke out in 1939 and once more Charles Edward opposed the land of his birth. His three sons fought for Germany and one, Prince Hubertus, was killed on the Eastern Front. At the end of the war Charles Edward was captured by the Americans and interned. Brought to trial for war crimes, he pleaded 'Not Guilty', and while dubiety was expressed he was 'exonerated of complicity in actual war crimes', but his estates were confiscated and he was fined heavily forcing him into poverty.

Charles Edward died at Coburg on 6 March 1954. Ironically, his sister Princess Alice, Countess of Athlone, became one of the best loved of British royal ladies. She was deeply distressed at her brother's death but outlived him by some thirty years; she died in 1981 aged 98.

Other members of the Windsor's German family tree went along with Hitler, others held back. Queen Victoria's great-grandson Wilhelm of Prussia (b.1882), son of Queen Victoria's grandson Kaiser Wilhelm II of Germany, served in the 1st Infantry Regiment at Koningsberg; he played a role in the invasion of Poland but died from internal injuries in 1940 during an attack on the French positions at Valenciennes. His funeral at Potsdam drew a crowd in excess of 50,000 which displeased Hitler. The Crown Prince's brother Prince August Wilhelm (1887–1949), became a keen member of the *Nationalsozialistische Deutsche Arbeiterpartei* (National Socialist German Workers party). At first Hitler was happy to accept the help and exploit the positions of German royalty, but by 1943 he turned against them and stripped all members of the Hohenzollern and Habsburg families of their titles and commissions. August Wilhelm was expelled from the Nazi party and arrested. Another who was thrown out was Queen Victoria's great-grandson Prince Wilhelm-Karl von Preussen (1922–2007), but a further three of Queen Victoria's great-grandsons were more committed Nazi supporters: the princes Van Hessen.

Prince Christoph (1901–43), his twin brother Richard (1901–69), Philipp (1896–1980) and his twin Wolfgang (1896–1989) had as their grandmother Princess Victoria (1840–1901), eldest daughter of Queen Victoria; she married Emperor Frederick II (1831–88) of Germany, King of Prussia. The princes' mother was Princess Margaret ('Mossy', 1872–1954), the youngest child of the Empress Frederick, who married Prince Frederick Charles of Hesse in January 1893.

Prince Christoph married Princess Sophia (1914–2000) of Greece and Denmark on 15 December 1930. Her train was carried by her 9-year-old brother Philip (later Duke of Edinburgh). Christoph joined the Nazi party in 1931 and the *Schutzstaffel* (SS) in 1932; he was attached to Reichsführer SS Heinrich Himmler's personal staff and became head of Reichsmarschall Herman Göring's security service the *Forshungstamt*. Prince Richard joined the Nazi party in 1932 and the *Sturmbateilung* (SA) the same year. Prince Philipp joined the Nazi party in 1930 and the SA in 1932. Prince Wolfgang, also a party member, became Oberpresedent (governor) of Hessen-Nassau.

Queen Elizabeth II's marriage to Lt Philip Mountbatten (formerly Schleswig-Holstein-Sonderburg-Glucksberg), son of the bisexual Prince Andrew of Greece and Princess Alice of Hesse-Darmstadt, was almost scuppered by Philip's links with Hitler's henchmen. Leading the opposition to Philip, whose suit with the infatuated Princess Elizabeth was being doggedly pursued by Philip's uncle Lord Mountbatten, was his future mother-in-law Queen Elizabeth (better known today as the Queen Mother). One of her brothers had been killed during the First World War and she had a dislike of Germans, despite the fact that her own mother-in-law Queen Mary was wholly German. Nevertheless, she was opposed to her daughter marrying a man whose four sisters had married Germans and whose brothers-in-law fought for Hitler. Princess Elizabeth's deep infatuation for Philip Mountbatten meant that her parents, with serious misgivings, consented to the marriage. Philip's sisters and their husbands were not invited to the marriage ceremony.

At the diamond wedding anniversary celebrations of Queen Elizabeth II and Prince Philip, in November 2007, in the congregation at the Westminster Abbey service were a small group of Prince Philip's German relations; they were the prince's nieces and nephews, the children of his sisters.

Another link with the Nazi's came when Prince Michael of Kent married Marie-Christine daughter of Baron Gunther von Reibnitz. The baron had honorary membership of Himmler's SS, but in the postwar de-Nazification, most honorary-SS members were dubbed only *Mitlaufer* (fellow-travellers) and any public fuss concerning the marriage soon died down.

◆◆◆

It was during the Nazi threat to Britain that Queen Elizabeth, the Queen Mother, became a sharp shooter. Apart from medieval monarchs who were brought up to bear arms, few modern British sovereigns have been marksmen off the hunting field. George V, Edward VIII and George VI all had naval training and were familiar with firearms. During the Second World War George VI learned how to use a hand gun and a sten gun. It is said that wherever he went during the war years the sten gun went too. From the early days of the war the Queen Mother was taught how to use a pistol, causing her to remark, 'Now I shall not go down like all the others'.

♦ Did the House of Windsor leave their Russian royal cousins to be murdered?

'Ever your devoted cousin and friend.'

'God bless you good old Nicky.'

'You can always depend on me your greatest friend.'

Sentiments in letters from George V to his cousin Tsar Nicholas II of Russia.

Secrecy in the Royal Family has been honed to a fine art. Yet often this concealing of the truth has led to misunderstandings and false rumours. One such 'cover-up' cited by historians is the supposed betrayal by George V of his cousins the Romanovs.

Shot at the Ipatiev House – the 'House of Special Purpose' – at Ekaterinburg, Siberia, on 17 July 1918, their bodies dumped in a mineshaft but later moved and buried; so died Tsar Nicholas II, his wife Tsarina Alexandra Feodorovna, granddaughter of Queen Victoria, and their five children. Their murders by communists have been well documented; and their exhumation in 1991 and reburial on 17 July 1998 in St Catherine's Chapel of St Peter and St Paul, St Petersburg, received international media coverage. But the role of the British Royal Family in offering help to their Russian cousins remains hazy.

In the weeks that followed Nicholas II's abdication of the Russian throne, for himself and his heir the Tsarevich Alexei, the future of the Imperial Russian Royal Family became a political and diplomatic conundrum. On 19 March 1917 the British ambassador in Petrograd (modern St Petersburg) was instructed to inform the Russian Foreign Minister, Paul Miliukov, that 'any violence done to the Emperor and his family would have a most deplorable effect and would deeply shock public opinion in [the United Kingdom]'. Miliukov enquired if the British government would grant the Imperial Russian Royal Family asylum in Britain. The matter was discussed by Prime Minister David Lloyd-George, Chancellor of the Exchequer Andrew Bonar Law, George V's private secretary Lord Stamfordham and Foreign Office Minister Lord Hardinge. On 22 March signals were sent to the British ambassador to inform the Russian provisional government that the British would grant the Romanovs sanctuary for the duration of the war. These last few words were to be a clue as to the ultimate fate of the Romanovs.

Tsar Nicholas and his family took the offer at its face value; official discussions were made for the Romanovs to go to England. The family started to pack, expecting the call to embark at Petrograd quickly. Things were delayed as the royal children caught the measles. Back in Britain George V was having second thoughts. He was willing to arrange for his imperial cousins to seek sanctuary in say Switzerland or Denmark, but was increasingly 'doubtful' about them coming to England. George feared that temporary sanctuary would lead to permanent asylum. Once news had got out about the possible sanctuary offer, George received 'many abusive letters' from socialists and communist sympathisers and feared his kingdom might be plunged into bloody revolution. Sir George Buchanan, the British ambassador at Petrograd also 'pointed out that the presence of the Imperial Family in England would assuredly be exploited to our detriment by extremists as well as by the German agents in Russia'.

An alternative sanctuary in France was proposed and agreed by the British government, but not acted upon. The tide of events had quickened in Russia. On 22 March 1917, the Romanovs were moved to Tsarskoe Selo, near Petrograd, then to Tobolsk, Siberia, and then even further away to Ekaterinburg in the Ural Moutains.

In 2006 a diary was discovered that shed new light on a plot by the British Secret Services (then under 'C' – Sir Mansfield Cumming) to rescue the Romanovs. The diary belonged to Captain Stephen Alley (d. 1969, aged 93), second in command at the British International Mission at Petrograd; in those days Alley was employed by MI1, later MI6. The diary shows that Alley positioned a team of six fluent Russian-speaking agents ready to go to Ekaterinburg to rescue the Romanovs, codenamed 'The Valuables'. The plan was formulated to spring the Romanovs and take them by train to Murmansk and then on by Royal Navy vessel. The logistics were worked out but were never activated. Why? Historians believe, based on papers in the Russian State Archives, that Alley's telegrams detailing the rescue operation were intercepted by the communists (i.e. Bolsheviks) resulting in the house at Ekaterinburg becoming an impregnable fortress. Such a mission then would be military suicide. The Romanovs were left to their fate.

The British government had offered too little too late, and George V has never been exonerated for his part in procrastinating about what to do with his cousins. When Lloyd-George was writing his war memoirs in 1934, pressure was put on him to delete 'the chapter on the future residence of the deposed Tsar'. Lloyd-George complied. Did George V finally veto his cousins' rescue? The Royal Family still keep the answer secret. As Kenneth Rose wrote in his 1983 biography of George V: '... it is significant that the Royal Archives at Windsor contain hardly any documents dealing with the imprisonment of the Imperial Family between April 1917 and May 1918 ...' So is it any wonder that researchers believe that another 'royal cover-up' was enacted to save George V's honour?

When it comes to the murdered Romanovs there has been some cooperation between the Royal Family and the scientists in trying to identify the re-discovered remains. When these remains were unearthed Prince Philip supplied DNA to help identify the skeletons. The Tsarina's niece Princess Alice of Greece was Prince Philip's mother. Even so, two skeletons were missing: those of the Tsarevich Alexei and his sister Maria. In 2007 more supposed Romanov remains were discovered near the original burial site. Prince Philip's DNA has been cited again to prove that all the murdered Romanovs have now been identified.

Two postscripts to this story are of interest. One event is cited by some to underline what they consider to be King George V's 'hypocracy' in the matter of his cousins' murder. Writing in her memoirs *My Dear Marquis* Agnes, Baroness de Stoeckl, the former Miss Agnes Barron, wife of Sasha, a member of the Imperial Russian Diplomatic Corps wrote how Grand Duchess George of Russia (sister-in-law of

Nicholas II) wished to hold a service in memory of her relatives at the Russian chapel in London's Welbeck Street. She wrote:

> King George and Queen Mary wished to attend.
>
> The little chapel was full when we arrived, all rose and bowed as the Grand Duchess George of Russia entered with her daughters and took her place on the right side of the Iconastasis [a screen shutting off the sanctuary on which icons were placed]. Seats placed next to her were reserved for their Majesties. We stood immediately behind her. She had asked for this.
>
> We were all in the deepest mourning, wearing the regulation Russian headdress, a Marie Stuart cap, the peak edged with white, a long crepe veil covering us from head to foot.
>
> Their Majesties entered, escorted by Sasha.
>
> The priests in their black and silver vestments appeared, they bowed low to the King and Queen then to the Grand Duchess ...
>
> The beauty of the liturgy was too much for the loyal Russians who had come to pay their last homage to their beloved Emperor and all that he represented. They broke into sobs. . . . Their Majesties were much moved and at the end, when the choir sang a prayer to the Virgin in farewell to the soul which had fled, tears were running down the Queen's face.

There were those in the congregation who thought the tears were 'crocodile tears'.

The British ambassador at St Petersburg, Sir George Buchanan, was criticised at the time for 'bungling' the safe passage of the Russian Imperial Family to Britain. Others thought that he was 'far too gullible' and had been 'hoodwinked' by the leaders of the Russian Revolution into believing that the Imperial Family would be safe.

Buchanan was humiliated and returned to England in 1918. He was warned by the Foreign Office to make no comment on the fate of the Russian Imperial Family or George V's role in it. If he did he would be charged with infringing the Official Secrets Act and would lose his pension. Although he went on to be ambassador to Rome from 1919–21, Buchanan was denied an expected peerage. He died in 1924 much embittered by his treatment over the fate of the Imperial Family; his relatives believed that he too had been muzzled to protect George V.

◆ Which queen was rumoured to have become the first British royal to undergo fertility treatment?

The King has no information to suggest that King Olav was not the son of King Haakon.

Official statement by King Harald V of Norway, 2004, cousin of Queen Elizabeth II.

From the House of Normandy to the House of Windsor there have been forty reigning monarchs of England, then the United Kingdom since 1603. Only eight of them bore no legitimate children: William II, Richard I, Richard II, Edward V, Edward VI, Mary I, Elizabeth I and Edward VIII; count nine if Jane 'The Nine Days Queen' is included. So fecundity has not been a problem in royal family trees from 1066–2008; a point also proved by the scores of royal illegitimates. Yet one royal dynasty with its roots in Britain offers an intriguing insight into infertility.

In 2004 respected Norwegian writer Tor Bomann-Larsen in his biography of Queen Elizabeth II's great-aunt Maud, *Folket* (The People) offered an astonishing theory which, said the international press, 'sent shockwaves across Scandinavia'. According to the author Queen Elizabeth's close relatives in Norway perpetuated their dynasty by way of artificial insemination.

Princess Maud Charlotte Mary Victoria, fifth child and youngest daughter of Edward VII and Queen Alexandra was born at Marlborough House, London, on 26 November 1869. On 22 July 1896 at Buckingham Palace she married her younger cousin Prince Christian Carl Frederick of Denmark (1872–1957). The prince was elected King of Norway after the country broke away from Sweden in 1905; he ruled as King Haakon VII.

Six years passed and to the disappointment of her husband, mother and father, Maud had not become pregnant. Maud was immensely proud of her tiny 18in waist; this gave rise to uninformed court gossip that she was unable to conceive. 'What could be done about the situation?' Edward VII consulted Dr Sir Francis Laking who had been his physician-in-ordinary and surgeon apothecary since he was Prince of Wales. Some time in late 1902 Maud made a secret visit to a London clinic where she was put under the care of Sir Francis. Nine months later Maud gave birth in London to Prince Alexander Edward Christian Frederick on 2 July 1903; in 1957 he succeeded as King Olav V of Norway (d.1991) and became a close friend of the British Royal Family.

It has been suggested that Prince Carl may have been rendered infertile through a childhood illness and Maud, who had many ills from pains and rashes to debility and depression, possibly had the 'royal malady' porphyria. So what was Sir Francis's role in Maud's pregnancy – if any?

No one in Denmark had seen Maud pregnant and Tor Bomann-Larsen's theory is that she was made pregnant by royal doctor Laking or his son Guy. There is no suggestion of adultery, but rather a pregnancy through artificial insemination with sperm donated by one of the Lakings. After all, the technique had been successfully carried out in the 1890s. Bomann-Larsen draws attention, too, to the 'striking physical resemblance' between Crown Prince Alexander and Sir Francis Laking. Furthermore, it is pointed out that when the baby prince was conceived Prince Carl was 'away at sea and only visited [Maud] once'.

Maud was a shy, unassuming and unworldly character and it is thought that Laking's 'process' would not have been discussed with her. Yet it is certain that any procedure would have been talked over with, and agreed to, by Edward VII, if not Prince Carl.

Maud spent a great deal of time in England; she died in London on 20 November 1938, just before her 69th birthday. Sir Francis Laking died in 1914 and his son Sir Guy Francis Laking (b.1875), became Keeper of the King's Armoury at Windsor in 1902, a post created for him by Edward VII, and later he became first keeper of the London Museum. Sir Guy married and fathered two children; he died in 1919. Since the publication of Bomann-Larsen's book, the reviews have been largely dismissive, describing his 'evidence' as shaky. If the truth of King Olav V's biological parentage needs to be known, only a DNA test could reveal the reality.

◆ Why was George V's son called 'The Lost Prince'?

HRH Prince John, who has since infancy suffered from epileptic fits, which have lately become more frequent and severe, passed away in his sleep following an attack this afternoon at Sandringham.
Court circular bulletin from surgeon apothecary Sir Alan Reeve Manby (1848–1925), 18 January 1919, Sandringham House.

Enter the lych-gate of St Mary Magdalene Church, Sandringham, Norfolk, walk forward and you will find him. His grave lies next to that of his baby uncle, another Prince John, the stillborn son of Edward VII and Queen Alexandra, of 16 June 1890. Who was this Prince John so interred in a grave that is remarkably un-royal and who biographers have called 'The Little Prince the Nation Forgot?'

Prince John Charles Francis was born at 3.05 a.m. at York Cottage, Sandringham, on 12 July 1905, the sixth and last child of Prince George and Princess Mary of Teck, the future George V and Queen Mary. All of the royal couple's children exhibited characteristic oddities. Prince Edward (the future Edward VIII) suffered from deafness inherited from his grandmother Queen Alexandra and was also a severe depressive, with the 'Hanoverian melancholic gene' inherited from his grandmother Queen Victoria. Prince Albert (later King George VI) had a distressing stutter and congenitally malformed knees. He would fly into uncontrollable rages. Prince Henry, Duke of Gloucester, had unfathomable fits of tears, interlarded with episodes of nervous giggling and was declared 'mentally backward'. Prince George, Duke of Kent howled whenever he saw his mother, was of a 'frenetic character' and in adulthood was absorbed into a milieu of homosexuality and drugs. Princess Mary, later the Princess Royal suffered from a crippling shyness, but had to be removed from her brothers' schoolroom for being a 'disruptive influence'. Alas, Prince John showed early signs of mental retardation. At the age of 4 he began to suffer from fits, which the royal doctors diagnosed as epilepsy originating after conception (genetic epilepsy). His fits could render him violent and unpredictable, and when the royal children were out on the hills above Balmoral, for instance, Loeila Ponsonby noted, Prince John had to be roped to his nanny as a precaution against self-harm.

In an age when 'mental afflictions' were obscured from public view, it was noted that the Royal Family, said Garry Jenkins, 'wanted nothing more than to bury the memory of Prince John as an embarrassing footnote in their history'. Prince Edward, Prince of Wales considered his afflicted brother a 'regrettable nuisance' and scarcely mentions him in his ghosted autobiography *A King's Story* (1951). Reginald Baliol Brett, 2nd Viscount Esher, political and royal go-between, noted Prince John's increasing unpredictability in his diary entry for 21 August 1910. On one occasion at lunch with the king and queen at Balmoral, wrote Esher, Prince John continually ran round the dining table 'all the while they ate'. Regularly he would slip from his nanny's notice to appear unannounced at his parents' official gatherings and make a 'scene'. As his behaviour became more eccentric, the king and queen realised that he was not controllable as 'normal' children; they were particularly concerned that John would have a fit in public. So, said the court gossips, John was packed off to Sandringham estate in the care of royal nanny Mrs Lalla Bill.

It is a popular royal description that George V and Queen Mary were unfeeling parents. Certainly the Duke of Windsor (the former Edward VIII) wrote to the Earl of Dudley after Queen Mary's death: 'I'm afraid the fluids in her veins have always been as icy cold as they are now in death.' Again, while jumping to the queen's defence, her lady-in-waiting of over fifty years, Mabell, Countess of Airlie, openly agreed that the queen 'had no interest in her children as babies'. Both George and Mary had a keen sense of public duty and in protecting the monarchy and this caused them to be secretive about John. He was moved to Wood Farm in 1916, on the edge of the Sandringham estate, near Wolferton. There, as far as the public were concerned, he became the forgotten member of the Royal Family. Perhaps the last family album photograph of him to appear in the public milieu was the one taken by Prince Edward at Balmoral in 1912, wherein Prince John is pictured riding in a metal royal car and sporting a white sailor suit. Despite the royal gossip about Queen Mary's coldness towards her children there is evidence that Queen Mary spent a lot of time with John at Sandringham, and his grandmother Queen Alexandra showed him much compassion. Despite her crippling deafness and rheumatism, she would send her car to Wood Farm to bring the 'dear and precious little boy' to her at Sandringham for afternoon tea, music and games.

Early on the morning of 18 January 1919, Dr Sir Alan Manby was called to John's bedside. Through the preceding night his condition had worsened after an epileptic fit. That afternoon Dr Manby recorded that John had succumbed to 'a severe seizure'. In her Sandringham diary Queen Mary wrote this:

> At 5.30 Lalla Bill telephoned to me from Wood Farm, Wolferton, that our poor darling little Johnnie had passed away suddenly after one of his attacks. The news gave me a great shock, tho' for the poor little boy's restless soul, death came as a great release. I broke the news to George & we motored down to Wood Farm. Found poor Lalla very resigned but heartbroken. Little Johnnie looked very peaceful lying there.

The Queen penned another memory to her friend Miss Emily Alcock on 2 February 1919:

> For him it is a great release as his malady was becoming worse as he grew older, & he has thus been spared much suffering. I cannot say how grateful we feel to God for having taken him in such a peaceful way, he just slept quietly into his heavenly home, no pain, no struggle, just peace for the poor little troubled spirit which had been a great anxiety to us for many years, ever since he was four years old. . . . The first break in the family circle is hard to bear but people have been so kind & sympathetic & this has helped us much.

It is true to say that in an age of non-technological media, when newspapers were more reverential towards the Royal Family than today, by 1919 half of Britain had forgotten Prince John existed, while the other half had never heard of him. It is likely that Prince John had had the best care as prescribed by the medical and social criteria of the day. It is the modern interpretation of these criteria that makes John's 'exile' to Sandringham seem a chapter of royal embarrassment.

A little anecdote on Prince John comes from the memoirs of Baroness de Stoeckl:

> One day [Princess Victoria, the second daughter of Edward VII] was in the nursery playing with her nephews and niece, the children of King George V. Prince John, the youngest, was only a baby, he had been given a piece of biscuit which he had sucked thoroughly, then scraped on the floor, finally he gave it to the dog to lick. At this moment, King Edward came in and stood looking down at the child. The latter held up the biscuit and said, 'Grandpa eat!' Before Princess Victoria could intervene, the biscuit had been swallowed by the affectionate grandfather. The princess, having seen the adventures of that biscuit, promptly left the room and was sick.

ACKNOWLEDGEMENTS

Each quotation in the text is acknowledged in situ and sourced in the Bibliography. In the compilation of the book many supplementary sources, too many to acknowledge separately, have been studied. In particular special mention is made of the author's gratitude to a sight of the biographical work on royalty undertaken by Mike Ashley and Dr Julian Lock in their *British Monarchs* (Robinson, 1998), and David Williamson in *Brewer's British Royalty* (Cassell, 1996). Royal anecdotes abound and the late Elizabeth Longford's *The Oxford Book of Royal Anecdotes* (Oxford University Press, 1989), and Deborah and Gerald Strober's selection of the oral history of Queen Elizabeth II, *The Monarchy* (Hutchinson, 2002) have been a useful source of reflection.

Every effort has been made to trace literary heirs of copyright material, but death of authors, reversion of rights and long forgotten publishing sources make the task more difficult. To all, though, many thanks are due.

BIBLIOGRAPHY

Texts to 1800

Andre, Friar Bernard, *Vita Henrici Septimi*.
Anglo Saxon Chronicle.
Anon., *Boke of Kervynge*, Wynkyn de Worde, 1508.
Bacon, Francis, *History of the reign of King Henry VII*, 1622.
Boorde, Andrew, *Brevyary of Health*, 1547.
Camden, William, *Annales Rerum Anglicarum, et Hibernicarum, regnante Elizabetha, ad Annum Salutis 1589*, London, 1615.
Capgrave, Friar John (1393–1464), *Chronicle*.
Chronicle of Pierre de Longtoft.
Chronicle of Walter of Guisborough.
Gaimar, Geoffrey (fl.1140), *Lestorie des Engles*.
Goscelin (fl.1099), *Translatio Sancti Mildrethe Virginis*.
—— (fl.1080), *Life of Saint Edward*.
Harrington, Sir John, *Metamorphosis of Ajax*, 1596.
Hazlitt, William, *Travel Notes*.
Holinshed, Raphael, *Chronicles*, (England to 1535).
James I/VI, *Christis Kirk on the Green*.
Le Baker, Geoffrey, *Chronicle, c.* 1341.
Leland, John, *Collectaria*, pre-1548.
More, Hannah, *Daniel*.
More, Sir Thomas, *History of Richard III*.
Oglander, Sir John (1585–1655), *Diary*.
Paris, Matthew, *Chronica Majora*, (to the year 1253).
Philippe de Commynes, *Memoirs, c.* 1498.
Robert of Lewis, Bishop of Bath, *Gesta Stephani*.
Rous, J., *Historia Regum Angliae*.
Scalacronica.
Skelton, John, *Speculum Principis, c.*1499.
Vergil, Polydore, *Anglicae Historiae*.
W.A., *A Book of Cookynge Very necessary for all such as delight therein*, Edward Allde, 1588.
Wace, *Roman du Rou*.
Wavrin, Jean de, *Chronique d'Angleterre*.
William of Malmesbury, *Gesta Regum Anglorum*.
Wolcot, John (Peter Pindar), *Poems*, 1791.
Worcester analyst, *Chronicle of the age of the Church*.

Selected Reading

Anand, Sushila, *Indian Sahib: Queen Victoria's Dear Abdul*, Duckworth, 1996.

Ashley, Maurice, *The English Civil War: A Concise History*, Thames and Hudson, 1974.

Barber, Richard, *Edward, Prince of Wales and Aquitaine: A Biography of the Black Prince*, Woodbridge, The Boydell Press, 2002.

Barlow, Frank, *Thomas Becket*, Weidenfeld & Nicolson, 1986.

Barrow, G.W.S., *Robert Bruce*, Edinburgh University Press, 1976.

Beatty, Laura, *Lily Langtry: Manners, Masks and Morals*, Chatto & Windus, 1999.

Benson, A.C. and Esher, Viscount, *The Letters of Queen Victoria 1837–1861*, John Murray, 1908.

Benson, E.F., *Queen Victoria*, New York, Barnes & Noble, 1992.

Bird, Anthony, *The Damnable Duke of Cumberland*, Barrie & Rockliff, 1966.

Bloch, Marc, *The Royal Touch: Monarchy and Miracles in France and England*, New York, Dorset Press, 1989.

Bomann-Larsen, Tor, *Folket*, Oslo, Cappelan, 2004.

Bradford, Sarah, *George VI*, Weidenfeld & Nicolson, 1989.

Brewer, Clifford, *The Death of Kings*, Abson Books, 2000.

Brewer, Revd E. Cobham, *Dictionary of Phrase & Fable*, Odhams Press, n.d.

Bridgeman, Harriet and Drury, Elizabeth, *Society Scandals*, David & Charles, 1977.

Broad, Lewis, *Queens, Crowns and Coronations*, Hutchinson, 1952.

Brodhurst, J. Penderel, *King Edward VII*, Virtue & Co., 1911.

Brown, Craig and Cunliffe, Lesley, *The Book of Royal Lists*, Routledge & Kegal Paul, 1982.

Chambers, James, *The Norman Kings*, Weidenfeld & Nicolson, 1981.

Chancellor, John, *The Life & Times of Edward I*, Weidenfeld & Nicolson, 1981.

Charlot, Monica, *Victoria: The Young Queen*, Blackwell, 1991.

Cheetham, Anthony, *Life & Times of Richard III*, Weidenfeld & Nicolson, 1972.

Cornwallis-West, George, *Edwardian Hey-Days*, Putnam, 1930.

De la Noy, Michael, *Windsor Castle: Past & Present*, Headline, 1990.

Dobson, Aidan, *The Royal Tombs of Great Britain*, Duckworth, 2004.

Doherty, Paul, *Isabella and the Strange Death of Edward II*, Constable & Robertson, 2003.

Dyson, Hope and Tennyson, Charles, *Dear and Honoured Lady: The Correspondence of Queen Victoria and Alfred Tennyson*, Macmillan, 1969.

Earle, Peter, *The Life and Times of James II*, Weidenfeld & Nicolson, 1972.

Field, Ophelia, *The Favourite: Sarah Duchess of Marlborough*, Hodder & Stoughton, 2002.

Fitzgerald, Percy, *Dukes and Princesses …*, London, 1882.

Fleming, G.H., *Lady Colin Campbell: Victorian 'Sex Goddess'*, The Windrush Press, 1989.

Fraser, Antonia, *King Charles II*, Weidenfeld & Nicolson, 1979.

—— *The Warrior queens: Boadicea's Chariot*, Weidenfeld & Nicolson, 1969.

—— *Mary, Queen of Scots*, Weidenfeld & Nicolson, 1969.

—— *King James*, Weidenfeld & Nicolson, 1974.

Fraser, Flora, *Princesses: The Six Daughters of George III*, John Murray, 2004.

Frazer, Sir J.G., *The Golden Bough*, 1890.

Gairdner, James, *History of the Life & Reign of Richard III*, 1898.

Gillingham, John, *The Life & Times of Richard I*, Weidenfeld & Nicolson, 1973.

Green, David, *Queen Anne*, Collins, 1970.

Green, Shirley, *The Curious History of Contraception*, Ebury Press, 1971.

Grinnell-Milne, Duncan, *The Killing of William Rufus*, David & Charles, 1968.

Gristwood, Sarah, *Arabella: England's Lost Queen*, Bantam Press, 2003.

Gordon, Sophie, *Noble Hounds and Dear Companions*, Royal Collection Publications, 2007.

Hallan, E. (ed), *The Plantagenet Chronicles*, Phoebe Philips Editions, 1986.

Hanrahan, David C., *Colonel Blood: The Man Who Stole the Crown Jewels*, Sutton Publishing, 2003.

Hibbert, Christopher, *George IV: Regent and King*, Allen Lane, 1975.

—— *Edward VII*, Allen Lane, 1976.

—— *George III: A Personal History*, Viking, 1998.

Hingley, Richard and Unwin, Christina, *Boudica: Iron Age Warrior Queen*, Hambledon & London, 2005.

Humble, Richard, *The Saxon Kings*, Weidenfeld & Nicolson, 1980.

Hutchinson, Robert, *The Last Days of Henry VIII*, Weidenfeld & Nicolson, 2005.

Kinnaird, George (ed), *My Dear Marquis: Baroness de Stoeckl*, John Murray, 1952.

Lamont-Brown, Raymond, *Edward VII's Last Loves*, Sutton Publishing, 1998.

—— *Royal Murder Mysteries*, Weidenfeld & Nicolson, 1990.

—— *John Brown: Queen Victoria's Highland Servant*, Sutton Publishing, 2000.

—— *Royal Poxes and Potions: The Lives of Court Physicians, Surgeons and Apothecaries*, Sutton Publishing, 2001.

Lawson, M.K., *Cnut: England's Viking King*, Tempus Publishing, 2004.

Lee, Sir Sydney, *Queen Victoria*, Smith Elder, 1902.

—— *Edward VII*, Macmillan, 1925.

Leslie, Anita, *The Marlborough House Set*, New York, Doubleday & Co., 1972.

—— *Edwardians in Love*, Hutchinson, 1972.

Lindsay, John, *The Lovely Quaker*, 1939.

Loades, David (gen ed), *Chronicles of the Tudor Kings*, Greenwich Editions, 2002.

Longford, Elizabeth, *Victoria RI*, Weidenfeld & Nicolson, 1964.

—— (ed), *The Oxford Book of Royal Anecdotes*, Oxford University Press, 1989.

Lowe John, *Edward James: A Surrealist Life*, Collins, 1991.

Luke, Mary, *The Nine Days Queen: A Portrait of Lady Jane Grey*, New York, Morrow & Co. Inc, 1986.

McClintock, J. Dewar, *Royal Motoring*, G.T. Foulis & Co. Ltd, 1962.

Macdougal, Norman, *James IV*, Tuckwell Press, 1997.

Madge, Tom, *Royal Yachts of the World*, Thomas Reid Publications, 1997.

Marlow, Joseph, *George I*, Weidenfeld & Nicolson, 1973.

Mason, Emma, *William II: Rufus, The Red King*, Tempus Publishing, 2005.

Masters, Brian, *The Mistresses of Charles II*, Blond & Briggs, 1979.

Menkes, Suzy, *The Royal Jewels*, Guild Publishing, 1985.

Melville, Sir John, *Memoires*, 1827.

Miller, John, *The Life and Times of William & Mary*, Weidenfeld & Nicolson, 1974.

Montague, Lord, *The Motoring Montagues*.

Morillo, Stephen, *The Battle of Hastings*, Boydell & Brewer, 1996.

Munson, James, *Maria Fitzherbert: The Secret Wife of George IV*, Constable, 2001.

Nicholson, Harold, *King George V: The Life & Reign*, Constable 1952.

Parissien, Steven, *George IV: The Grand Entertainment*, John Murray, 2001.

Pendered, Mary Lucy, *The Fair Quaker: Hannah Lightfoot and her Relations with George III*, 1910.

Petropoulos, Jonathan, *Royals and the Reich: The Princes Van Hessen in Nazi Germany*, Oxford University Press, 2006.

Plowden, Alison, *Caroline & Charlotte: The Regent's wife & daughter, 1795–1821*, Sidgwick & Jackson, 1989.

Ponsonby, Sir Frederick, *Recollections of Three Reigns*, Eyre & Spottiswoode, 1957.

Prebble, John, *The King's Jaunt: George IV in Scotland, 1822*, Collins, 1988.

Priestley, J.B., *The Prince of Pleasure and His Regency*, Heinemann, 1969.

Reid, Michaela, *Ask Sir James*, Hodder & Stoughton, 1987.

Ridley, Jasper, *Napoleon III and Eugenie*, Constable, 1979.

Roots, Ivan, *Speeches of Oliver Cromwell*, Everyman Classics, 1989.

Rose, Kenneth, *King George V*, Weidenfeld & Nicolson, 1983.

St Albyn, Giles, *Queen Victoria: A Portrait*, Sinclair-Stevenson, 1991.

Seward, Desmond, *Richard III: England's Black Legend*, Hamlyn, 1983.

Sheppard, Edgar, *George, Duke of Cumberland: A Memoir of his Private Life*, Longmans, Green & Co., 1901.

Somerset, Anne, *Elizabeth I*, Weidenfeld & Nicolson, 1991.

Starkey, David, *The Reign of Henry VIII: Personalities and Politics*, George Philip, 1985.
—— *Elizabeth*, Chatto & Windus, 2000.
—— *Six Wives: The Queens of Henry VIII*, Chatto & Windus, 2003.

Stewart, Alan, *The Cradle King: A Life of James VI & I*, Chatto & Windus, 2003.

Steuart, A. Francis, *The Exiled Bourbons in Scotland*, William Brown, 1908.

Stoney, Benita and Weltzein, Heinrich C. (eds), *My Mistress the Queen: The Letters of Frieda Arnold, Dresser to Queen Victoria*, Weidenfeld & Nicolson, 1994.

Strickland, Agnes, *Lives of the Queens of England*, 1840–48.

Strober, Deborah and Gerald, *The Monarchy: An Oral History of Elizabeth II*, Hutchinson, 2002.

Taylor, Anthony, *Down with the Crown: British Anti-monarchism and Debates about Royalty since 1790*, Reaktion Books, 1999.

Thornton, Michael, *Royal Feud: The Queen Mother and the Duchess of Windsor*, Michael Joseph, 1985.

Tisdall, E.E.P., *Queen Victoria's John Brown*, Stanley Paul, 1938.

Tout, F.T., *Edward I*, 1890.

Turner, E.S., *The Court of St James's*, Michael Joseph, 1953.

Van Der Kiste, John and Jordaan, Bee, *Dearest Affie: Alfred Duke of Edinburgh, Queen Victoria's Second Son,* Sutton Publishing, 1984.

Walvin, James, *Victorian Values*, Andre Deutsch, 1987.

Warren, W.L., *King John*, Eyre Methuen, 1961.

Warwick, Christopher, *Abdication*, Sidgwick & Jackson, 1986.

Watson, Francis, *Dawson of Penn*, Chatto & Windus, 1951.

Wedgewood, C.V., *The Trial of Charles I*, Collins, 1964.

Weir, Alison, *Elizabeth The Queen*, Jonathan Cape, 1998.

Williams, Ethel Carleton, *Anne of Denmark*, Longman, 1970.

Willson, D.H., *King James VI & I*, Jonathan Cape, 1956.

Windsor, The Duke of, *A King's Story*, Cassell, 1951.

Woodruff, Douglas, *The Life & Times of Alfred the Great*, Weidenfeld & Nicolson, 1974.

INDEX